ANARCHISM
AND
ANARCHO-SYNDICALISM

BY

KARL MARX
FREDERICK ENGELS
V. I. LENIN

Fredonia Books
Amsterdam, The Netherlands

Anarchism and Anarcho-Syndicalism

by
Karl Marx
Frederick Engels
V. I. Lenin

ISBN: 1-4101-0141-X

Reprinted from the 1972 edition

Fredonia Books
Amsterdam, The Netherlands
http://www.fredoniabooks.com

CONTENTS

1*

PREFACE

Anarchism, by class nature a petty-bourgeois socio-political trend, took shape from the 1840s to the 1860s, but its ideas have much earlier origins. For all the diversity of its trends, and the differences in the views of its ideologists, of whom the most important were Max Stirner (the pseudonym of Johann Kaspar Schmidt), Pierre Joseph Proudhon and Mikhail Bakunin, they all had some common features. It was above all denial of any state power and the claim to absolute freedom for the individual. The anarchists' extreme individualism and subjectivism were a reflection of the petty-bourgeois protest against the development of large-scale capitalist production, which tended to ruin the petty bourgeoisie, against the exploiting essence of the state, which safeguarded the interests of big capital, and against the capitalist forms of the industrial revolution. With the anarchists this protest became an abstract denial of the state, which they believed *per se*, quite independently of its class nature and essence, to be the root of all evil, and this led them to deny centralisation in any form and to preach a boundless autonomy. What all anarchist trends have in common is a utopian vision of setting up a society without state and exploiting classes through a spontaneous rebellion by the masses and instant abolition of state power and all its institutions, instead of thorough political struggle by the working class, socialist revolution, and establishment of a proletarian dictatorship.

Anarchism, an outgrowth of petty-bourgeois revolutionism, has had some influence on the working-class movement as well, especially at its early stages. The anarchist ideology spread when the working class was immature and lacked experience in struggle. This was expressed in the emergence of specific trends in the working-class movement: Proudhonism, which denied the state but preached a peaceful resolution of social conflicts; Bakuninism, with its characteristic ultra-revolutionary catchwords; anarcho-syndicalism, which appeared a little later, and which confined the working-class struggle to economic struggle, and denied the role and importance of political parties, and so on. It was also expressed in the penetration of some anarchist propositions, especially on tactics, into working-class party programmes, and the appearance within Marxist parties of "Left" deviations, which were always as dangerous as reformism and revisionism.

This class doctrine, alien to the proletariat, which substitutes the dogmatic catchword for the revolutionary idea, sectarianism for true proletarian organisation, adventurism springing from voluntarist conceptions for well-conceived tactics based on a sober view of the objective factors, and utopian visions about absolute individual freedom for the scientific analysis of the laws of social development, has done and continues to do a great deal of harm to the world working-class movement. For all these reasons the founders of Marxism, and Lenin after them, have carried on a relentless struggle against every brand of anarchist ideology and all its manifestations of influence on the working class.

It is almost a hundred years since Marx and Engels in their joint work, *Fictitious Splits in the International*, directed against the anarchists, said that "in every new historical phase old mistakes reappear momentarily".* Even then anarchism was already an "old mistake", and events in the intervening period have borne out this view. Although Marx and Engels, and Lenin after them, showed anarchism to be scientifically untenable, its strategy and tactics faulty, and its views harmful to the revolutionary proletarian move-

* See p. 73 of this volume.—*Ed.*

ment and all liberation struggle in general—and this has been confirmed by life itself and the practice of everyday struggle—the old mistakes do indeed tend to recur both in the sphere of social thought and mankind's spiritual development, and in the sphere of practical revolutionary struggle.

The writings of Marx and Engels show that scientific communism emerged and took shape in sharp and relentless criticism of and separation from the set of ideas which subsequently constituted the body of anarchist views.

As they elaborated their world outlook, putting forward and substantiating the idea of the decisive role the masses have to play in history, and of the proletariat's historical mission being determined by socio-economic factors, Marx and Engels of necessity sharply criticised the subjective idealism and individualism which many radicals among the German intellectuals at the time displayed. It was in *The German Ideology* that Marx and Engels fully exposed the "Left" petty-bourgeois trends as being hostile to the proletariat's scientific revolutionary outlook, and drew the final line of demarcation between them. One reason why Marx and Engels wrote their joint work, apart from the need to formulate their views, in contrast to the existing philosophical systems, was the appearance in October 1844 of Stirner's book, *The Unique and His Property*, and a number of articles. The appearance of Stirner's book meant that anarchism was taking shape as a definite ideological trend, summing up its credo. *The German Ideology* was the first systematic exposition of the new world outlook, the materialist view of history, which had been formulated in sharp polemics with different philosophical systems, including anarchism. From the standpoint of the new outlook, Marx and Engels subjected Stirner's conception to a comprehensive critique. They stressed that his idealistic constructions were completely irrelevant to the actual laws of social development. They stressed that "people won freedom for themselves each time to the extent that was dictated and permitted not by their ideal of man, but by the existing productive forces."* In contrast to the extreme individualism propounded by anarchism, Marx and Engels substantiated the proposi-

* K. Marx and F. Engels, *The German Ideology*, Moscow, 1964, p. 475.—*Ed.*

tion of the proletariat's historical mission, as the only class which in virtue of its nature takes revolutionary action to transform the world and is eventually to lead society to the construction of a communist system, under which every individual would find the best conditions for giving the fullest development to all his capacities. They stressed that "only in community with others has each individual the means of cultivating his gifts in all directions; only in the community, therefore, is personal freedom possible."* *The German Ideology* not only exposed Stirner's specious revolutionary views, but for the first time laid bare the class roots of anarchism as an essentially petty-bourgeois ideology.

From the very start of their revolutionary activity, Marx and Engels directed their efforts to uniting the progressive representatives of the working-class movement, and equipping them with a scientific theory, which meant the establishment of a proletarian party. A most important element in solving this historic task was the struggle against "Left" sectarian and anarchist ideas, and the efforts to overcome the disjunction and isolation of the working-class movement. Beginning with the first proletarian organisation they set up—the Brussels Communist Correspondents' Committee— Marx and Engels tirelessly fought against the elements of anarchist ideology, which saw the revolution as a spontaneous riot, and denied the need for the proletariat's participation in political struggle, spreading the idea of a primitive egalitarian communism. What Marx and Engels most sharply opposed was dogmatism, the denial of the need to make a scientific analysis of reality as the basis of all revolutionary activity, and a scornful attitude to the masses. Addressing a sitting of the Brussels Committee, Marx said: "To address the working man without a strictly scientific idea and a positive doctrine is to engage in an empty and dishonest preaching game, which assumes an inspired prophet, on the one hand, and nothing but asses listening to him with gaping mouths, on the other.... Ignorance has never yet helped anyone!"**

* K. Marx and F. Engels, *The German Ideology*, Moscow, 1964, p. 91.—*Ed.*
** *Reminiscences about K. Marx and F. Engels*, Moscow, 1956, pp. 281, 282.—*Ed.*

Marx's book, *The Poverty of Philosophy*, aimed against Proudhon's views, had an important part to play in the struggle against petty-bourgeois socialism, and in the spread of scientific communism. In criticising Proudhon's petty-bourgeois reformist views, Marx also laid considerable emphasis on criticising his anarchist views, above all his negative attitude to workers' strike action, and struggle to improve their material condition. Marx showed Proudhon's views—constituting something like a peaceful variant of anarchism—to be antithetical to and incompatible with the scientific outlook, with special emphasis on a critique of dogmatism as the common feature of every brand of petty-bourgeois socialism.

The activity of Marx and Engels in the League of Communists and on the editorial board of the *Neue Rheinische Zeitung* during the 1848-1849 revolution marked a whole epoch in the development of the working-class movement, and an important stage in bringing together scientific communism and the working-class movement. An important feature of their activity was the struggle against "Left" sectarianism and "Left" rhetoric. The very establishment of the Communist League signified a break with the old forms of workers' organisation and the traditions of the conspiratorial groups and sects, something that was clearly evident even as the Rules of the League were adopted. It was based, for the first time, on organisational principles which were in line with the principles of scientific communism, and which were fundamentally different from those workers' and socialist organisations had been guided by until then.

In that period, Marx and Engels directed their struggle to overcoming the "Left" sectarian views of the proletariat's attitude to bourgeois-democratic changes, and the proletariat's role and place in a bourgeois-democratic revolution in the historical conditions at the time. In their articles written in that period, Marx and Engels showed that the working class stood to gain from completing the bourgeois changes, and giving society a democratic structure, and opposed every attempt to isolate the working class from the general democratic camp.

After the defeat of the 1848-1849 revolution, the struggle against "Left" sectarian views became extremely important.

Marx saw the situation as a forced lull in the revolutionary
struggle and put forward the task of rallying together the
leading fighters under the banner of scientific communism,
restoring and expanding the ties disrupted by the victory
of the reaction, and organising and preparing the revolutionary fighters for the coming battles. In these conditions,
adventurism and refusal to reckon with the realities of the
situation could merely compound the losses suffered by the
working-class movement. Marx and Engels said the petty-
bourgeois conspirators were "alchemists of the revolution",
and showed their aim to be a forced acceleration of revolutionary process through action by individuals, instead of
organising massive revolutionary struggle. Marx and Engels
vigorously fought against those who advocated such tactics
in the Communist League, the "Left" faction of Willich and
Schapper. The discussion in the League showed that the
tactical differences stemmed from profound theoretical differences. Willich denied the need to determine the material
prerequisites for establishing communism, and the need to
tackle the tasks of bourgeois-democratic changes before
going on to communist construction. Marx showed the connection between the failure to understand that revolution
was a complex and drawn-out process, and the neglect of
the fundamental laws of social development by the "Left"
sectarians, and said: "The German national outlook, which
flatters the national feelings of German artisans, is substituted for the Manifesto's universal views. The idealistic
view is put forward in place of the Manifesto's materialist
view. The *will* is set up in place of the actual relations as
the main thing in revolution. While we say to the workers:
'You will perhaps need to go through another 15, 20 or 50
years of civil war to change the existing conditions and
make yourselves capable of exercising domination,' they are
told instead: 'We must take over *at once*, and if not, then we
can all go to sleep'."*

The struggle against anarchism attained the highest pitch
in the First International—the International Working Men's
Association—the first massive international organisation of
the proletariat, whose activity was a turning point in the

---

* Marx/Engels, *Werke*, Bd. 8, S. 598.—*Ed.*

history of the world working-class movement. In that period, a great stride forward was made in bringing together scientific theory and the mass movement, and the ideological and organisational foundation laid for the establishment of proletarian parties. The First International was capable of fulfilling this historic mission because of the tireless struggle of Marx and Engels, the founders and true leaders of the Association, against every brand of anarchist ideology, a struggle which they carried to an organisational demarcation between the truly revolutionary majority of the Association and anarchist organisations.

During the early years of the First International, anarchism had not yet taken shape as an independent and formalised movement within the Association. Anarchist views were variously shared by Proudhon's French followers, who also propounded utopian reformist ideas, by the Belgian collectivist Proudhonists, and some Swiss members of the International, all of whom took the typical anarchist view of the state as the root-cause of all evil, denied the importance of political struggle, and the importance for the working-class movement of the national-liberation struggle, and so on. Many anarchist ideas were exploded at the early congresses of the International and the discussions within its local sections, with the development of the proletariat's struggle and Marx's summing up of its experience as the basis of the ideological struggle and the education of the masses acting as the crucial factor in this process.

It was the emergence in the International of Bakuninism, a new adversary of scientific communism, that led to more intense struggle against anarchism, and increased the danger of this brand of petty-bourgeois ideas.

Bakuninism, a brand of pre-Marxian petty-bourgeois socialism, was the most pronounced expression of anarchist ideas. Bakunin's theory was a reflection of the backward economic conditions in Russia after the 1861 reform, and of the conditions prevailing in the economically less developed countries of Western Europe, and it is this that gave it an international character.

Bakunin's anarchism expressed the desperate mood of the downtrodden and deprived masses, the peasantry and the urban petty bourgeoisie, who had lost faith in the political leaders of various bourgeois parties, and who were unable to find their way towards organised class struggle. Hence the sharp criticism of inequality, oppression and exploitation, the impassioned advocacy of socialism, and the calls to world revolution and the destruction of all the institutions of the old society, all of which went hand in hand with the preaching of extreme individualism, claims that society was opposed to the individual, and demands of absolute freedom for the individual and abolition of all authority, subordination and discipline.

From its inception, Bakuninism was avowedly hostile to the theory and tactics of scientific communism. From the outset, Bakunin and his followers set themselves the task of fighting the influence of Marxism, and taking over leadership in the International, setting up for that purpose their own organisations—the International Alliance of Socialist Democracy, which claimed membership in the International, while retaining its own programme and rules, and a secret Alliance, to carry on subversive operations within the Association. From 1868 on, with the establishment of the Alliance, an acute ideological struggle developed in the International, in the course of which Marx and Engels attacked Bakuninism and gave a comprehensive critique of the anarchist outlook as a whole of its strategy and tactics, exposed the Bakuninists' splitting activity and showed that Bakuninism was petty-bourgeois and alien to the working-class movement.

The important thing is to note the nature of this criticism: Marx and Engels countered the declarative and speculative anarchist propositions and their dogmatism and idealism with a concrete analysis of reality and the experience of the working-class movement (with the summed-up experience of the Paris Commune being of tremendous importance in this respect), and showed the dialectical laws of the mass revolutionary struggle. They countered the revolutionary rhetoric with a scientific solution of the fundamental problems in the revolutionary transformation of the world.

Marx and Engels criticised the characteristic anarchist approach of detaching the national-liberation movement from the proletarian struggle, and proved that the struggle of the oppressed peoples and the working class of the metropolitan countries must be merged in a single revolutionary tide, that the proletariat had a vital stake in the solution of the national problem, and that there could be no fundamental solution to this problem without its active participation.

Marx and Engels showed the need for an alliance of the working class and the peasantry, and the great complexity of the problem of drawing the peasantry into socialist revolution and—what was most important—restructuring its economy on socialist lines. At the same time, they proved that this was the only way ultimately meeting the interests of the peasantry itself. This dealt a blow at the efforts to idealise peasant revolutionism, in contrast to the proletarian revolutionary attitude, and at the voluntarist declaration about the possibility of decreeing the socialist transformation of the countryside immediately after the revolution.

Marx and Engels showed the importance and interconnection of all the forms of proletarian struggle—economic, political and ideological—and proved that to ignore any of these meant keeping the working class passive, and actually refusing to struggle for the revolutionary transformation of society, regardless of the ultra-revolutionary catchwords that were used.

Marx and Engels demonstrated that the anarchist dogmas about "abolishing the state" as the first step in the revolution, destroying authority of every kind, and introducing total decentralisation as a necessary condition of the revolution, were quite untenable. They countered all these theories with a materialist analysis of the nature and essence of the state, and established the proposition that the bourgeois state machine had to be broken up and replaced by the proletarian dictatorship, as the state of the transition period. Marx and Engels said the dictatorship of the proletariat could be a temporary one, a stage in the withering away of the political state, and wrote about the state system of the future communist society, meaning above all the need to manage social large-scale production. In contrast to the anarchist view of the proletarian dictatorship as being coercion pure and simple, Marx and Engels emphasised the creative functions of the proletarian dictatorship and its role in building the new society as its main function.

The form of organisation of the revolutionary forces, above all the need to set up an independent party of the working class in every country, and the forms and methods of working-class struggle, were problems of especial importance in the polemics with the anarchists in the period of the First International. They were central at the 1871 London Conference, and the 1872 Hague Congress of the International. During the discussion at the Conference, Marx and Engels drew on the experience of the Paris Commune to explode the anarchist view that there was no need for political struggle and parties, and that craft unions would do as well. In his well-known speech at the London Conference on September 21, Engels said: "We want the abolition of classes. How can this be achieved? By the political dominion of the proletariat. ... But revolution is the supreme political act; he who desires it must desire also the means, the political action that prepares it, that gives the workers their education in revolution. ... But the politics that must be conducted are workers' politics; the workers' party must be not merely an appendage of some of the bourgeois parties, but a fully independent party which has its goal and its own policy."* Marx added: "We must tell the governments: we know you to be an armed force directed against the proletarians; we shall act against you peacefully wherever possible, and use arms whenever necessary".**

This was a blow at the whole anarchist concept of political struggle, the voluntarist approach to revolution, and denial of the need for a proletarian dictatorship. The resolutions adopted by the Conference and later by the Hague Congress proclaimed the need to set up proletarian parties, outlined the fundamental propositions on the party's organisational forms and strategy, and provided the ideological basis for the fight against anarchism. They defined, in general terms, the tasks before the working-class movement for a whole period of its development.

However, the battle was joined not only on theoretical lines. The Bakuninists opposed the principles of the proletarian party approach, which, thanks to the tireless efforts of Marx and Engels, were making headway in the working-class movement, and in a sense provided the basis for the organi-

---

* See pp. 51-52 of this volume.—*Ed.*
** Marx/Engels, *Werke*, Bd. 17, S. 652.—*Ed.*

sation of the International. The Bakuninists opposed this creative search for new, proletarian forms of organisation, by putting forward essentially old forms and methods of organisation, which had been accepted by petty-bourgeois conspiratorial societies, an organisation which Bakunin himself compared with that of the "Society of Jesus". This was an attempt, springing from lack of faith in the revolutionary consciousness of the masses, to destroy the massive working-class organisations and to set up a kind of bureaucracy of functionaries,. which was absolutely unaccountable to the masses, and which acted entirely on orders issued from above, from the movement's secret centre.

All of this the Bakuninists sought to realise within the International, using the organisations it had already set up, and capitalising on the prestige it enjoyed among the workers. To attain their ends, they attacked the organisational principles of the Association itself, principles whose defence Marx and Engels closely bound up with their critique of the Bakuninists' ideological constructions. An important aspect of the writings and correspondence of Marx and Engels, especially after they had learned of the existence of the secret Alliance (April 1872), was exposure of the Bakuninists' splitting activity, which revealed the methods of struggle characteristic of "Left" sectarianism. Putting emphasis on the most important fact—that the Bakuninists tried to rally all the forces hostile to scientific communism behind a screen of revolutionary declarations, Engels wrote: "For the first time in the history of the working-class struggles, we stumble over a secret conspiracy plotted in the midst of that class, and intended to undermine, not the existing capitalist *régime*, but the very Association in which that *régime* finds its most energetic opponent. It is a conspiracy got up to hamper the proletarian movement."* In their critique of anarchism, Marx and Engels stressed the fact that the Bakuninists were trying to split the working-class movement and to demolish the unity that had already been gained, a unity that was the earnest of victories for the proletariat.

Characterising the activity of the secret Alliance, they wrote: "Here we have a society which, under the mask of

---

* See p. 81 of this volume.—*Ed.*

the most extreme anarchism, directs its blows not against the existing governments but against the revolutionaries who refuse to accept its dogma and leadership ... it infiltrates the ranks of the international organisation of the working class, at first attempts to dominate it and, when this plan fails, sets to work to disorganise it. It brazenly substitutes its sectarian programme and narrow ideas for the broad programme and great aspirations of our Association; it organises within the public sections of the International its own little secret sections which obey the same instructions ... in its newspapers it publicly attacks all those who refuse to submit to its will, and by its own avowal provokes open warfare within our ranks. It resorts to any means, any disloyalty to achieve its ends."* Historians of every trend—both anarchist and Social-Democratic—have repeatedly reproached Marx and Engels for having described in their writings, especially in "The Alliance of Socialist Democracy and the International Working Men's Association", these "means", which included the use of physical force against those who did not accept their views, and frauds and hoaxes. Indeed, Marx and Engels succeeded in exposing the anarchists' revolutionary rhetoric and showed that their methods naturally sprang from their lack of faith in the proletariat's revolutionary potential, and from the whole system of "Left" sectarian views and their petty-bourgeois character.

It was not only the triumph of the programme and organisational principles of Marxism at the Hague Congress of the First International, but also the organisational separation from the anarchists, which Marx and Engels secured, that was an important success for the working-class movement and an earnest of its further advance.

But the victory scored in the First International did not signify an end to the struggle against anarchism and "Left" sectarianism. In the period of the First International Marx and Engels confronted anarchism as a relatively massive movement, but later on they were to face a new phenomenon, the influence of anarchist ideology on members of Social-Democratic parties, the emergence of "Left"-sectarian groups within them (like the so-called "Young" within the German

---

* See p. 106 of this volume.—*Ed.*

Social-Democratic Party), with anarchist mistakes made by some party leaders. In guiding the Social-Democratic parties of the Second International, Engels constantly warned against the danger of sectarianism and "Left" opportunism, emphasising that if the adventurism and voluntarism displayed by these party members won out they could well "ruin even the strongest party with millions in its ranks, to the well-merited applause of the whole hostile world".* Engels repeatedly stressed that such "theories" had nothing in common with scientific communism.

A great contribution in implementing the ideas of Marx and Engels was made by Lenin, the founder and leader of the Bolshevik Party. He developed Marxism in the new historical conditions and formulated the theory, strategy and tactics of the international communist movement on the basis of his generalisation of new economic and political phenomena in the epoch of imperialism, and the vast experience of the international working-class movement. The whole of Lenin's activity in preparing the working class for the epoch-making exploit—the Great October Socialist Revolution, which ushered in a new epoch in the history of mankind—in carrying out the revolution, in laying the foundations of socialism, and in uniting the communist movement throughout the world was closely connected and interwoven with his tireless struggle against any departure from Marxism.

Lenin took an open stand not only against reformism and its influence on the working-class movement, but also against the influence and spread of the anarchist ideology. In so doing he had to attack not so much avowed anarchist trends and groups, like the S.R.s, who exerted no great influence on the working class of Russia, as the spread of essentially anarchist views camouflaged as "true", "revolutionary" Marxism.

From the very start of his activity as theorist and practitioner of the revolutionary proletarian movement, Lenin fought against the dogmatic view of Marxism, and in his own activity always took the creative approach to Marxism as a living and constantly developing doctrine. Lenin insisted

* Marx/Engels, *Werke*, Bd. 22, S. 69.—*Ed.*

on loyalty to the principles of scientific communism, but rejected every cliché and dogma, and always criticised attempts to use the letter of Marxism as a cover for repudiating its living spirit and the demands of the time.

The Marxist, Lenin said, must "take cognisance of real life, of the true facts of *reality*, and not cling to a theory of yesterday, which, like all theories, at best only outlines the main and the general, only *comes near* to embracing life in all its complexity."*

It was this implacable attitude to dogmatism, to the neglect of dialectics, to those who "regard 'slogans', not as a practical conclusion from a class analysis and assessment of a particular moment in history, but as a charm with which a party or a tendency has been provided once and for all,"** that was the key factor behind the emergence and development of Bolshevism, and the development of the international communist movement. Lenin said that "Bolshevism took shape, developed and became steeled in the long years of struggle against *petty-bourgeois revolutionism*, which smacks of anarchism, or borrows something from the latter and, in all essential matters, does not measure up to the conditions and requirements of a consistently proletarian class struggle".***

Lenin constantly criticised avowed anarchist trends, "Left" rhetoric and the "infantile disorder" of "Leftism" in the young Communist Parties. He laid bare the social roots of petty-bourgeois revolutionism, and the reasons for its influence on the working-class movement, which consisted in the fact that the proletariat was surrounded by petty-bourgeois elements, and this has caused and continues to cause relapses into petty-bourgeois individualism, anarchism, vacillation and adventurism. At the same time, Lenin showed that the spread and influence of "Left" rhetoric was due to inadequate experience, and the error of treating some forms and methods of struggle as an absolute. Lenin wrote: "True revolutionaries have mostly come a cropper when they began to write 'revolution' with a capital R, to elevate 'revolution' to something almost divine, to lose their heads, to lose the abi-

* V. I. Lenin, *Collected Works*, Vol. 24, p. 45.—*Ed.*
** Ibid., Vol. 15, p. 154.—*Ed.*
*** See p. 304 of this volume.—*Ed.*

lity to reflect, weigh and ascertain in the coolest and most dispassionate manner at what moment, under what circumstances and in which sphere of action you must act in a revolutionary manner, and at what moment, under what circumstances and in which sphere you must turn to reformist action."*

The Bolshevik Party's strength and fighting capacity were largely due to Lenin's implacable attitude to ideological vacillations, to the influence of alien views, and to the efforts to revise Marxism from Right or "Left".

In 1908, an acute ideological struggle flared up within the Party against a group of otzovists over the participation in the reactionary parliament and legal workers' organisations. These men had been tantalised by revolutionary catchwords and ignored the changes that had taken place in the situation, so that their calls for staying out of parliament and organisations in fact deprived the Party of the possibility of exerting an influence on the masses through the use of legal means. Lenin said this was the worst kind of "caricature of Bolshevism". The otzovist leaders were expelled from the Party, but the struggle against the trend continued. In the course of it Lenin showed that behind all this talk about loyalty to Marxism, etc., lurked anarchism, an anti-Marxist doctrine which did harm to the working-class movement. Lenin took the otzovists as an example to illustrate one of the worst flaws of anarchist tactics, when he wrote: "In what lies the fallacy of the anarchists' argument? It lies in the fact that, owing to their radically incorrect ideas of the course of social development, they are unable to take into account those peculiarities of the concrete political (and economic) situation in different countries which determine the specific significance of one or another means of struggle *for a given period of time*."**

In 1918, one of the most trying periods of the young Soviet Republic, an acute ideological struggle flared up in the Party against a "Left"-wing deviation from Marxism over the conclusion of the peace of Brest-Litovsk, an "ignominious" peace, as Lenin called it, but one which was being imposed on the

---

* V. I. Lenin, *Collected Works*, Vol. 33, p. 111.—*Ed.*
** See p. 236 of this volume.—*Ed.*

Soviet power. Both the Trotskyites and the Left-Communist group, displaying great enthusiasm over "Leftist" talk about a "world revolution", and so on, came out against the conclusion of the peace. Lenin attacked the phrase-mongers, those who were infected with the "itch of the revolutionary phrase", and taught the Communists to make a strict reckoning of the forces, showing that "Leftist" talk covered up lack of faith in the revolutionary potential of the masses, and that Trotskyism and honest Party members who were confused on that issue were inviting the Party to abandon its realistic policy and to take adventurist action which was counselled by despair and was sure to end in defeat. Warning against this concrete danger to the Party line, Lenin attacked "Leftist" phrase-mongering and adventurism as a whole and showed that it had petty-bourgeois class roots. He wrote: "We must fight against the revolutionary phrase, we have to fight it, we absolutely must fight it, so that at some future time people will not say of us the bitter truth that 'a revolutionary phrase about revolutionary war ruined the revolution'."* His work, *Left-Wing Childishness and the Petty-Bourgeois Mentality*, is part of the treasury of Marxist writings against "Left" opportunism.

Lenin played an exceptional role in fostering the young cadres of the newly established Communist Parties and in helping them to formulate the correct strategy and tactics. The activity of Lenin and the Bolsheviks in establishing the Communist International, as a direct continuation of the struggle Lenin had carried on in the international arena to unite all true revolutionary forces within the international working-class movement, had a great part to play in developing the communist movement. The activity of the Third International was all geared to the tasks of strengthening this movement ideologically and organisationally, tasks which were solved in ideological struggle against revisionism and reformism, and in overcoming "Left" sectarianism. Naturally, as a kind of backlash to the sway of the reformists, sectarianism could well become a serious obstacle in the way of the Communist Parties' developing into massive revolutionary parties of the working class. Erroneous views on the Party's

---

* V. I. Lenin, *Collected Works*, Vol. 27, p. 29.—*Ed.*

attitude to the class and the masses, to Communists' participation in reactionary trade unions and bourgeois parliaments, and denial in some instances that compromises and agreements were admissible and necessary, in fact led to isolation of the Communists, although in the early stages this "Left" danger met the mood among some sections of the working class. By 1920, the "Leftist" mistakes made by some Parties became quite considerable, and a natural source of alarm.

The task of formulating truly Marxist-Leninist programmes and tactical and organisational principles for the movement was fulfilled by the Second and Third Congresses of the Comintern, which were important milestones in the cohesion of the Communist Parties and the triumph of the truly revolutionary doctrine. The deliberations of the Second Congress and its decisions were entirely based on Lenin's famous book, *"Left-Wing" Communism—an Infantile Disorder* (1920), which became an invaluable weapon in the struggle for consistent revolutionary tactics, and against the doctrinaire and sectarian approach.

It dealt with the most important theoretical questions of Marxism and the practice of the working-class movement, the problem of the socialist revolution. Summing up the vast experience of the Bolsheviks and of the revolutionary struggle of the masses, Lenin showed how the revolution was to be prepared and carried forward to victory, with special emphasis on the role of the Party, and what Party can lead the working class to victory.

He wrote: "Without a party of iron that has been tempered in the struggle, a party enjoying the confidence of all honest people in the class in question, a party capable of watching and influencing the mood of the masses, such a struggle cannot be waged successfully."* He argued that the Party must show constant concern for the purity of its theory, warding off ideological attacks against Marxism from both Right and "Left". He stressed that the Party could not become the leading force of the working class unless it administered an ideological defeat on anarchism and overcame "Leftist" attitudes. In the light of this basic stand, he examined all the concrete aspects of the disorder in the movement.

---

* Ibid., Vol. 31, pp. 44-45.—*Ed.*

Lenin oriented the Communist Parties towards winning over the masses, and showed the ways and means. The Second Congress of the Comintern, helped by Lenin's tireless efforts in raising the movement's theoretical level, played a great role in establishing the principles of truly revolutionary Marxism, and dealt a heavy blow at the "Leftist" danger. However, "Leftist" sectarianism was not to be overcome at one blow. In fact, it became even more dangerous towards the end of 1920 and the beginning of 1921, as the revolutionary tide ebbed. The struggle against it was continued by the Third Congress of the Comintern, on the eve of which Lenin wrote: "If the Congress is not going to wage a vigorous offensive against... 'Leftist' stupidities, the whole movement is doomed."*

The Congress sharply condemned "Left" sectarianism. By formulating a concrete slogan—"Into the masses!"—it showed the practical way of overcoming it, set before the Communist Parties an exceptionally important task, and determined the main line of their activity.

The tireless activity of Lenin and the Bolshevik Party in fighting both Right and "Left" opportunism laid the foundation for the great successes of the present-day communist movement, the most powerful movement of our day. The more than a century experience in the development of the working-class movement and of Marxist theory shows that any attack on scientific communism and the strategy and tactics of the communist movement, regardless of how "Leftist" and ultra-revolutionary the catchwords used as a cover, is bound to fail, and that Marxism-Leninism has been proved correct by the experience of the movement and by life itself. Experience shows that the masses are never carried away by the "Leftist" phrase for very long, and that the working class and all the truly revolutionary forces soon come to see the pseudo-revolutionary conjurers for the charlatans that they are, leaving them marooned from the powerful tide of massive revolutionary struggle to transform the world. The writings of the Marxist-Leninist classics have been and remain a powerful weapon in overcoming "Left" sectarianism.

N. Y. Kolpinsky

---

* V. I. Lenin, *Collected Works*, Vol. 32, p. 468.—*Ed.*

Karl Marx
and
Frederick Engels

FREDERICK ENGELS

THE CATCHWORD: "ABOLITION OF THE STATE" AND THE GERMAN "FRIENDS OF ANARCHY"[1]

"For Communists abolition of the state makes sense only as the necessary result of the abolition of classes, with whose disappearance the need for the organised power of one class for the purpose of holding down the other classes will automatically disappear. The abolition of the state in *bourgeois* countries means the reduction of state power to the North American level. Class contradictions there are not fully developed, and class conflicts are always palliated by the outflow of the proletarian surplus population to the West; state interference is reduced to a minimum in the East and entirely absent in the West. Abolition of the state in *feudal* countries means the abolition of feudalism and the establishment of a conventional bourgeois state. In *Germany* the slogan conceals either a cowardly flight from actual concrete struggles, the extravagant bogus transformation of *bourgeois* liberty into absolute freedom and independence of the *individual*, or finally the indifference of the bourgeois towards any form of state so long as it does not hamper the development of bourgeois interests. The fact that the abolition of the state 'in the higher sense' is advocated in so absurd a manner is of course no fault of the Berliners Stirner and Faucher. La plus belle fille de la France ne peut donner que ce qu'elle a."* (*Neue Rheinische Zeitung. Politisch-ökonomische Revue*, Heft IV, p. 58.[2])

---

* The most beautiful girl in France cannot give more than she has.—*Ed.*

Abolition of the State, *anarchy*, has meanwhile become a widely used catchword in Germany. A few German followers of Proudhon[3], Berlin's "superior" democrats and even the forgotten "most noble minds of the nation", members of the Stuttgart Parliament and the Imperial Regency,[4] have —each in his own way—adopted this wild-sounding catchword.

All these factions agree in their desire to maintain the existing *bourgeois society*. Since they uphold bourgeois society they are bound to uphold the rule of the bourgeoisie and in Germany even the winning of this rule by the bourgeoisie; they differ from the real members of the bourgeoisie only in the matter of unusual form, which gives them the semblance of "going further", of "going further than anyone else". This semblance vanishes on all real conflicts; in every case these exponents of anarchy did their utmost to stem anarchy when faced with the *real* anarchy of revolutionary crises, when the masses fought with "brute force". In the final analysis this much praised "anarchy" amounts in substance to what in more advanced countries is termed "order". The "friends of anarchy" in Germany find themselves in complete and friendly agreement with the "friends of order" in France.

In so far as the friends of anarchy do not depend on the ideas of the Frenchmen Proudhon and Girardin, in so far as their views are of Germanic origin, they all stem from one common source—*Stirner*. The period of decline of German philosophy has in general provided the Democratic Party in Germany with most of its stock phrases. Even before the February revolution[5], the concepts and phrases of the latest German men of letters, especially of Feuerbach and Stirner, had, in a rather diluted form, become part of the general literary knowledge and of journalism, and these in their turn were the main sources of the democratic spokesmen in the post-March[6] period. In particular Stirner's advocacy of statelessness was eminently suited to impart to Proudhon's anarchy and Girardin's abolition of the state the "higher solemnity" of German philosophy. Although Stirner's book *Der Einzige und sein Eigenthum* is forgotten, his notions and especially his critique of the State reappear among the friends of anarchy. Having already examined the sources upon which these gentlemen draw, in so far as they were of French origin[7], we now have to plunge once more into the depths of antediluvian German philosophy in order to examine their German sources. If one is obliged to deal with current German polemics it is more pleasant to rely on the original inventor of a particular mode of thought than on the dealers in second-hand goods.

> O Muses, saddle Pegasus for me once more
> To ride forth to the ancient land of romance.[8]

Before turning to the above-mentioned book of Stirner we must carry our thoughts back to the "old romantic land" and the forgotten period in which the book was published. Taking advantage of the government's financial difficulties, the Prussian bourgeoisie began to win political power, and alongside the bourgeois-constitutional movement, the communist movement was steadily spreading among the proletariat. The bourgeois elements of society, who still needed the support of the proletarians to attain their own goal, were everywhere forced to affect a certain brand of socialism; the conservative and feudal party was also obliged to make promises to the proletariat. Side by side with the struggle of the bourgeoisie and peasantry against the feudal nobility and the bureaucracy there was the struggle of the workers against the bourgeoisie, and in between these a number of intermediate forms embracing all species of socialism— reactionary, petty-bourgeois and bourgeois socialism. All these struggles and aspirations were held down and prevented from being given expression by the authorities, the censorship, and the ban on association and assembly. Such was the position of the parties at the time when German philosophy was celebrating its last and rather meagre successes.

From the very outset the censorship compelled all more or less undesirable elements to use a mode of expression that was as abstract as possible; German philosophical tradition, which had just reached the stage of the complete dissolution of the Hegelian school, provided such a terminology. The struggle against religion still continued. The more difficult it became to wage a political struggle in the press against the existing regime, the more eagerly was it carried on in the form of a religious and philosophical fight. German philosophy in its most diluted form became the common possession of "the educated", and the more it became so the more diluted, incoherent and trite did the philosophers' views become, and the more did this dissolution and triteness raise them in the estimation of the "educated" public.

The muddle in the minds of "the educated" was appalling and grew steadily worse. It was a veritable medley of German, French and English ideas, ancient, medieval and modern. The muddle was all the greater for all these ideas having been taken from second, third or fourth hands and circulated in so garbled a form as to make them almost unrecognisable. This fate overtook not only the ideas of French and English liberals and socialists but also those of Germans, e.g. Hegel. The entire literature of that period and, as we shall see, Stirner's work in particular provide numerous proofs of this, and contemporary German literature is today still suffering badly from the consequences.

The philosophical shadow-boxing that went on below the surface of this confusion was a reflection of the real struggle. Every new philosophical trend attracted the general attention of "the educated" who in Germany consisted of a multitude of idle minds, young lawyers, aspirants to teacher's posts, frustrated theologians, penniless physicians, writers, etc., etc. For these people each of these "new turns" meant a historical phase discarded and disposed of for good. For instance, as soon as bourgeois liberalism was criticised in any way by some philosopher or other, it was dead, expunged from the pages of history and destroyed for all practical purposes as well. The same applies to republicanism, socialism, etc. The extent to which these stages of development were "destroyed", "disintegrated" and "disposed of" was revealed later, during the revolution, when they played a leading part, while the philosophers who had destroyed them were no longer remembered.

The muddled form and content, the arrogant banality and bombastic drivel, the abysmal triviality and dialectical poverty of the latest German philosophy surpasses everything that ever appeared in this field, and is matched only by the amazing gullibility of the public, which took all this at its face value, regarding it as the latest word, as "something unheard of". The German nation, the "thorough"...*

Written in October 1850

First published in the journal
Pod znamenem marksizma, No. 6, 1927

Translated from
the German

* The manuscript ends here.—*Ed.*

MARX TO ENGELS IN MANCHESTER

[London], August 8, 1851

... Now to the *Idée générale de la Révolution au XIX*
siècle par P. J. Proudhon.[9] When I first wrote to you about
the book, I had read only excerpts from it—often garbled
ones. I can send you now an σκελετὸν.* To start with:
the book contains well-written attacks on Rousseau,
Robespierre, the Mountain,[10] etc. The force of the actual
development, to use the language of the immortal Ruge, is
as follows:

First essay. Only the reaction brought about the development of the revolution.

*Second essay. Are there sufficient grounds for a revolu-
tion in the nineteenth century?*

The revolution of 1789 overthrew the old regime, but it
neglected to create a new society or to create society anew.
Instead of thinking about political economy they were thinking only of politics. At present there is "anarchy of the economic forces" and consequently a "tendency towards an
impoverished society". This can be seen in the division of
labour, in machinery, competition and the credit system. The
growth of pauperism and crime. Furthermore, the importance of the *state* (l'état) has steadily grown; it has been
endowed with all the attributes of the absolute; its indepen-

---

* Outline.—*Ed.*

dence and power has increased. Growth of the national debt. The state supports wealth against poverty. Corruption. The State enslaves society. A new revolution is necessary. It is the task of the revolution to change, to rectify the harmful trend of society. Society itself must not be affected. Arbitrary reorganisation of society is out of the question.

Third essay. The principle of association.

Association is not an economic force but a tenet. It is not something organic and productive as are the division of labour, commerce, exchange, etc. Association must not be confused with collective power. Collective power is an impersonal action, association a voluntary commitment. Association is by its very nature sterile, even harmful, since it restricts the freedom of the worker. People have ascribed to the social contract powers which are due only to the division of labour, exchange, the collective power. When associations are set up to carry through important enterprises, then the accomplishment of the latter is due not to the *principle* of the association but to its *measures*. People will submit to the association only if they receive a satisfactory compensation. The productive association is of benefit only to weak or lazy members. It stands for solidarity and common responsibility towards others. In general association is only applicable under certain conditions which depend on the means at its disposal. An association based on family ties and on the law of sacrifice and formed quite irrespective of any external economic considerations—i.e. association for the sake of association—is a purely religious act, a supernatural tie of no practical value, nothing but a myth. Association must not be confused with the new relations which are likely to result from the interdependence of producers and consumers. Association levels the contracting parties, subordinates their freedom to their social duty and divests them of their individuality.

Fourth essay. The principle of authority.

The concept of governmentalism is rooted in family habits and domestic experience. Democracy is the ultimate expression of the evolution of government. The concept of government is contraposed to that of contract. The truly revolutionary motto is—No government! *Absolute power* is very soon compelled to negate itself and to accept limitations in the shape of *laws* and *institutions*. Legislative acts become as innumerable as the interests which they outwardly define. They lapse into the bad infinity. The law is a fetter imposed on the individual from without. *Constitutional monarchy.* A hybrid absurdity. *Universal suffrage.* The prophetic intuition of the multitude is an absurdity. I need neither attorneys nor deputies. Elections, votes, even unanimous ones, decide nothing. According to the voting by universal suffrage Bonaparte is the right man, etc. *Pure democracy or direct government*—invented by Rittinghausen, Considérant, Ledru-Rollin—is an impossibility and an absurdity. Thus this concept of the state carried to extremes demonstrates how nonsensical it is.

Fifth essay. Social liquidation.

1. *National bank.* The Bank of France is to be abolished by decree. It is not to be turned into a national bank, but into a public utility. Interest will be reduced to 1/2 or 1/4 of one per cent.

2. *National debt.* By this measure private capitals are deprived of the discount business; they flow to the stock exchange, the State pays only 1/2 or 1/4 of one per cent, thus putting an end to the interest in interest. The State pays yearly instalments instead of interest, i.e., it reimburses the borrowed capital in annual instalments. Or in other words, it decrees that the interest the State pays in yearly instalments is to be deducted from the principal.

3. *Debts on mortgages. Simple debentures.*

"Interest payable on all debts, mortgages, I.O.U.s, and shares of joint stock companies, is fixed at 1/4 or 1/2 of one per cent. Repayment can only be demanded in the form of yearly instalments. The annual instalment will be 10 per cent for amounts below 2,000 frs., and 5 per cent for amounts above 2,000 frs. To facilitate the repayment of outstanding debts, and to replace the former money-lenders, one of the offices of the national discount bank will be converted into a land mortgage bank; it will be able to grant loans up to a total of 500 million per annum."

4. *Real estate; buildings.*

Decree: "All rent payments will be treated as payments made on account of the property, whose value is assumed to be twenty times that of the rent. With every payment of

rent the tenant acquires a proportional and joint share in
the house he occupies and in all the buildings let as dwellings to citizens. The property thus repaid gradually passes
to the local administration, which as a result of the repayment takes over the mortgage and prerogatives in the name
of the body of tenants, and ensures their right to live at
their dwelling place indefinitely at cost price. The local administration can negotiate separate agreements with the
property owners for the purpose of immediately liquidating
and redeeming the leased properties. In this case and in
order that the present generation be able to enjoy reduced
rents, these local administrations can immediately introduce
a reduction in rent on houses for which they have signed
agreements; the reduction is to be calculated in such a way
that amortisation will take place within thirty years. With
regard to the repair, management and maintenance of the
buildings and the construction of new ones, the local authorities will have to deal with building organisations or associations of building workers according to the principles and
rules of the new social contract. Owners who are the sole
occupiers of their houses may retain their property as long
as they think it is in their interest to do so."

5. *Landed property.*

"By paying rent for the use of a land lot the tenant farmer
acquires a share in the property tantamount to a mortgage.
As soon as the land is fully paid off it is taken over by the
commune, which takes the place of the former owner and
shares with the farmer the ownership rights and the net
product. The communes may conclude agreements with
property owners who wish to do so with a view to redeeming
rents and immediately repaying the property owners. In
this case the communes will have to attend to the settlement
of cultivators and the delimitation of their land, taking care
to offset as far as possible differences in the size of the plots
by the quality of the land, and to fix the rent in accordance
with the yield. As soon as the land is completely paid off,
all the communes of the republic will have to come to an
arrangement for equalising differences in the quality of the
land lots and also variations in their cultivation. The part
of the rent due to them from the plots in their area is to be
used for this compensation and as a general insurance fund.

From this time on, the old owners who had retained their property rights because they cultivated their land themselves, will be placed on the same footing as the new ones, they will have to pay the same rent and receive the same rights, so that no one is favoured by the chance of location or inheritance and the conditions of farming are equal for all. Land tax is to be abolished. The functions of the rural police are to be taken over by the local councils."

Sixth essay. Organisation of the economic forces.

1. *Credit.* The above-mentioned national bank with its branches. Gradual withdrawal from circulation of gold and silver. Their replacement by paper money. As regards *personal credit*, its fields of application are to be the workers' associations and agricultural and trade societies.

2. *Property.* See "Landed property" described earlier. Given the above-mentioned conditions, one can without the slightest hesitation permit the owners to sell, transfer, alienate or put their property into circulation as they please.... Repayment by yearly instalments being made easy, the value of a real estate may be endlessly divided, exchanged or undergo any conceivable change, without in the least affecting the real estate itself. Agricultural work is opposed to the collective mode.

3. *Division of labour, collective power, machines. Workers' associations.*

Any industry, factory or enterprise which by its nature requires the simultaneous employment of a large number of workers of different trades is to become the seat of a workers' association or corporation. But where the goods can be produced without the combined operation of diverse types of skill, by one individual or one family, there is no room for association. Hence, no associations in small workshops, the handicrafts, shoemaking, tailoring, etc., and among shopkeepers, etc. Associations in *large-scale industry;* here, therefore, *workers' corporations* will be set up. Every member of the association has a joint right to the property of the corporation; he has the right to successively hold all posts in the corporation; his education, tuition and apprenticeship must be organised in such a way that while he is made to carry out his share of the unpleasant and difficult duties, he performs a series of tasks and gains experience, so that when he reaches maturity he has attained an all-round proficiency and receives a sufficient income. The posts are elective and the rules are adopted by the members of the association; wages depend on the nature of the work, the ability and degree of responsibility; both the profits and expenses of the corporation are shared by all members in accordance with the work they perform; everyone is at liberty to leave the association whenever he wishes, to settle his account and relinquish his rights; the corporation in its turn is free to accept new members at any time.... This solves two problems: those of collective power and of division of labour.... During the transition period these workshops are managed by manufacturers, etc.

4. *The determination of value; the organisation of a cheap market.* Remedies have to be taken against the high prices of commodities and their arbitrary fixation. The *fair price* corresponds exactly to (a) the costs of production according to the officially established average costs of the free producers; (b) the wages of the tradesman, or compensation for the advantages the seller forgoes by parting with the article. To induce the tradesman to sell he must be given a guarantee. This can be done in various ways; either the consumers who want to pay a fair price and who are also producers undertake to sell their own products to the tradesman on equal terms—this is already customary among various workers' associations in Paris—or these consumers merely promise the dealer a premium or else a turnover sufficiently large to provide him with an income. For example, in order to make certain that all pay a fair price and receive goods and services of good quality, the State, on behalf of the interests it temporarily represents, and the departments and Communes on behalf of the inhabitants of their respective areas, undertake to guarantee that the entrepreneurs offering the most favourable terms receive either a definite rate of interest on the capital and the material resources used in their enterprises, or a fixed salary, or in appropriate cases are given a sufficient number of orders. In return the tendering parties promise to meet all consumers' requests for the goods and services they have undertaken to supply. For the rest, full scope is left for competition. They have to state the component parts of their prices, the mode of del-

ivery, the duration of their contract and the means of fulfilling it. The sealed tenders submitted within the appointed
time are opened and made public—according to the importance of the contract—8 days, 15 days, one month, or three
months before the award is due to be made. Upon the ex-
piration of each contract new tenders will be invited.

5. *Foreign trade.* As soon as the rate of interest is reduced
tariffs must be reduced, and when interest is done away with
or has dropped to 1/4 or 1/2 of one per cent customs duties
must be abolished.

*Seventh essay. The dissolution of the government in the
economic structure.*

Society without authority. Abolition of cults, the judiciary,
the administration, the police, public education, war, the
navy, etc.—everything couched in the appropriate Stirnerian
language.

Please let me know in detail what you think of this recipe. Greetings.

Yours,

K. Marx

First published in *Der Briefwechsel*
zwischen F. Engels und K. Marx.
Bd. I, Stuttgart, 1913

Translated from
the German and French

ENGELS TO MARX IN LONDON

M[anchester], August 21, 1851

...I am half through Pr[oudhon's] book[11] and think that
your opinion is completely justified.* His appeal to the bourgeoisie, his return to Saint-Simon and a hundred other things
in the critical part alone confirm that he regards the industrial class, the bourgeoisie and proletariat, as intrinsically
identical and brought into contradiction only by the non-
completion of the revolution. The pseudo-philosophical interpretation of history is quite obvious: before the revolution
the industrial class was in the *an sich* state; between 1789
and 1848 in a state of contradiction, negation; Proudhon's
synthesis is to wind up the whole with a flourish.** I have
the impression that the whole thing is a last attempt to defend the bourgeoisie theoretically. Our propositions that the
historically decisive impetus comes from material production,
the class struggle, etc., have been largely accepted, mostly
in a distorted form, and on this—by means of pseudo-He-
gelian jugglery—the experiment is based of seemingly merging the proletariat once more in the bourgeoisie. I have not
yet read the synthetical part. His attacks on Louis Blanc,
Robespierre and Rousseau contain rather nice things here
and there, but on the whole there is nothing more pretentious and superficial than his critique of politics, e.g., where

---

* See pp. 32-38 of this volume.—*Ed.*
** The last eight words are in English in the original. —*Ed.*

he deals with democracy and, like the *Neue Preussische Zeitung*[12] and the entire old historical school, advances the number of persons as an argument and is not ashamed to use petty practical considerations worthy of a schoolboy to construct his systems. And what a grand idea to show that Authority and Freedom are irreconcilable contradictions, and that no form of government can give him a sufficient moral reason why *he* should obey it! Great heavens, why indeed is power needed?

Incidentally, I am convinced that Herr Ewerbeck has let him have his translation of the *Manifesto*,[13] and perhaps secretly also translations of your articles in the *Revue*.[14] Some of the points are definitely stolen from this source, e.g., that government is nothing but the power of one class for suppressing the others, and that it will disappear together with the disappearance of class contradictions. Also many points about the French movement since 1848. I don't think that he found all this in your book against him[15]....

First published in
*Der Briefwechsel zwischen
F. Engels und K. Marx.*
Bd. I, Stuttgart, 1913

Translated from
the German

MARX TO ENGELS IN MANCHESTER

[London], June 20, 1866

... Yesterday there was a discussion in the International Council on the present war.[16] The question had been announced beforehand and our room was very crowded. The Italian gentry too had sent delegates. The discussion wound up, as was to be foreseen, with the question of "nationality" in general and the attitude we take towards it. This subject was adjourned till next Tuesday.

The French, who were numerously represented, gave vent to their cordial dislike of the Italians.

Moreover, the representatives of the "*Young France*" (*nonworkers*) came out with the announcement that all nationalities and even nations were "antiquated prejudices". Proudhonised Stirnerism. Everything is to be dissolved into small "groups" or "communes", which in turn are to form an "association", but no state. And this "individualisation" of humanity and the corresponding "mutualism" are to go on while history comes to a stop in all other countries and the whole world waits until the French are ripe for a social revolution. Then they will demonstrate the experiment to us, and the rest of the world, overwhelmed by the force of their example, will follow suit. Exactly what Fourier expected of his model phalanstery.[17] Anyhow, whoever encumbers the "social" question with the "superstitions" of the old world is a "reactionary".

The English laughed very much when I began my speech by saying that our friend Lafargue and others, who had done away with nationalities, had spoken *"French"* to us, i.e., a language which nine-tenths of the audience did not understand. I also suggested that by the negation of nationalities he appeared, quite unconsciously, to understand their absorption by the model French nation.

As for the rest the situation is difficult now, because on the one hand silly English Italianism and on the other the erroneous French polemics against it must be equally combated. In particular every demonstration that would involve our Association in a one-sided course must be prevented.

Greetings.

Yours,
K. M.

First published in
*Der Briefwechsel zwischen
F. Engels und K. Marx.*
Bd. III, Stuttgart, 1913

Translated from
the German

MARX TO L. KUGELMANN IN HANOVER

London, October* 9, 1866

I had great fears for the first Congress at Geneva.[18] On the whole however it turned out better than I expected. The effect in France, England and America was unhoped for. I could not, and did not want to go there, but wrote the programme for the London delegates. I deliberately restricted it to those points which allow of immediate agreement and concerted action by the workers, and give direct nourishment and impetus to the requirements of the class struggle and the organisation of the workers into a class. The Parisian gentlemen had their heads full of the emptiest Proudhonist phrases. They babble about science and know nothing. They scorn all *revolutionary* action, that is, action arising out of the class struggle itself, all concentrated, social movements, and therefore also those which can be carried through by *political means* (for instance the *legal* shortening of the working day). Under the *pretext of freedom*, and of anti-governmentalism or anti-authoritarian individualism, these gentlemen—who for sixteen years have so quietly endured the most miserable despotism, and still endure it!—actually preach ordinary bourgeois economy, only Proudhonistically idealised! Proudhon did enormous mischief. His sham criticism and sham opposition to the utopians (he himself is only a petty-bourgeois utopian,

---

* In the original a misprint: November.—*Ed.*

whereas in the utopias of a Fourier, an Owen, etc., there is the anticipation and imaginative expression of a new world) attracted and corrupted first the *jeunesse brilliante*, the students, and then the workmen, particularly those of Paris, who as workers in luxury trades are strongly attached, without knowing it, to the old rubbish. Ignorant, vain, presumptuous, talkative, blusteringly arrogant, they were on the point of spoiling everything, for they rushed to the Congress in numbers which bore no relation whatever to the number of their members. In the report I shall, incidentally, rap them on the knuckles. . . .

First published
in the magazine
Die Neue Zeit,
Bd. 2. No. 2. 1901-1902

Translated from
the German

MARX TO P. LAFARGUE IN PARIS

London, April 19, 1870

...But Bakounine's programme was "*the* theory". It consisted, in fact of 3 points.

1) That the first requirement of the social Revolution was —*the abolition of inheritance*, vieillerie St. Simoniste,[19] dont le charlatan et *l'ignoramus* Bakounine se faisait l'éditeur responsable.* It is evident: If you have had the power to make the social Revolution in one day, par décret plébiscitaire, you would abolish at once landed property and capital, and would therefore have no occasion at all to occupy yourselves with *le droit d'héritage.* On the other hand, if you have not that power (and it is of course foolish to suppose such a power), the proclamation of the *abolition of inheritance* would be not a serious act, but a foolish menace, rallying the whole peasantry and the whole small middle-class round the reaction. Suppose f.i. that the Yankees had not had the power to abolish slavery by the sword. What an imbecility it would have been to proclaim the *abolition of inheritance in slaves!* The whole thing rests on a superannuated idealism, which considers the actual jurisprudence as the basis of our economical state, instead of seeing that our economical state is the basis and source of our jurisprud-

---

* Saint-Simonist nonsense, of which the charlatan and ignoramus Bakunin became a responsible publisher.—*Ed.*

ence! As to Bakounine, all he wanted was to improvise a programme of his own making. Voilà tout. C'était un programme d'occasion.*

2) "*l'égalité* des différentes *classes*".** To suppose on the one hand the continued existence of *classes*, and on the other hand the *égalité* of the members belonging to them, this blunder shows you at once the shameless ignorance and superficiality of that fellow who made it his "special mission" to enlighten us on "theory".

3) The working class must not occupy itself with *politics*. They must only organise themselves by trades-unions. One fine day, by means of the *Internationale* they will supplant the place of all existing states. You see what a caricature he has made of my doctrines! As the transformation of the existing States into Associations is our last end, we must allow the governments, these great Trade-Unions of the ruling classes, to do as they like, because to occupy ourselves with them is to acknowledge them. Why! In the same way the old socialists said: You must not occupy yourselves with the wages question, because you want to abolish wages labour, and to struggle with the capitalist about the rate of wages is to acknowledge the wages system! The ass has not even seen that every class movement *as* a class movement, is necessarily and was always a *political* movement.

This then is the whole theoretical baggage of Mahomet-Bakounine, a Mahomet without a Koran. . . .

First published   Written in English
in the symposium
Annali an. 1, Milano, 1958

---

* A haphazard programme.—*Ed.*
** Equality of different classes.—*Ed.*

ENGELS TO C. CAFIERO[20]
IN BARLETTA

London, July 1[-3], 1871

...Bakunin has a theory of his own, consisting more or less of a mixture of Communism and Proudhonism. The wish to unite these two theories in one shows that he is completely ignorant of political economy. From Proudhon he has adopted, among other phrases, anarchy as the final state of society. He is opposed to all political action by the working class, since it would in fact involve recognition of the existing state. Moreover, in his opinion all political acts are "authoritarian". But how he hopes the present political oppression and the tyranny of capital will be broken, or how he means to advance his pet ideas of abolishing the right of inheritance without "authoritarian acts" he does not explain. Yet an uprising having been forcibly pushed through in Lyons in September 1870, he decreed from the Hotel de Ville the abolition of the State without taking any measures against the bourgeois of the National Guard, who walked calmly into the Hotel de Ville, chased Bakunin out and re-established the State in less than an hour.[21] Nevertheless Bakunin with his theories has founded a sect to which a small part of the French and Swiss workers adhere as well as many of our people in Spain and some in Italy, among the latter Caporusso and his friends. Caporusso thus lives up to his name, for he indeed has a Russian as his chief.*

---

* A pun: Capo in Italian means "chief".—*Ed.*

Now our Association* is established to afford a central medium of communication between the working men's societies existing in the different countries and aiming at the same end, that is, the protection, advancement and complete emancipation of the working classes (first rule of the Association). Wherever the special theories of Bakunin and his friends were limited to these ends, there would be no objection to accepting them as members of the Association and allowing them to propagate their ideas by any suitable means. We have all kinds of people in the Association—Communists, Proudhonists, unionists, trade unionists, co-operators, Bakuninists, etc.—and have men of quite different opinions even in our General Council. As soon as the Association became a sect it would be lost. Our strength lies in the breadth with which the first rule is interpreted, i.e., in that all men who aim for the complete emancipation of the working class are admitted. Unfortunately, the Bakuninists, with the narrow-mindedness common to all sects, were not content with this. According to them, the General Council was composed of reactionaries and the Association's programme was not sufficiently clear. Atheism and materialism—which Bakunin himself learnt from us Germans—should be made obligatory and the abolition of the right of inheritance and the State, etc., should be included in our programme. Now Marx and I are just as good old atheists and materialists as Bakunin, as indeed are most of our members, and we know as well as he does how senseless this right of inheritance is, although we differ from him as regards the importance and usefulness of presenting its abolition as deliverance from all evil. "The Abolition of the State" is an old German philosophical phrase which we were wont to make great use of in our boyhood. But to include all these things in our programme would mean to drive away a vast number of members, and to divide instead of uniting the European proletariat. When all the efforts to secure the adoption of the Bakuninist programme as the programme of the Association had failed, an attempt was made to drive the Association onto that path by indirect means.

Bakunin formed an *Alliance of Socialist Democracy*[22] in

* The International Working Men's Association.—*Ed.*

Geneva, which was to be an international association separate from our own. The most radical minds of our sections,
the Bakuninists, were to form everywhere sections of this
Alliance, and these sections were to be subject to a separate
General Council in Geneva (Bakunin) and have National
Councils distinct from our own. At our General Congress,
the *Alliance* was to attend our congress in the morning and
hold its own separate congress in the afternoon.

This gracious plan was submitted to the General Council
in November 1868, but on December 22, 1868, the General
Council rejected these rules as contrary to the General Rules
of our Association and declared that the sections of the
Alliance could only be admitted individually and that the
Alliance must dissolve itself or cease to belong to the International. On March 9, 1869, the General Council informed
the Alliance that "there exists, therefore, no obstacle to the
transformation of the sections of the Alliance into sections
of the International Working Men's Association. The dissolution of the Alliance, and the entrance of its sections into
the International Working Men's Association once settled,
it would, according to our Regulations, become necessary to
inform the General Council of the residence and the numer-
ical strength of each new section".* These conditions were
never properly fulfilled. The Alliance itself was condemned
everywhere except in France and Switzerland, where it ended
up by creating a split, whereas about a thousand Bakuninists—less than one-tenth of our people—withdrew from
the French and Swiss Federations and now call upon the
Council to be recognised as a separate federation, which the
Council is not likely to oppose. From which you can see
that the main result of the Bakuninists' action has been to
create a split in our ranks. Nobody opposed their special
dogma, but they were not content with that and wanted to
command, and impose their doctrines upon all our members.

We have resisted, as was our duty, and if they wish to
agree to stand calmly in line with our other members, we

---

* This quotation was distorted by the police, some words were
missing and the phrase was illegible. The text was restored according
to the document: K. Marx, *The General Council of the International
Working Men's Association to the International Alliance of Socialist
Democracy* [London, 9 March, 1869].—*Ed.*

have neither the right nor the wish to exclude them. But it remains to be seen whether it is wise to attach importance to such elements, and if we can win the Italian sections that are not imbued with this special fanaticism, we shall certainly be able to work together better. You will be able to judge for yourself from the situation you find in Naples....

First published   Translated from
in the magazine   the Italian
La Società No. 4, 1951

FREDERICK ENGELS

ON POLITICAL ACTION
OF THE WORKING CLASS

NOTES OF A SPEECH DELIVERED ON SEPTEMBER 21, 1871,
AT A SESSION OF THE LONDON CONFERENCE[33]

Absolute abstention in political matters is impossible, so all the abstentionist journals are actually engaging in politics. The only point is how this should be done and what policy should be adopted. Apart from that, abstention for us is impossible. The workers' party already exists as a political party in most countries. It is not for us to ruin it by preaching abstention. Experience of real life, political oppression which is imposed on them by the existing governments, for either political or social ends, force the workers to engage in politics whether they like it or not. To preach abstention to them would be to drive them into the arms of bourgeois politics. Particularly after the Paris Commune, which has placed political action by the proletariat on the agenda, abstention is quite impossible.

We want the abolition of classes. How can this be achieved? By the political dominion of the proletariat. And when this has been universally acknowledged, we are told not to meddle in politics! All the abstentionists call themselves revolutionaries, and even revolutionaries above all. But revolution is the supreme political act; he who desires it must desire also the means, the political action that prepares it, that gives the workers their education in revolution without which the workers on the very next day after the struggle will always be duped by the Favres and the Pyats. But the politics that must be conducted are workers' politics; the workers' party must be not merely an appendage of some of the bourgeois parties, but a fully independent party which has its goal and its own policy.

The political freedoms, the right of assembly and association and the freedom of the press, these are our weapons. Are we to fold our arms and abstain if they seek to deprive us of them? We are told that any political act implies recognition of the existing state of affairs. But when this state of affairs gives us the means to protest against it, the use of such means is not recognition of the existing state of affairs.

First published in full in the magazine
The Communist International
No. 29. 1934

Translated from
the French

KARL MARX and FREDERICK ENGELS

From RESOLUTIONS OF THE CONFERENCE
OF DELEGATES OF THE INTERNATIONAL
WORKING MEN'S ASSOCIATION

ASSEMBLED AT LONDON
FROM 17TH TO 23RD SEPTEMBER 1871

IX

POLITICAL ACTION OF THE WORKING CLASS[24]

Considering the following passage of the preamble to the Rules: "The economical emancipation of the working classes is the great end to which every political movement ought to be subordinate as a means";[25]

That the Inaugural Address of the International Working Men's Association (1864) states: "The lords of land and the lords of capital will always use their political privileges for the defence and perpetuation of their economical monopolies. So far from promoting, they will continue to lay every possible impediment in the way of the emancipation of labour.... To conquer political power has therefore become the great duty of the working classes";[26]

That the Congress of Lausanne (1867) has passed this resolution: "The social emancipation of the workmen is inseparable from their political emancipation";[27]

That the declaration of the General Council relative to the pretended plot of the French Internationals on the eve of the plebiscite[28] (1870) says: "Certainly by the tenor of our Statutes, all our branches in England, on the Continent, and in America have the special mission not only to serve as centres for the militant organisation of the working class, but also to support, in their respective countries, every political movement tending towards the accomplishment of our ultimate end—the economical emancipation of the working class";

That false translations of the original Statutes have given rise to various interpretations which were mischievous to the development and action of the International Working Men's Association;

In presence of an unbridled reaction which violently crushes every effort at emancipation on the part of the working men, and pretends to maintain by brute force the distinction of classes and the political domination of the propertied classes resulting from it;

Considering, that against this collective power of the propertied classes the working class cannot act, as a class, except by constituting itself into a political party, distinct from, and opposed to, all old parties formed by the propertied classes;

That this constitution of the working class into a political party is indispensable in order to ensure the triumph of the Social Revolution and its ultimate end—the abolition of classes;

That the combination of forces which the working class has already effected by its economical struggles ought at the same time to serve as a lever for its struggles against the political power of landlords and capitalists—

The Conference recalls to the members of the *International*:

That in the militant state of the working class, its economical movement and its political action are indissolubly united.

Drawn up, edited and
prepared for the publication
by K. Marx and F. Engels
in September-October 1871

Printed according to the
text of the English
pamphlet

Published in pamphlet form
in English, German and French
and in several organs
of the International in
November-December 1871

MARX TO F. BOLTE
IN NEW YORK

[London], November 23, 1871

...The *International* was founded in order to replace the socialist or semi-socialist sects by a real organisation of the working class for struggle. The original Rules and the Inaugural Address show this at a glance. On the other hand the International could not have maintained itself if the course of history had not already smashed sectarianism. The development of socialist sectarianism and that of the real working-class movement always stand in inverse ratio to each other. Sects are justified (historically) so long as the working class is not yet ripe for an independent historical movement. As soon as it has attained this maturity all sects are essentially reactionary. Nevertheless, what history exhibits everywhere was repeated in the history of the International. What is antiquated tries to re-establish itself and maintain its position within the newly acquired form.

And the history of the International was a *continual struggle of the General Council* against the sects and amateur experiments, which sought to assert themselves within the International against the real movement of the working class. This struggle was conducted at the *congresses*, but far more in the private negotiations between the General Council and the individual sections.

In Paris, as the Proudhonists (Mutualists) were cofounders of the Association, they naturally held the reins there

for the first few years. Later, of course, collectivist, positiv-
ist, etc., groups were formed there in opposition to them.

In Germany—the Lassalle clique. I myself corresponded
with the notorious Schweitzer for two years and proved to
him irrefutably that Lassalle's organisation was a mere
sectarian organisation and, as such, hostile to the organisation of the *real* workers' movement striven for by the International. He had his "reasons" for not understanding.

At the end of 1868 the Russian Bakunin joined the *International* with the aim of forming inside it *a second International* under the name of *"Alliance de la Démocratie Socialiste" and with himself as leader*. He—a man devoid of all
theoretical knowledge—laid claim to representing in that
separate body the *scientific* propaganda of the International, and wanted to make such propaganda the special
function of that second *International within the International.*

His programme was a hash superficially scraped together
from the Right and from the Left—*equality of classes* (!),
abolition of the right of inheritance as the *starting point* of
the social movement (St. Simonist nonsense), *atheism* as a
dogma dictated to the members, etc., and as the main dogma
(Proudhonist): abstention from the political movement.

This children's primer found favour (and still has a certain hold) in Italy and Spain, where the real conditions for
the workers' movement are as yet little developed, and
among a few vain, ambitious, and empty doctrinaires in
Latin Switzerland and in Belgium.

To Mr. Bakunin doctrine (the mess he has brewed from
bits of Proudhon, St. Simon, and others) was and is a
secondary matter—merely a means to his personal self-
assertion. Though a nonentity as a theoretician he is in his
element as an intriguer.

For years the General Council had to fight against his
conspiracy (supported up to a certain point by the French
Proudhonists, especially in the *South of France*). At last, by
means of Conference Resolutions 1, 2 and 3, IX, XVI, and
XVII, it delivered its long-prepared blow.[29]

It goes without saying that the General Council does not
support in America what it combats in Europe. Resolutions
1, 2, 3 and IX now give the New York Committee the legal

weapons with which to put an end to all sectarianism and amateur groups, and, if necessary, to expel them. . . .

Nota bene: *On the political movement*:

The political movement of the working class has as its ultimate object, of course, the conquest of political power for this class, and this naturally requires a previous organisation of the working class developed up to a certain point and arising precisely from its economic struggles.

On the other hand, however, every movement in which the working class comes out as a *class* against the ruling classes and tries to coerce them by pressure from without is a political movement. For instance, the attempt in a particular factory or even in a particular trade to force a shorter working day out of individual capitalists by strikes, etc., is a purely economic movement. On the other hand the movement to force through an eight-hour, etc., *law*, is a *political* movement. And in this way, out of the separate economic movements of the workers there grows up everywhere a *political* movement, that is to say, a movement of the *class*, with the object of enforcing its interests in a general form, in a form possessing general, socially coercive force. While these movements presuppose a certain degree of previous organisation, they are in turn equally a means of developing this organisation.

Where the working class is not yet far enough advanced in its organisation to undertake a decisive campaign against the collective power, i.e., the political power of the ruling classes, it must at any rate be trained for this by continual agitation against this power and by a hostile attitude toward the policies of the ruling classes. Otherwise it remains a plaything in their hands, as the September revolution in France[30] showed, and as is also proved to a certain extent by the game that Messrs. Gladstone & Co. have been successfully engaged in in England up to the present time. . . .

First published in abridged form
in the book: *Briefe und Auszüge
aus Briefen von Joh. Phil. Becker,
Jos. Dietzgen, Friedrich Engels,
Karl Marx u. A. an F. A. Sorge und
Andere*, Stuttgart, 1906 and in
full in K. Marx, F. Engels, *Works*,
1st Russ. Edition. Vol. XXVI. 1935

Translated from
the German

ENGELS TO P. LAFARGUE
IN MADRID

London, December 30, 1871

Our Spanish friends will realise now how these gentlemen misuse the word *authoritarian*. As soon as something displeases the Bakuninists, they say: it's *authoritarian*, and thereby they imagine they have damned it forever. If they were workers instead of bourgeois, journalists, etc., or if they had but given a little study to economic questions and conditions in modern industry, they would know that no joint action of any sort is possible without imposing on some an extraneous will, i.e., an authority. Whether it be the will of a majority of voters, of a leading committee, or of one man, it is still a will imposed on the dissentients; but without that single and directing will, no co-operation is possible. Go and run one of the big Barcelona factories without direction, that is, without authority! Or administer a railway without the certainty that every engine-driver, fireman, etc., will be at his post at precisely the time when he should be there! I should very much like to know whether the gallant Bakunin would entrust his large person to a railway carriage if that railway were administered according to principles by which nobody would be at his post if he did not please to submit to the authority of the regulations far more authoritarian in any possible state of society than those of the Basle Congress![31] All these fine ultra-radical and revolutionary phrases merely serve to conceal the utter poverty of ideas and the most complete ignorance of the conditions in which the daily life of society is carried on. Go and abolish "all authority, even with consent", amongst the sailors on a ship! ...

First published in
F. Engels, P. et L. Lafargue,
Correspondance, T. I, Paris, 1956

Translated from
the French

FREDERICK ENGELS

THE CONGRESS OF SONVILLIER AND THE INTERNATIONAL[32]

It is hardly necessary to enlarge upon the present position of the International Working Men's Association. On the one hand, owing to the tremendous events in Paris,[33] it has become stronger and more widespread than ever before; on the other we find almost all the European governments united against it—Thiers and Gorchakov, Bismarck and Beust, Victor Emanuel and the Pope,* Spain and Belgium. A general drive against the International has been launched, all the powers of the old world, the courts-martial and civil courts, the police and the press, squires from the backwoods and bourgeois, vie with each other in persecuting it, and there is hardly a spot on the entire continent where every means is not used to outlaw this fear-inspiring great brotherhood of workers.

At this very moment of general and inevitable disorganisation caused by the forces of the old society, when unity and solidarity are more indispensable than ever, at this very moment a small number of sections—whose number by their own admission is steadily diminishing—in some corner of Switzerland has chosen to throw an apple of discord in the shape of a public circular among the members of the International. These people—they call themselves the *Fede-*

---

* Pius IX.—*Ed.*

ration of the Jura—are essentially the same who under the leadership of Bakunin have continuously undermined the unity in the French-speaking part of Switzerland for more than two years and who through their assiduous private correspondence with kindred notabilities in various countries have obstructed concerted action in the International. So long as these intrigues were confined to Switzerland or done on the quiet we did not want to give them wide publicity, but this circular compels us to speak.

Because this year the General Council has not convened a Congress but a Conference,[34] a circular to all sections of the International has been adopted by the Federation of the Jura at its Congress at Sonvillier on November 12. Large numbers of the circular were printed and mailed in all directions requesting all sections to press for the immediate convocation of a Congress. Why a conference *had to* take the place of a Congress is perfectly clear, at least to us in Germany and Austria. If we had been represented at a Congress our delegates on their return would have been immediately apprehended and placed into safe custody, and the delegates from Spain, Italy and France would have been in the same position. But a conference which held no public debates but only committee meetings could very well take place, for the names of the delegates would not be published. It had the disadvantage that it could not decide fundamental issues or make any changes in the General Rules, that it had no legislative power at all and could pass merely administrative decisions designed to facilitate the putting into practice of the organisational measures laid down by the General Rules and Congress resolutions. But nothing more was required under the circumstances, it was merely a question of adopting measures to deal with the present emergency, and a conference was sufficient for the purpose.

The attacks on the conference and its decisions, however, were merely a pretext. In fact, the present circular only makes passing mention of them. It considers, on the contrary, that the evil is far more deep-rooted. It asserts that according to the General Rules and the original Congress Resolutions the International is nothing but "a free federation of autonomous" (independent) "sections", whose aim is the emancipation of the workers by the workers themselves "without any directing authority, even if set up by voluntary agreement".

The General Council therefore was nothing but "a simple statistical and correspondence bureau". But this original basis was very soon distorted, first by conferring on the General Council the right to co-opt new members, and even more by the Resolutions of the Basle Congress, which gave the General Council the right to suspend individual sections till the next Congress and to decide controversies provisionally until the Congress adopted a relevant resolution. This placed dangerous powers in the hands of the General Council and turned the free association of independent sections into a hierarchical and authoritarian organisation of "disciplined sections", so that

"the sections are entirely under the control of the General Council, which can arbitrarily either refuse to admit them or suspend their work".

To our German readers, who know only too well the value of an organisation that is able to defend itself, all this will seem very strange. And this is quite natural, for Mr Bakunin's theories, which appear here in their full splendour, have not yet penetrated into Germany. A workers' association which has inscribed upon its banner the motto of struggle for the emancipation of the working class is to be headed, not by an executive committee, but merely by a statistical and correspondence bureau! For Bakunin and his companions, however, the struggle for the emancipation of the working class is a mere pretext; their real aim is quite different.

"The future society is to be nothing but the generalised form of organisation adopted by the International. We must therefore see to it that this organisation approximates as closely as possible to our ideal.... The International, the nucleus of the future human society, should already now be the true image of our principles of freedom and federalism, and should banish all principles which tend to lead to authority and dictatorship."

We Germans have earned a bad name for our mysticism, but we have never gone the length of such mysticism. The International is to be the prototype of a future society in which there will be no executions à la Versailles,[35] no courts-martial, no standing armies, no inspection of private correspondence, and no Brunswick criminal court![36] Just now, when we have to defend ourselves with all the means at our disposal, the proletariat is told to organise not in accordance with the requirements of the struggle it is daily and hourly compelled to wage, but according to the vague notions of a future society entertained by some dreamers. Let us try to imagine what our own German organisation would look like according to this pattern. Instead of fighting the government and the bourgeoisie, it would meditate on whether each paragraph of our General Rules and each resolution passed by the Congress presented a true image of the future society. In place of our executive committee there would be a simple statistical and correspondence bureau; it would have to deal as best it knew with the independent sections, which are so independent that they can accept no steering authority, be it even one set up by their own free decision; for they would thus violate their primary duty—that of being a true model of the future society. Co-ordination of forces and joint action are no longer mentioned. If in each individual section the minority submits to the decision of the majority, it commits a crime against the principles of freedom and accepts a principle which leads to authority and dictatorship! If Stieber and all his associates, if the entire black cabinet,[37] if all Prussian officers were ordered to join the Social-Democratic organisation in order to wreck it, the committee, or rather the statistical correspondence bureau, must by no means keep them out, for this would amount to establishing a hierarchical and authoritarian organisation! And above all, there should be no disciplined sections! Indeed, no party discipline, no centralisation of forces at a particular point, no weapons of struggle! For what, then, would happen to the model of the future society? In short, where would this new organisation get us? To the cowardly, servile organisation of the early Christians, those slaves who gratefully accepted every kick and whose grovelling did indeed after 300 years win them the victory of their religion—a method of revolution which the proletariat will surely not imitate! Like the early Christians, who took heaven as they imagined it as the model for their organisation, so we are to take Mr Bakunin's heaven of the future society as a model, and are to pray and hope instead of

fighting. And the people who preach this nonsense pretend
to be the only true revolutionaries!

As far as the International is concerned, all this is still a
long way off. Until the Congress passes new decisions it is the
duty of the General Council to carry out the Basle resolutions and it will do its duty. Just as it did not hesitate to
expel the Tolains and Durands, so it will see to it that
Stieber & Co. will not be admitted into the International,
even if Mr Bakunin should consider this dictatorial.

But how did these reprehensible Basle resolutions come
into being? Very simply. The Belgian delegates proposed
them, and *no one supported them more ardently than Bakunin and his friends,* especially Schwitzguébel and Guillaume,
who signed the circular in question! But then matters were
of course quite different. These gentlemen then hoped to
secure a majority and that the General Council would be
dominated by them. At that time they wanted to make the
General Council as strong as possible. And now—now it is
quite a different matter. Now the grapes are sour, and the
Council is to be reduced to a simple statistical correspondence bureau, so that Bakunin's chaste future society should
not have to blush.

These people, professional sectarians, who, with all their
mystical early-Christian doctrines, form an insignificant
minority in the International, have the effrontery to reproach
the General Council and its members with wanting

"to make their particular programme, their personal tenets the pre-
dominant ones in the International; they regard their private ideas
as the official theory which alone should be entitled to full recognition in the Association."

This is indeed bold language. Anyone who has been able
to follow the internal history of the International knows
that for nearly three years now these people have been
mainly occupied in trying to force their sectarian doctrine
on the Association as its general programme, and having
failed in this they underhandedly seek to pass off Bakunin's
phrases as the general programme of the International.
Nevertheless, the General Council protested only against this
insinuation but has so far never challenged their right to
belong to the International or freely to propagate their sec-

tarian humbug as such. How the General Council will look upon their latest circular is yet to be seen.

These people have themselves brilliantly demonstrated what they have achieved by their new organisation. Wherever the International did not encounter the violent resistance of reactionary governments, it has made enormous advances since the Paris Commune. What do we see, on the other hand, in the Swiss Jura, where these gentlemen were free to run things their own way during the last eighteen months? Their own report to the Sonvillier Congress (printed in the Geneva journal *La Révolution Sociale* of November 23) says:

"These terrible events could not but exert a *partly demoralising* and partly beneficial influence on our sections.... Then the gigantic struggle which the proletariat has to wage against the bourgeoisie will begin, and that makes people think ... some withdraw (s'en vont) and hide their cowardice, others rally closer than ever in support of the regenerating principle of the International. This is at present the dominant fact of the internal history of the International in general and of our Federation in particular."

What is new here is the statement that this happened in the International in general, where just the opposite took place. It is true that this happened in the Jura Federation. According to these gentlemen themselves, the Moutier Section has suffered least of all, but has achieved nothing:

"Though no new sections were set up, it is to be hoped that, etc." ... and this section was after all "in a particularly favourable position because of the excellent temper of the population".... "the Grange Section has been reduced to a small nucleus of workers."

Two sections in Biel never answered the letters of the Committee, and the same applies to the sections in Neuchâtel and one in Locle; the third section in Biel is

"for the time being dead" ... although "there is still some hope of the International in Biel reviving".

The Saint-Blaise Section is dead; that of Val de Ruz has vanished, no one knows how; after a prolonged agony the central Section at Locle was dissolved, but has managed to reconstitute itself, evidently for the purpose of the Congress elections; that of La-Chaux-de-Fonds is in a critical position; the watch-makers' section in Courtelary is now trans-

forming itself into a trades association and adopting the
rules of the association of Swiss watch-makers; it thus adopts
the rules of an organisation which is not part of the International; the central Section at Courtelary has suspended
its activities because its members have formed separate
Sections at Saint-Imier and Sonvillier (which has not prevented this central section from sending two delegates to the
Congress, in addition to the delegates from Saint-Imier and
Sonvillier); after an outstanding career the Catébat Section
had to dissolve itself as a result of intrigues by the local
bourgeois, and the same happened to the Corgémont Section; finally in Geneva one Section is still in existence.

That is what in eighteen months the representatives of a
free federation of independent sections headed by a statistical and correspondence bureau have done to a flourishing,
though not widespread or numerous, Federation. And that
in a country where they had complete freedom of action,
and at a time when everywhere else the International had
made gigantic advances. And at the very moment when
they themselves paint this picture of their miserable failure,
this expression of utter helplessness and dissolution, they
demand that we should divert the International from the
course it has hitherto followed, a course which has made it
what it is now, and lead it along the path which brought
the Jura Federation from a comparatively flourishing state
to complete dissolution.

Written   Translated from
ca. January 3, 1872   the German

First published in
Der Volksstaat No. 3,
January 10, 1872

ENGELS TO C. TERZAGHI
IN TURIN

(Second Variant)

[*Draft*]

London, [about January 14[-15], 1872]

...But the Jura Circular[38] discloses the evil intent of the authors.

At first they picked a quarrel with us on the pretext of the Conference[39]; now they attack us because we are carrying out the resolutions of the Basle Congress, resolutions which we are *obliged* to carry out. They do not want any authority exercised through the General Council even if *it were freely assented to by all.* I would very much like to know how without that authority (as they call it) it would have been possible to bring the Tolains, Durands and Nechayevs to account and how the intrusion of Mardocheans* and traitors is going to be prevented by your fine phrase, autonomy of the sections, as is explained in the circular. No one, to be sure, disputes the autonomy of the sections, but federation is not possible without ceding certain powers to the federal committees and, in the last instance, to the General Council.

But do you know who the authors and protagonists of these *authoritarian* resolutions were? The delegates of the General Council? By no means. Those authoritarian measures were proposed by the Belgian delegates, and the

---

* Secret police agents.—*Ed.*

3*

Schwitzguébels, the Guillaumes and the Bakunins were their *most ardent defenders. That's how things are.*

I believe the terms "Authority" and centralisation are being greatly abused. I know nothing more authoritarian than a revolution, and when one's will is imposed on others with bombs and bullets, as in every revolution, it seems to me an act of authority is being committed. It was the lack of centralisation and authority that cost the Paris Commune its life. Do what you like with authority, etc., after the victory, but for the struggle we must unite all our forces in one *fascio** and concentrate them at one point of attack. And when I am told that authority and centralisation are two things that should be condemned under all possible circumstances it seems to me that those who say so either do not know what a revolution is or are revolutionaries in name only....

First published in
K. Marx, F. Engels, *Works*,
2nd Russ. ed., Vol. 33

Translated from
the Italian and
the German

---

* A fist.—*Ed.*

ENGELS TO T. CUNO
IN MILAN

London, January 24, 1872

... Bakunin, who up to 1868 had intrigued against the International, joined it after he had suffered a fiasco at the Berne Peace Congress[40] and at once began to conspire *within it* against the General Council. Bakunin has a peculiar theory of his own, a medley of Proudhonism and communism. The chief point concerning the former is that he does not regard capital, i.e., the class antagonism between capitalists and wage workers which has arisen through social development, but the *state* as the main evil to be abolished. While the great mass of the Social-Democratic workers hold our view that state power is nothing more than the organisation which the ruling classes—landowners and capitalists—have provided for themselves in order to protect their social privileges, Bakunin maintains that it is the *state* which has created capital, that the capitalist has his capital *only by the grace of the state*. As, therefore, the state is the chief evil, it is above all the state which must be done away with and then capitalism will go to blazes of itself. We, on the contrary, say: Do away with capital, the concentration of all means of production in the hands of the few, and the state will fall of itself. The difference is an essential one: Without a previous social revolution the abolition of the state is nonsense; the abolition of capital *is* precisely the social revolution and involves a change in the whole mode of production. Now

then, inasmuch as to Bakunin the state is the main evil,
nothing must be done which can keep the state—that is, any
state, whether it be a republic, a monarchy or anything else
—alive. Hence *complete abstention from all politics.* To
commit a political act, especially to take part in an election,
would be a betrayal of principle. The thing to do is to carry
on propaganda, heap abuse upon the state, organise, and
when *all* the workers, hence the majority, are won over,
depose all the authorities, abolish the state and replace it
with the organisation of the International. This great act, with
which the millennium begins, is called *social liquidation.*

All this sounds extremely radical and is so simple that it
can be learnt by heart in five minutes; that is why the Bakuninist theory has speedily found favour also in Italy and
Spain among young lawyers, doctors, and other doctrinaires.
But the mass of the workers will never allow itself to be
persuaded that the public affairs of their countries are not
also their own affairs; they are naturally *politically-minded*
and whoever tries to make them believe that they should
leave politics alone will in the end be left in the lurch. To
preach to the workers that they should in all circumstances
abstain from politics is to drive them into the arms of the
priests or the bourgeois republicans.

Now, as the International, according to Bakunin, was not
formed for political struggle but to replace the old state
organisation as soon as social liquidation takes place, it follows that it must come as near as possible to the Bakuninist
ideal of future society. In this society there will above all
be no *authority,* for authority=state=absolute evil. (How
these people propose to run a factory, operate a railway or
steer a ship without a will that decides in the last resort,
without single management, they of course do not tell us.)
The authority of the majority over the minority also ceases.
Every individual and every community is autonomous; but
as to how a society of even only two people is possible
unless each gives up some of his autonomy, Bakunin again
maintains silence.

And so the International too must be arranged according
to this pattern. Every section, and in every section every
individual, is to be autonomous. To hell with the *Basle resolutions*[41], which confer upon the General Council a perni-

cious authority demoralising even to itself! Even if this authority is conferred *voluntarily* it must cease just *because* it is authority!

Here you have in brief the main points of this swindle....

First published in abriged form
in the book: F. Engels, *Politisches
Vermächtnis. Aus unveröffentlichten
Briefen.* Berlin, 1920 and in full in
the journal *Die Gesellschaft* No. 11,
Berlin. 1925

Translated from
the German

KARL MARX and FREDERICK ENGELS

From FICTITIOUS SPLITS
IN THE INTERNATIONAL

CIRCULAR FROM THE GENERAL COUNCIL
OF THE INTERNATIONAL WORKING MEN'S ASSOCIATION[41]

...We now pass on to the sectarian sections:

The first phase of the proletariat's struggle against the bourgeoisie is marked by a sectarian movement. That is logical at a time when the proletariat has not yet developed sufficiently to act as a class. Certain thinkers criticise social antagonisms and suggest fantastic solutions thereof, which the mass of workers is left to accept, preach and put into practice. The sects formed by these initiators are abstentionist by their very nature, i.e., alien to all real action, politics, strikes, coalitions, or, in a word, to any united movement. The mass of the proletariat always remains indifferent or even hostile to their propaganda. The Paris and Lyons workers did not want the Saint-Simonians, the Fourierists, the Icarians,[43] any more than the Chartists and the English trades unionists wanted the Owenists. These sects act as levers of the movement in the beginning, but become an obstruction as soon as the movement outgrows them; after which they become reactionary. Witness the sects in France and England, and lately the Lassalleans in Germany who, after having hindered the proletariat's organisation for several years, ended by becoming simple instruments of the police. To sum up, we have here the infancy of the proletarian movement, just as astrology and alchemy are the infancy of science. If the International were to be founded it was necessary that the proletariat would go through this phase.

Contrary to the sectarian organisations with their vagaries and rivalries, the International is a genuine and militant organisation of the proletarian class of all countries united in their common struggle against the capitalists and the landowners, against their class power organised in the state. The International's Rules, therefore, speak of only simple "workers' societies", all following the same goal and accepting the same programme, which presents a general outline of the proletarian movement, while leaving its theoretical elaboration to be guided by the needs of the practical struggle and the exchange of ideas in the sections, unrestrictedly admitting all shades of socialist convictions in their organs and Congresses.

Just as in every new historical phase old mistakes reappear momentarily only to disappear forthwith, so within the International there followed a resurrection of sectarian sections, though in a less obvious form.

The Alliance, while considering the resurrection of the sects a great step forward, is in itself conclusive proof that their time is over: for, if initially they contained elements of progress, the programme of the Alliance, in tow of a "Mohammed without the Koran"*, is nothing but a heap of pompously worded ideas long since dead and capable only of frightening bourgeois idiots or serving as evidence to be used by the Bonapartist or other prosecutors against members of the International.**

The Conference, at which all shades of socialism were represented, unanimously acclaimed the resolution against sectarian sections, fully convinced that this resolution, stressing once again the International's true character, would mark a new stage of its development. The Alliance supporters,

---

* Bakunin.—*Ed.*
** Recent police publications on the International, including the Jules Favre circular to foreign powers and the report of Sacase, a deputy in the Rural Assembly, on the Dufaure project, are full of quotations from the Alliance's pompous manifestos.[44] The phraseology of these sectarians, whose radicalism is wholly restricted to verbiage, is extremely useful for promoting the aims of the reactionaries.

whom this resolution dealt a fatal blow, construed it only as the General Council's victory over the International....

Anarchy, then, is the great war-horse of their master Bakunin, who has taken nothing from the socialist systems except a set of slogans. What all socialists understand by anarchy is this: once the aim of the proletarian movement, the abolition of classes, has been attained, the power of the State, which serves to keep the great majority of producers under the yoke of a numerically small exploiting minority, disappears, and the functions of government are transformed into simple administrative functions. The Alliance puts matters the other way round. It proclaims anarchy in the proletarian ranks as the surest means of breaking the powerful concentration of social and political forces in the hands of the exploiters. Under this pretext it demands of the International, at the very moment when the old world is seeking to crush it, that it should replace its organisation by anarchy....

Written between mid-January
and March 5, 1872

Published as a pamphlet
in Geneva in 1872

Translated from
the French

ENGELS TO L. PIO
IN COPENHAGEN

[London], March 7, 1872

During your stay in Geneva and Leipzig you will have
heard of the attempt by a few dissidents led by Bakunin
to indict the General Council at a specially convened Congress.[45] The attitude of the International towards politics
lies at the root of the matter. These gentlemen demand *complete abstention from all political action*, and in particular
from all elections, whereas from the beginning the slogan of
the International was the winning of political power by the
working class as a means to social emancipation,[46] and the
General Council upheld this. Resolution IX of the Conference* started the fight; but since resolutions of the Conference dealing with fundamental issues have no binding
force until confirmed by the Federations, it is important to
receive the decision of the Danish Federal Council endorc-
ing this resolution. I do not speak about the subject matter
itself—this would be an affront towards a politically so
advanced people. . . .

First published
in *Die Neue Zeit*
No. 23, Bd. I, Stuttgart, 1921

Translated from
the German

* See pp. 53-54 of this volume.—*Ed.*

MARX TO P. LAFARGUE
IN MADRID

London, March 21, 1872

My dear Toole,

I am sending you herewith an excerpt from our circular against the dissidents,* concerning the functions of the General Council.

All the General Council can do to apply the General Rules and the Congress resolutions to a concrete case is to pass a decision like a tribunal. But whether it is carried out depends in each country entirely on the particular section of the International. From the moment, therefore, that the Council ceases to act as *an instrument of the general interests* of the International, it will become an utterly powerless cipher. On the other hand, the General Council is itself one of the active forces of the Association essential for maintaining its unity and preventing its being taken over by hostile elements. The moral influence which the present Council (notwithstanding all its shortcomings)** has been able to gain in face of the common enemy has wounded the egotism of these people, who always regarded the International merely as an instrument of their personal ambition.

Above all one must bear in mind that our Association is the *militant organisation* of the proletariat, and by no means a society for the advancement of doctrinaire amateurs.

---

* See pp. 72-74 of this volume.—*Ed.*
** The words in brackets are written in English by Marx.—*Ed.*

To destroy our organisation at this moment would be an act of resignation. Both the bourgeoisie and the governments could wish for nothing better. Read the report of the backwoodsman Sacase on Dufaure's draft.[47] What aspect of the Association does he admire and fear most of all? "Its organisation."

We have made excellent progress since the London Conference.

New Federations have been set up in Denmark, New Zealand and Portugal. The organisation has greatly expanded in the *United States, France* (where, as they themselves admit, Malon and Co. do not have a single Section), *Germany*, Hungary, and Britain (since the formation of the British Federal Council). *Irish* Sections have been set up quite recently. In Italy the only important sections, those in Milan and Turin, belong to us; the others are led by lawyers, journalists and other doctrinaire bourgeois. (Incidentally, one of Bakunin's personal grievances against me is that he has lost all influence in Russia, where the revolutionary youth are for me.)

The resolutions of the London Conference have already been accepted in France, America, Britain, Ireland, Denmark, Holland, Germany, Austria, Hungary, Switzerland (apart from the Jurassians), by the genuine workers' sections in Italy, and finally by the Russians and the Poles. Those who do not recognise them will in no way alter this fact, but they will be compelled to isolate themselves from the overwhelming majority of the International.

First published in Russian
in the journal *Voprosy
istorii KPSS*,
1962, No. 3

Translated from
the French

ENGELS TO C. CAFIERO
IN NAPLES

[Record of Contents]

London, June 14, 1872

Since May 16th, I have received no newspapers although have sent off *Eastern Post* etc. regularly. Why?* Can it be more than a coincidence that at the same time (May 10) the *Bulletin Jurassien* boasts of having in its possession private letters written by me to friends in Italy full of vile slander[48] etc., etc.? In any case, I have written to no one but you in Italy, and it must be to my letters to you that *Schwitzguébel's* paper refers. You owe me an explanation on this matter and I am expecting you to give me one. I am amazed that you did not do so as soon as this was published.

My letters need not fear publication, but it is a point of honour *for you* that I should know if they have been passed to my enemies with or without your consent. If with your consent, then I can only draw one conclusion: that you have let yourself be persuaded into joining the *Bakuninist secret society, the Alliance*, which, preaching the disorganisation of the International to the uninitiated, under the mask of autonomy, anarchy, and anti-authoritarianism, practices absolute authoritarianism with the initiated, with the aim of taking over leadership of the Association, treating the working masses as a flock of sheep blindly following a few initiated

---

* Up to this point in German in the manuscript.—*Ed.*

leaders, and imitating in the International the role of the Jesuits in the Catholic Church.

If my conjectures are well founded, I must congratulate you on having placed your precious "autonomy" in permanent safe-keeping, abandoning it entirely into the hands of Pope Bakunin. But I cannot believe that you, a pure anarchist and anti-authoritarian, have renounced your dearest principles to such a degree, and even less that you could have behaved so basely towards me when I have always treated you with extreme sincerity and confidence. But you must now announce your position in this matter and without delay.

Greetings and emancipation.

Yours truly,
F. E.

First published in the book:
M. Nettlau, *Bakunin e l'Internazionale in Italia. Dal 1864 al 1872*, Ginevra. 1928

Translated from the Italian and German

FREDERICK ENGELS

From the Address THE GENERAL COUNCIL
TO ALL THE MEMBERS
OF THE INTERNATIONAL
WORKING MEN'S ASSOCIATION[49]

... And now, three years later, we are put in possession of documents which prove irrefragably that this same Alliance of Socialist Democracy, in spite of its formal promise, has continued and does continue to exist as an international body within the International, and that in the shape of a secret society; that it is still directed by M. Bakounine; that its ends are still the same, and that all the attacks which for the last twelve months have been directed apparently against the London Conference and the General Council, but in reality against the whole of our organisation, have had their source in this Alliance. The same men who accuse the General Council of authoritativeness without ever having been able to specify one single authoritative act on its part, who talk at every opportunity of the autonomy of sections, of the free federation of groups; who charge the General Council with the intention of forcing upon the International its own official and orthodox doctrine and to transform our Association into a hierarchically constituted organisation—these very same men, in practice, constitute themselves as a secret society with a hierarchical organisation, and under a, not merely authoritative, but absolutely dictatorial leadership; they trample under their feet every vestige of autonomy of sections and federations; they aim at forcing upon the International, by means of this secret organisation, the personal and orthodox doctrines of M. Bakounine. While they demand that the International should be organised from below upwards, they themselves, as members of the Alliance, humbly submit to the word of command which is handed down to them from above. . . .

For the first time in the history of the working-class struggles, we stumble over a secret conspiracy plotted in the midst of that class, and intended to undermine, not the existing capitalist *régime*, but the very Association in which that *régime* finds its most energetic opponent. It is a conspiracy got up to hamper the proletarian movement. Thus, wherever we meet it, we find it preaching the emasculating doctrine of absolute abstention from political action; and while the plain profane Internationals are persecuted and imprisoned over nearly all Europe, the valiant members of the Alliance enjoy a quite exceptional immunity.

Citizens, it is for you to choose. What is at stake at this moment, is neither the autonomy of sections, nor the free federation of groups, nor the organisation from below upwards, nor any other formula equally pretentious and sonorous; the question today is this: Do you want your central organs composed of men who recognise no other mandate but yours, or do you want them composed of men elected by surprise, and who accept your mandate with the resolution to lead you, like a flock of sheep, as they may be directed by secret instructions emanating from a mysterious personage in Switzerland?

To unveil the existence of this secret society of dupers, is to crush its power. The men of the Alliance themselves are not foolish enough to expect that the great mass of the Internationals would knowingly submit to an organisation like theirs, its existence once made known. Yet there is complete incompatibility between the dupers and those who are intended for the dupes, between the Alliance and the International.

Moreover, it is time once and for all to put a stop to those internal quarrels provoked every day afresh within our Association, by the presence of this parasite body. These quarrels only serve to squander forces which ought to be employed in fighting the present middle-class *régime*. The Alliance, in so far as it paralyses the action of the International against the enemies of the working class, serves admirably the middle class and the governments.

For these reasons, the General Council will call upon the Congress of The Hague to expel from the International all and every member of the Alliance and to give the Council such powers as shall enable it effectually to prevent the recurrence of similar conspiracies.

Written August 4-6, 1872

First published in Russian
in K. Marx, F. Engels, *Works*,
1st ed., Vol. XIII, Part II, 1940

Printed according to
*The General Council of
the First International,
1871-1872, Minutes,*
Moscow, pp. 440-41,
444-45

KARL MARX and FREDERICK ENGELS

From THE RESOLUTIONS OF THE GENERAL CONGRESS HELD IN THE HAGUE[50]

SEPTEMBER 2-7, 1872

I

RESOLUTION ON THE RULES

That the following article summing up the content of Resolution IX of the London Conference (September 1871)* be included in the Rules after Article 7.

Article 7a. In its struggle against the collective power of the possessing classes the proletariat can act as a class only by constituting itself a distinct political party, opposed to all the old parties formed by the possessing classes.

This constitution of the proletariat into a political party is indispensable to ensure the triumph of the social revolution and of its ultimate goal: the abolition of classes.

The coalition of the forces of the working class, already achieved by the economic struggle, must also serve, in the hands of this class, as a lever in its struggle against the political power of its exploiters.

As the lords of the land and of capital always make use of their political privileges to defend and perpetuate their economic monopolies and to enslave labour, the conquest of political power becomes the great duty of the proletariat. . . .

Adopted by 29 votes against 8 abstaining.

Drawn up by K. Marx and F. Engels

Translated from the French

Published as a pamphlet:
Résolutions du congrès général tenu a la Haye du 2 au 7 septembre 1872, Londres, 1872, and in the newspapers *La Emancipacion* No. 72, November 2, 1872 and *The International Herald* No. 37, December 14, 1872

---

* See pp. 53-54 of this volume.—*Ed.*

KARL MARX

THE HAGUE CONGRESS

REPORTER'S RECORD
OF THE SPEECH MADE AT THE MEETING HELD
IN AMSTERDAM ON SEPTEMBER 8, 1872[31]

The Hague Congress did three principal things:

It proclaimed the necessity for the working classes to fight, in the political as well as the social sphere, against the old society, a society which is collapsing; and we are happy to see that the resolution of the London Conference is from now on included in our Rules.* A group had formed in our midst advocating the workers' abstention from politics.

We have thought it important to point out how very dangerous and baneful to our cause we considered these principles to be.

The worker will some day have to win political supremacy in order to organise labour along new lines; he will have to defeat the old policy supporting old institutions, under penalty—as in the case of the ancient Christians, who neglected and scorned it—of never seeing their kingdom on earth.

But we have by no means affirmed that this goal would be achieved by identical means.

We know of the allowances we must make for the institutions, customs and traditions of the various countries; and we do not deny that there are countries such as America, England, and I would add Holland if I knew your institutions better, where the working people may achieve their goal by peaceful means. If that is true, we must also recognise

---

* See pp. 51-52 and 83 of this volume.—*Ed.*

that in most of the continental countries it is force that will
have to be the lever of our revolutions; it is force that we
shall some day have to resort to in order to establish a reign
of labour.

Published in the newspapers   Translated from
La Liberté No. 37,   the French
September 15, 1872 and *Der Volksstaat*
No. 79, October 2, 1872

From THE IMPERATIVE MANDATES TO THE HAGUE CONGRESS[52]

... The *Jura* mandate gives rise to yet other reflections. It reveals the whole situation which prevails in the Alliance, where despite all the phrases about *anarchy, autonomy, free federation*, etc., there are really only two things: *authority* and *obedience*. A few weeks before Schwitzguébel and Guillaume drew up their mandate abolishing the *General Rules* except for the preamble, their friends outside the International, delegates to the Rimini Conference, drew up the Statutes of the so-called Italian Federation, consisting of the preamble to the General Rules and Federal Regulations. The General Rules were thus *abolished* in the organisation elected by the Rimini Conference. One can see that the men of the Alliance always act in obedience to secret and uniform instructions. And *La Federación*[53] of Barcelona was no doubt obeying these secret orders when it suddenly started pressing for discord in the International. For our Association's strong organisation in Spain has begun to represent a danger to the secret leaders of the Alliance. This organisation gives too much power to the working class, and thus creates difficulties for the secret rule of the gentlemen of the Alliance, who know all about the advantages of fishing in troubled waters.

Destroy the organisation and you'll find the waters as troubled as you could wish. Destroy above all the Trade Unions, declare war on strikes, reduce working-class solidarity to an empty phrase, and you will find yourself with a free field for your pompous, empty, doctrinaire phrases. Pro-

vided the workers of our region permit you to destroy what
has cost them four years of great effort to build, and what
is, undoubtedly, the best organisation in the whole International.

Written at the beginning of October 1872

Published in *La Emancipacion*
No. 69. October 13. 1872

Translated from
the Spanish

From THE HOUSING QUESTION[54]

Part Three
SUPPLEMENT ON PROUDHON
AND THE HOUSING QUESTION

I

In No. 86 of the *Volksstaat*, A. Mülberger reveals himself as the author of the articles criticised by me in No. 51 and subsequent numbers of the paper. In his answer he overwhelms me with such a series of reproaches, and at the same time confuses all the issues to such an extent that willy-nilly I am compelled to reply to him. I shall attempt to give my reply, which to my regret must be made to a large extent in the field of personal polemics enjoined upon me by Mülberger himself, a general interest by presenting the chief points once again and if possible more clearly than before, even at the risk of being told once more by Mülberger that all this "contains nothing essentially new either for him or for the other readers of the *Volksstaat*".

Mülberger complains of the form and content of my criticism. As far as the form is concerned it will be sufficient to reply that at the time I did not even know who had written the articles in question. There can, therefore, be no question of any personal "prejudice" against their author; against the solution of the housing problem put forward in the articles I was of course in so far "prejudiced" as I was long ago acquainted with it from Proudhon and my opinion on it was firmly fixed.

I am not going to quarrel with friend Mülberger about the "tone" of my criticism. When one has been so long in the movement as I have, one develops a fairly thick skin against attacks, and therefore one easily presumes the existence of the same in others. In order to compensate Mülberger I shall endeavour this time to bring my "tone" into the right relation to the sensitiveness of his epidermis.

Mülberger complains with particular bitterness that I said he was a Proudhonist, and he protests that he is not. Naturally I must believe him, but I shall adduce proof that the articles in question—and I had to do with them alone—contain nothing but undiluted Proudhonism.

But according to Mülberger I have also criticised Proudhon "frivolously" and have done him a serious injustice.

"The doctrine of the petty bourgeois Proudhon has become an accepted dogma in Germany, which is even proclaimed by many who have never read a line of him."

When I express regret that for twenty years the workers speaking Romance languages have had no other mental pabulum than the works of Proudhon, Mülberger answers that as far as the Latin workers are concerned, "the principles formulated by Proudhon are almost everywhere the driving spirit of the movement". This I must deny. First of all, the "driving spirit" of the working-class movement nowhere lies in "principles", but everywhere in the development of large-scale industry and its effects, the accumulation and concentration of capital, on the one hand, and of the proletariat, on the other. Secondly, it is not correct to say that in the Latin countries Proudhon's so-called "principles" play the decisive role ascribed to them by Mülberger; that "the principles of anarchism, of the organisation of the *forces économiques*, of the *liquidation sociale*, etc., have there ... become the true bearers of the revolutionary movement". Not to speak of Spain and Italy, where the Proudhonist panacea has gained some influence only in the still more botched form presented by Bakunin, it is a notorious fact for anyone who knows the international working-class movement that in France the Proudhonists form a numerically rather insignificant sect, while the mass of the French workers refuses to have anything to do with the social reform plan drawn up by Proudhon under the titles of *Liquidation sociale* and *Organisation des forces économiques*. This was shown, among other things, in the Commune. Although the Proudhonists were strongly represented in the Commune, not

the slightest attempt was made to liquidate the old society
or to organise the economic forces according to Proudhon's
proposals. On the contrary, it does the Commune the greatest honour that in all its economic measures the "driving
spirit" was not any set of "principles", but simple, practical
needs. And therefore these measure —abolition of night
work in the bakeries, prohibition of monetary fines in the
factories, confiscation of shut-down factories and workshops
and handing them over to workers' associations—were not
at all in accordance with the spirit of Proudhonism but certainly in accordance with the spirit of German scientific
socialism. The only social measure which the Proudhonists
put through was the decision *not* to confiscate the Bank of
France, and this was partly responsible for the downfall of
the Commune. In the same way, when the so-called Blanquists[55] made an attempt to transform themselves from mere
political revolutionists into a socialist workers' faction with
a definite programme—as was done by the Blanquist fugitives in London in their manifesto, *Internationale et Révolution*—they did not proclaim the "principles" of the Proudhonist plan for the salvation of society, but adopted, and
almost literally at that, the views of German scientific socialism on the necessity of political action by the proletariat
and of its dictatorship as the transition to the abolition of
classes and, with them, of the state—views such as had
already been expressed in the *Communist Manifesto* and
since then on innumerable occasions. And if Mülberger even
draws the conclusion from the Germans' disdain of Proudhon that there has been a lack of understanding of the movement in the Latin countries "down to the Paris Commune,"
let him as proof of this lack tell us what work from the
Latin side has understood and described the Commune even
approximately as correctly as has the *Address of the General Council of the International on the Civil War in France*,
written by the German Marx.

The only country where the working-class movement is
directly under the influence of Proudhonist "principles" is
Belgium, and precisely as a result of this the Belgian movement comes, as Hegel would say, "from nothing through
nothing to nothing."[56]

When I consider it a misfortune that for twenty years the

workers of the Latin countries fed intellectually, directly or indirectly, exclusively on Proudhon, I do not mean that thoroughly mythical dominance of Proudhon's reform recipe —termed by Mülberger the "principles"—but the fact that their economic criticism of existing society was contaminated with absolutely false Proudhonist phrases and that their poli- tical actions were bungled by Proudhonist influence. Wheth- er thus the "Proudhonised workers of the Latin countries" "stand more in the revolution" than the German workers, who in any case understand the meaning of scientific Ger- man socialism infinitely better than the Latins understand their Proudhon, we shall be able to answer only after we have learnt what "to stand in the revolution" really means. We have heard talk of people who "stand in Christianity, in the true faith, in the grace of God," etc. But "standing" in the revolution, in the most violent of all movements? Is, then, "the revolution" a dogmatic religion in which one must believe?

Mülberger further reproaches me with having asserted, in defiance of the express wording of his articles, that he had declared the housing question to be an exclusively working- class question.

This time Mülberger is really right. I overlooked the passage in question. It was irresponsible of me to overlook it, for it is one most characteristic of the whole tendency of his disquisition. Mülberger actually writes in plain words:

"As we have been so frequently and largely exposed to the *absurd* charge of pursuing a *class policy*, of striving for *class domination*, and such like, we wish to stress first of all and expressly that the housing question is by no means a question which affects the proletariat exclu- sively, but that, *on the contrary*, it interests *to a quite prominent extent the middle classes proper*, the small tradesmen, the petty bourgeoisie, the whole bureaucracy.... The housing question is precisely that point of social reform which more than any other seems appropriate to reveal the *absolute inner identity of the interests of the proletariat*, on the one hand, and the interests of the *middle classes proper* of society, on the other. The middle classes suffer just as much as, and *perhaps even more* than, the proletariat under the oppressive fetters of the rented dwelling.... Today the middle classes proper of society are faced with the question of whether they ... can summon sufficient strength ... to participate in the process of the transformation of society in alliance with the youthful, vigorous and energetic workers' party, a transformation *whose blessings will be enjoyed above all by them.*"

Friend Mülberger thus makes the following points here:

1. "We" do not pursue any "class policy" and do not strive for "class domination". But the German Social-Democratic Workers' Party, just *because* it is a *workers' party*, necessarily pursues a "class policy", the policy of the working class. Since each political party sets out to establish its rule in the state, so the German Social-Democratic Workers' Party is necessarily striving to establish *its* rule, the rule of the working class, hence "class domination". Moreover, *every* real proletarian party, from the English Chartists onward, has put forward a class policy, the organisation of the proletariat as an independent political party, as the primary condition of its struggle, and the dictatorship of the proletariat as the immediate aim of the struggle. By declaring this to be "absurd", Mülberger puts himself outside the proletarian movement and inside the camp of petty-bourgeois socialism.

2. The housing question has the advantage that it is not an exclusively working-class question, but a question which "interests to a quite prominent extent" the petty bourgeoisie, in that "the middle classes proper" suffer from it "just as much as, and perhaps even more than", the proletariat. If anyone declares that the petty bourgeoisie suffers, even if in one respect only, "perhaps even more than the proletariat", he can hardly complain if one counts him among the petty-bourgeois Socialists. Has Mülberger therefore any grounds for complaint when I say:

"It is largely with just such sufferings as these, which the working class endures in common with other classes, and particularly the petty bourgeoisie, that petty-bourgeois socialism, to which Proudhon belongs, prefers to occupy itself. And thus it is not at all accidental that our German Proudhonist seizes chiefly upon the housing question, which, as we have seen, is by no means exclusively a working-class question."

3. There is an "absolute inner identity" between the interests of the "middle classes proper of society" and the interests of the proletariat, and it is not the proletariat, but these middle classes proper which will "enjoy above all" the "blessings" of the coming process of transformation of society.

The workers, therefore, are going to make the coming social revolution "above all" in the interests of the petty bourgeoisie. And furthermore, there is an absolute inner identity of the interests of the petty bourgeoisie and those of the proletariat. If the interests of the petty bourgeoisie have an inner identity with those of the workers, then those of the workers have an inner identity with those of the petty bourgeoisie. The petty-bourgeois standpoint has thus as much right to exist in the movement as the proletarian stand-point, and it is precisely the assertion of this equality of right that is called petty-bourgeois socialism.

It is therefore perfectly consistent when, on page 25 of the separate reprint,[57] Mülberger extols "petty industry" as the "actual *buttress* of society", "because in accordance with its very nature it combines within itself the three factors: labour—acquisition—possession, and because in the combi-nation of these three factors it places no bounds to the capa-city for development of the individual"; and when he re-proaches modern industry in particular with destroying this nursery for the production of normal human beings and "making out of a virile *class* continually reproducing itself an unconscious *heap* of humans who do not know whither to direct their anxious gaze". The petty bourgeois is thus Mül-berger's model human being and petty industry is Mülber-ger's model mode of production. Did I defame him, therefore, when I classed him among the petty-bourgeois Socialists?

As Mülberger rejects all responsibility for Proudhon, it would be superfluous to discuss here any further how Proud-hon's reform plans aim at transforming all members of so-ciety into petty bourgeois and small peasants. It will be just as unnecessary to deal with the alleged identity of interests of the petty bourgeoisie and the workers. What is necessary is to be found already in the *Communist Manifesto*. (Leip-zig Edition, 1872, pp. 12 and 21.)

The result of our examination is, therefore, that side by side with the "myth of the petty bourgeois Proudhon" appears the reality of the petty bourgeois Mülberger.

Written
in January 1873

Translated from
the German

Published in the newspaper
Der Volksstaat No. 12,
February 8, 1873

KARL MARX

INDIFFERENCE TO POLITICS

"The working class should not form a political party, and should not, under any circumstances, undertake political action, since to combat the State is to recognise the State, which is contrary to the eternal principles. The workers must not strike, since to make efforts to increase one's wages or prevent them from being reduced is to recognise *Wages*, which is contrary to the eternal principles of emancipation of the working class!

"If in the political struggle against the bourgeois State the workers only manage to wrest concessions, they are making compromises, which is contrary to the eternal principles. One must therefore scorn any peaceful movement, as the English and American workers have the bad habit of doing. The workers must make no effort to establish a legal limit to the working day, since this is like making compromises with the bosses, who could then only exploit them for ten to twelve hours instead of fourteen to sixteen. They must not even bother to have the employment of children below the age of ten in the factories forbidden by law, since in this way they are not putting an end to the exploitation of children under ten years of age, and are thus making another compromise, which prejudices the purity of the eternal principles.

"Still less should the workers desire that, as in the American Republic, the State whose *budget* is drawn from the working class should be obliged to provide elementary education for the children of workers because elementary education is not complete education. It is better that the working men and women should not know how to read and write or count, than that they should be taught by a teacher of a State school. Far better that the working class should be afflicted by ignorance and sixteen hour's drudgery than that the eternal principles should be violated!

"If the political struggle of the working class assumes violent forms, if the workers substitute their revolutionary dictatorship for the dictatorship of the bourgeois class, they are committing the terrible crime of lese-principle, for to satisfy their own base everyday needs and crush the resistance of the bourgeoisie, instead of laying down arms and abolishing the State they are giving it a revolutionary and transient form. The workers should not form individual unions for each trade, since they thereby perpetuate the division of social labour found in bourgeois society. This division which disunites the workers is really the basis of their present servitude.

"In a word, the workers should fold their arms and not waste their time in political and economic movements. These movements can only bring them immediate results. Like truly religious people, scornful of everyday needs, they should cry, full of faith: 'May our class be crucified, may our race perish, but may the eternal principles remain unstained!' They should, like pious Christians, believe in the words of the priest, despise earthly blessings and think only of earning Paradise. For Paradise read THE ABOLITION OF SOCIETY, which will one day arrive in some small corner of the world, no one knows how or by whose efforts, and the mystification will be exactly the same.

"Until this famous abolition of society arrives, the working class must behave decently, like a flock of well-fed sheep, leave the government in peace, fear the police, respect the laws, and provide cannon fodder without complaining.

"In practical everyday life the workers must be most obedient servants of the State, but inside themselves they must protest energetically against its existence, and show their profound theoretical disdain for it by purchasing and reading literary treatises on the abolition of the State. They must moreover take good care not to offer any resistance to

the capitalist order apart from holding forth on the society
of the future in which the odious order will have ceased to
exist!"

No one would deny that if the apostles of indifference
to politics were to express themselves in such a clear manner, the working class would soon tell them where to go and
would feel highly offended by these bourgeois doctrinaires
and displaced gentlefolk who are stupid or naive enough to
forbid them every real method of struggle because all the
arms to fight with must be taken from existing society, and
because the inevitable conditions of this struggle do not
unfortunately fit in with the idealist fantasies that these
doctors of *social science* have deified under the name of
Liberty, Autonomy and *Anarchy*. But the working-class
movement is so strong today that these philanthropic sectarians no longer dare to repeat for the economic struggle the
great truths they have incessantly proclaimed on the political struggle. They are too pusillanimous to apply them yet
to strikes, combinations, and trade unions, to the laws on
female and child labour, and on the reduction of working
hours, etc., etc.

Now, it remains to be seen whether they are capable of
appealing to the fine traditions, to modesty, to good faith
and the eternal principles!

Since the social conditions were not sufficiently developed
to permit the working class to form a militant class, the
first socialists (Fourier, Owen, Saint-Simon and others) were
inevitably bound to subscribe to dreams of the *ideal society*
of the future and condemn all such attempts as strikes, associations and political movements undertaken by the workers to bring some improvement to their lot. But if we have no
right to reject these patriarchs of socialism, just as the chem-
ists have no right to reject their fathers, the alchemists, we
must at least avoid repeating their mistakes, which if committed by us would be inexcusable.

Later, however—in 1839—when the working-class political and economic struggle had acquired a fairly marked
character in England, Bray—a disciple of Owen and one of
those who had found *mutualism* considerably earlier than
Proudhon—published a book entitled *Labour's Wrongs and
Labour's Remedy*.

In one of the chapters, which deals with the inefficacy *of all the remedies it is hoped will be achieved by the present struggle*, he submits to bitter criticism all the movements, whether political or economic, of the English working class, condemning the political movement, strikes, the reduction of working hours, legislation on female and child labour in the factories, since all this—according to him—instead of enabling us to pass out of the present state of society, keeps us there and only intensifies the antagonisms.

Now we come to the oracle of these doctors of social science, Proudhon. While the master had the courage to energetically condemn all economic movements (coalitions, strikes, etc.) that were contrary to the redeeming theories of his *mutualism*, he encouraged the working-class political movement by his writings and his own personal participation: his disciples do not dare to openly condemn the movement. In 1847, at the time when the master's major work *Système des contradictions économiques* ... appeared, I confuted his sophisms against the working-class movement.* Nevertheless, in 1864, after the Ollivier law, which accorded the French workers the right to combination in such a limited manner, Proudhon returned to his task in his book *Political Capacities of the Working Classes*, published a few days after his death.

The attacks of the master were so to the taste of the bourgeoisie that the *Times*, on the occasion of the big tailors' strike in London in 1866, did Proudhon the honour of translating him and condemning the strikers with his own words. Here are a few examples from it.

The miners of Reve-de-Gier had gone on strike and the soldiers had come hurrying to return them to reason.

"The authority that had the miners of Reve-de-Gier shot," Proudhon exclaims, "was in an unfortunate position. But it acted like the ancient Brutus standing between his paternal love and his duty as Consul: he had to sacrifice his sons in order to save the Republic. Brutus did not hesitate, and posterity dare not condemn him."**

As long as the proletariat has existed, one cannot recall

* See in the work *Misère de la philosophie. Réponse à la philosophie de la misère de M. Proudhon* (Paris, A. Frank, 1847) Chapter II, § 5 entitled "Les grèves et les coalitions des ouvriers".—*Ed.*

** P. Proudhon, *De la capacité politique des classes ouvrières*, Paris, Lacroix et Cie Editeurs, 1868, p. 327.—*Ed.*

a single case of a bourgeois having hesitated to sacrifice his workers to save his own interests. What Brutuses the bourgeois are!

"No, there is no right to combination, just as there is no right to fraud or theft, just as there is no right to incest or adultery."[*]

It must be said, however, that there is certainly the right to *stupidity*.

What then are the eternal principles in the name of which the master hurls his abracadabra excommunications?

First eternal principle:

"Wages determine prices".

Those who have not the faintest notion of political economy and do not know that the great bourgeois economist Ricardo in his *Principles of Political Economy*, published in 1817, refuted once and for all this traditional error know that remarkable fact of English industry, which can offer its products at a price greatly inferior to that of any other nation while the wages are relatively higher in England than in any other country in Europe.

Second eternal principle:

"The law authorising combinations is highly anti-juridical, anti-economic, contrary to every society and order."

In a word, it is "contrary to the economic *Right* of free competition".

If the master had been a little less of a chauvinist, he would have wondered how it was that forty years earlier a law so contrary to the *economic right of free competition* was promulgated in England, and how it is that as industry develops, and with it *free competition*, this law contrary to *every society and order* is imposing itself as a necessity upon the bourgeois states. He might have discovered that this Right (with a capital R) only exists in the *economic manuals* published by the Ignoramus Brothers of bourgeois political economy, in which manuals one finds such pearls as the following: "*Property is the fruit of labour*". They omitted to say "*of other people's*" labour.

---

* P. Proudhon, *De la capacité politique des classes ouvrières*, Paris, Lacroix et Cie Editeurs, 1868, p. 333.—*Ed.*

Third eternal principle:

"Thus, under the pretext of raising the working class from so-called social inferiority, it will be necessary to begin denouncing a whole class of citizens: the class of masters, entrepreneurs, bosses and bourgeois. It will be necessary to excite working-class democracy to scorn and hatred for these unworthy colleagues of the middle class, it will be necessary to prefer mercantile and industrial warfare to legal repression, and class antagonism to the State police."*

In order to prevent the working class from emerging from its so-called *social inferiority*, the boss condemns the associations formed by the working class which make it a class antagonistic to the respectable *category of the bosses, entrepreneurs and bourgeois* who certainly prefer, like Proudhon, *the State police to class antagonisms*. In order to avoid displeasing this respectable class in any way, the good Proudhon advises the workers (until the coming of the *mutualist society* and despite the great inconvenience caused them) "liberty or competition, our only guarantee."**

The master preached indifference to economics *in order to safeguard liberty or bourgeois competition*, our only guarantee. The disciples preach indifference to politics in order to safeguard bourgeois liberty, their only guarantee. If the early Christians, who also preached indifference to politics, needed the helping hand of an emperor to change them from oppressed into oppressors, the modern apostles of indifference to politics do not believe that their eternal principles oblige them to abstain from the pleasures of the world and the transient privileges of bourgeois society. And yet we must recognise that it is with a stoicism worthy of the Christian martyrs that they put up with the fourteen to sixteen hours of work with which the factory workers are overloaded!

London, January 1873

Published in December 1873
in *Almanacco Repubblicano
per l'anno 1874*

Translated from
the Italian

---

* Ibid., pp. 337-38.—*Ed.*
** Ibid., p. 334.—*Ed.*

4*

ON AUTHORITY

A number of Socialists have latterly launched a regular crusade against what they call the *principle of authority*. It suffices to tell them that this or that act is *authoritarian* for it to be condemned. This summary mode of procedure is being abused to such an extent that it has become necessary to look into the matter somewhat more closely. Authority, in the sense in which the word is used here, means: the imposition of the will of another upon ours; on the other hand, authority presupposes subordination. Now, since these two words sound bad and the relationship which they represent is disagreeable to the subordinated party, the question is to ascertain whether there is any way of dispensing with it, whether—given the conditions of present-day society—we could not create another social system, in which this authority would be given no scope any longer and would consequently have to disappear. On examining the economic, industrial and agricultural conditions which form the basis of present-day bourgeois society, we find that they tend more and more to replace isolated action by combined action of individuals. Modern industry with its big factories and mills, where hundreds of workers supervise complicated machines driven by steam, has superseded the small workshops of the separate producers; the carriages and wagons of the highways have been substituted by railway trains, just as the small schooners and sailing feluccas have been by steamboats. Even agriculture falls increasingly under the dominion of the machine and of steam, which slowly but relentlessly put in the place of the small proprietors big capitalists, who with the aid of hired workers cultivate vast stretches of land. Everywhere combined action, the complication of processes dependent upon each other, displaces independent action by individuals. But whoever mentions combined action speaks of organisation; now, is it possible to have organisation without authority?

Supposing a social revolution dethroned the capitalists, who now exercise their authority over the production and circulation of wealth. Supposing, to adopt entirely the point of view of the anti-authoritarians, that the land and the instruments of labour had become the collective property of the workers who use them. Will authority have disappeared or will it only have changed its form? Let us see.

Let us take by way of example a cotton spinning mill. The cotton must pass through at least six successive operations before it is reduced to the state of thread, and these operations take place for the most part in different rooms. Furthermore, keeping the machines going requires an engineer to look after the steam engine, mechanics to make the current repairs, and many other labourers, whose business it is to transfer the products from one room to another, and so forth. All these workers, men, women and children, are obliged to begin and finish their work at the hours fixed by the authority of the steam, which cares nothing for individual autonomy. The workers must, therefore, first come to an understanding on the hours of work; and these hours, once they are fixed, must be observed by all, without any exception. Thereafter particular questions arise in each room and at every moment concerning the mode of production, distribution of materials, etc., which must be settled at once on pain of seeing all production immediately stopped; whether they are settled by decision of a delegate placed at the head of each branch of labour or, if possible, by a majority vote, the will of the single individual will always have to subordinate itself, which means that questions are settled in an authoritarian way. The automatic machinery of a big factory is much more despotic than the small capitalists who employ workers ever have been. At least with regard to the hours of work one may write upon the portals of these factories: *Leave, ye that enter in, all autonomy behind*![58] If man, by dint of his knowledge and inventive genius, has subdued the forces of nature, the latter avenge themselves upon him by subjecting him, in so far as he employs them, to a veritable despotism independent of all social organisation. Wanting to abolish authority in large-scale industry is tantamount to wanting to abolish industry itself, to destroy the power loom in order to return to the spinning wheel.

Let us take another example—the railway. Here too the co-operation of an infinite number of individuals is absolutely necessary, and this co-operation must be practised during precisely fixed hours so that no accidents may happen. Here, too, the first condition of the job is a dominant will that settles all subordinate questions, whether this will is represented by a single delegate or a committee charged with the execution of the resolutions of the majority of persons interested. In either case there is very pronounced authority. Moreover, what would happen to the first train dispatched if the authority of the railway employees over the Hon. passengers were abolished?

But the necessity of authority, and of imperious authority at that, will nowhere be found more evident than on board a ship on the high seas. There, in time of danger, the lives of all depend on the instantaneous and absolute obedience of all to the will of one.

When I submitted arguments like these to the most rabid anti-authoritarians the only answer they were able to give me was the following: Yes, that's true, but here it is not a case of authority which we confer on our delegates, *but of a commission entrusted*! These gentlemen think that when they have changed the names of things they have changed the things themselves. This is how these profound thinkers mock at the whole world.

We have thus seen that, on the one hand, a certain authority, no matter how delegated, and, on the other hand, a certain subordination, are things which, independently of all social organisation, are imposed upon us together with the material conditions under which we produce and make products circulate.

We have seen, besides, that the material conditions of production and circulation inevitably develop with large-scale industry and large-scale agriculture, and increasingly tend to enlarge the scope of this authority. Hence it is absurd to speak of the principle of authority as being absolutely evil, and of the principle of autonomy as being absolutely good. Authority and autonomy are relative things whose spheres vary with the various phases of the development of society. If the autonomists confined themselves to saying that the social organisation of the future would restrict authority solely to the limits within which the conditions of production render it inevitable, we could understand each other; but they are blind to all facts that make the thing necessary, and they passionately fight the word.

Why do the anti-authoritarians not confine themselves to crying out against political authority, the state? All Socialists are agreed that the political state, and with it political authority, will disappear as a result of the coming social revolution, that is, that public functions will lose their political character and be transformed into the simple administrative functions of watching over the true interests of society. But the anti-authoritarians demand that the authoritarian political state be abolished at one stroke, even before the social conditions that gave birth to it have been destroyed. They demand that the first act of the social revolution shall be the abolition of authority. Have these gentlemen ever seen a revolution? A revolution is certainly the most authoritarian thing there is; it is the act whereby one part of the population imposes its will upon the other part by means of rifles, bayonets and cannon—authoritarian means, if such there be at all; and if the victorious party does not want to have fought in vain, it must maintain this rule by means of the terror which its arms inspire in the reactionaries. Would the Paris Commune have lasted a single day if it had not made use of this authority of the armed people against the bourgeois? Should we not, on the contrary, reproach it for not having used it freely enough? Therefore, either one of two things: either the anti-authoritarians don't know what they are talking about, in which case they are creating nothing but confusion; or they do know, and in that case they are betraying the movement of the proletariat. In either case they serve the reaction.

Written in October 1872-   Translated from
March 1873   the Italian

Published in December 1873
in the miscellany
*Almanacco Repubblicano
per l'anno 1874*

KARL MARX and FREDERICK ENGELS

From THE ALLIANCE OF SOCIALIST DEMOCRACY AND THE INTERNATIONAL WORKING MEN'S ASSOCIATION

REPORT AND DOCUMENTS PUBLISHED BY DECISION OF THE HAGUE CONGRESS OF THE INTERNATIONAL[59]

I

INTRODUCTION

The International Working Men's Association, in setting itself the aim of rallying under one banner the scattered forces of the world proletariat and thus becoming the living representative of the community of interests that unites the workers, was bound to open its doors to socialists of all shades. Its founders and the representatives of the workers' organisations of the Old and New worlds who at international congresses sanctioned the General Rules of the Association, forgot that the very breadth of its programme would allow the declassed elements to worm their way in and establish, at its very heart, secret organisations whose efforts, instead of being directed against the bourgeoisie and the existing governments, would be turned against the International itself. Such has been the case with the Alliance of Socialist Democracy.

At the Hague Congress, the General Council demanded an inquiry into this secret organisation. The Congress entrusted the task to a commission of five (citizens Cuno, Lucain, Splingard, Vichard, and Walter, who resigned), which delivered its report at the session of September 7th. The Congress passed the following resolution:

1. To expel from the International Mikhail Bakunin, as founder of the Alliance and also for an act committed on his own behalf;[60]

2. To expel James Guillaume, as a member of the Alliance;

3. To publish the documents relating to the Alliance....

Here we have a society which, under the mask of the most extreme anarchism, directs its blows not against the existing governments but against the revolutionaries who refuse to accept its dogma and leadership. Founded by a minority at a bourgeois congress,[61] it infiltrates the ranks of the international organisation of the working class, at first attempts to dominate it and, when this plan fails, sets to work to disorganise it. It brazenly substitutes its sectarian programme and narrow ideas for the broad programme and great aspirations of our Association; it organises within the public sections of the International its own little secret sections which obey the same instructions and in a good many instances succeed in gaining control of the public section by prearranged action; in its newspapers it publicly attacks all those who refuse to submit to its will, and by its own avowal provokes open warfare within our ranks. It resorts to any means, any disloyalty to achieve its ends; lies, slander, intimidation, the stab in the back—it finds them all equally suitable. Finally, in Russia it substitutes itself entirely for the International and commits, in its name, crimes against the common law, acts of fraud and an assassination for which the government and bourgeois press has blamed our Association. And the International must remain silent about all these acts because the society responsible for them is secret! The International has in its possession the statutes of this society, which is its mortal enemy; statutes in which it openly proclaims itself a modern Society of Jesus and declares that it has the right and the duty to practise all the methods employed by the Jesuits; statutes that explain in a flash the whole series of hostile acts to which the International has been subjected from this quarter; but the International must not make use of these statutes—that would be denouncing a secret society!

There is only one means of combating all these intrigues, but it will prove astonishingly effective; this means is complete publicity. Exposure of all these schemings in their entirety will render them utterly powerless. To protect them with our silence would be not only an act of naïveté that the leaders of the Alliance would be the first to ridicule; it would be sheer cowardice. What is more, it would be an act of treachery towards those Spanish members of the International who, while belonging to the secret Alliance, have not hesitated to divulge its existence and its mode of action, since it has set itself up in open hostility to the International. Besides, all that is contained in the secret statutes is to be found, in much more emphatic form, in the documents published in Russian by Bakunin and Nechayev themselves. The statutes are but their confirmation.

Let the ringleaders of the Alliance cry out that they have been denounced. We deliver them up to the scorn of the workers and the benevolence of the governments whom they have served so well in disorganising the proletarian movement. The Zurich *Tagwacht*, in a reply to Bakunin, had every right to say:

"If you are not a paid agent, the one thing quite certain is that a paid agent would never have succeeded in doing as much harm as you...."[62]

II

SECRET ALLIANCE

So far we have analysed the secret organisation designed to perpetuate the dictatorship of "Citizen B."*; now let us deal with his programme.[63]

"The association of international brothers aspires to a universal revolution, simultaneously social, philosophical, economic and political, so that of the present order of things, based on property, exploitation, and the principle of authority, whether religious, metaphysical, bourgeois-doctrinaire, or even Jacobin-revolutionary, not a stone will be left standing first in Europe and then in the rest of the world. With the cry of peace for the workers, liberty for all the oppressed and death to rulers, exploiters and guardians of all kinds, we seek to destroy all states and all churches along with all their institutions and laws, religious, political, juridical, financial, police, university, economic and social, so that the millions of deceived, enslaved, tormented and exploited human beings, liberated from all their directors and benefactors, official and officious, collective and individual, may breathe at last with complete freedom."

* Bakunin.—*Ed.*

Here indeed we have revolutionary revolutionism! The first condition for the achievement of this astounding goal is to refuse to fight the existing states and governments with the means employed by ordinary revolutionaries, but on the contrary to hurl resounding, grandiloquent phrases at

"the institution of the State and that which is both its consequence and foundation—i.e., private property."

Thus it is not the Bonapartist State, the Prussian or Russian State that has to be overthrown, but an abstract State, the State as such, a State that nowhere exists. But while the international brothers[64] in their desperate struggle against this State that is situated somewhere in the clouds know how to avoid the truncheons, the prison and the bullets that real States deal out to ordinary revolutionaries, we see on the other hand that they have reserved themselves the right, subject only to papal* dispensation, to profit by all the advantages offered by these real bourgeois states. Fanelli, an Italian deputy, Soriano, an employee of the government of Amadeus of Savoy, and perhaps Albert Richard and Gaspard Blanc, Bonapartist police agents, show how accommodating the Pope is in this respect.... That is why the police shows so little concern over "the Alliance or, to put it frankly, the conspiracy" of Citizen B. against the abstract idea of the State.

Well then, the first act of the revolution must be to decree the abolition of the State, as Bakunin did on September 28th in Lyons,[65] despite the fact that abolition of the State is of necessity an authoritarian act. By the State he means all power, political, revolutionary or reactionary,

"because it matters little to us whether this authority be called the church, the monarchy, the constitutional state, the bourgeois republic or even the revolutionary dictatorship. We detest them and reject them all in equal measure as unfailing sources of exploitation and despotism."

And he goes on to declare that all the revolutionaries who, on the day after the revolution, want "construction of a revolutionary State" are far more dangerous than all the existing governments put together, and that

"we, the international brothers, are the natural enemies of these revolutionaries"

---

* Bakunin's.—*Ed.*

because to disorganise the revolution is the first duty of the international brothers.

The reply to this bragging about the immediate abolition of the State and the establishment of anarchy has already been given in the last General Council's private circular on "Fictitious Splits in the International", of March 1872, page 37:

"Anarchy, then, is the great war-horse of their master Bakunin, who has taken nothing from the socialist systems except a set of slogans. What all socialists understand by anarchy is this: once the aim of the proletarian movement, the abolition of classes, has been attained, the power of the State, which serves to keep the great majority of producers under the yoke of a numerically small exploiting minority, disappears, and the functions of government are transformed into simple administrative functions. The Alliance puts matters the other way round. It proclaims anarchy in the proletarian ranks as the surest means of breaking the powerful concentration of social and political forces in the hands of the exploiters. Under this pretext it demands of the International, at the very moment when the old world is seeking to crush it, that it should replace its organisation by anarchy."*

Let us see, however, just what the consequences of the anarchist gospel are; let us suppose the State has been abolished by decree. According to Article 6, the consequences of this act will be: bankruptcy of the State, ending of state intervention to enforce payment of private debts, cessation of payment of all taxes and all tribute, disbandment of the army, the magistracy, the bureaucracy, the police and the clergy (!); abolition of official justice, accompanied by an auto-da-fé of all title deeds on property and all judicial and civil junk, confiscation of all productive capital and instruments of labour for the benefit of the workers' associations and an alliance of these associations, which "will constitute the Commune". This Commune will give individuals thus dispossessed the strict necessaries of life, while granting them freedom to earn more by their own labour.

What happened at Lyons has proved that merely decreeing the abolition of the State is far from sufficient to accomplish

* See p. 74 of this volume.—*Ed.*

all these fine promises. Two companies of the bourgeois National Guards proved quite sufficient, on the other hand, to shatter this splendid dream and send Bakunin hurrying back to Geneva with the miraculous decree in his pocket. Naturally he could not imagine his supporters to be so stupid that they need not be given some sort of plan of organisation that would put his decree into practical effect. Here is the plan:

"For the organisation of the Commune a federation of permanently functioning barricades and a Council of the Revolutionary Commune shall be set up by delegating one or two deputies from each barricade, one per street or per district, deputies vested with imperative mandates, responsible in all respects and subject to recall any time" (odd barricades, these barricades of the Alliance, where instead of fighting they spend their time writing mandates). "The *Commune Council*, thus organised, will be able to choose from its midst *Executive Committees*, a special one for each branch of the revolutionary administration of the Commune."

The insurgent capital, thus constituted as a Commune, then proclaims to the other communes of the country that it renounces all claim to govern them; it invites them to reorganise themselves in a revolutionary way and then to send their responsible and recallable deputies, vested with their imperative mandates, to an agreed place where they will set up a federation of insurgent associations, communes and provinces and organise a revolutionary *force* capable of triumphing over reaction. This organisation will not be confined to the communes of the insurgent country; other provinces or countries will be able to take part in it, while

"the provinces, communes, associations and individuals who take sides with reaction *will not be allowed to join it.*"

So the abolition of frontiers goes hand in hand with the most benevolent tolerance towards the reactionary provinces, which would not hesitate to resume the civil war.

Thus in this anarchistic organisation of the tribune-barricades we have first the Council of the Commune, then the executive committees which, to be able to do anything at all, must be vested with some power and supported by a police force; this is to be followed by nothing short of a federal *parliament*, whose principal object will be to organise this *police force*. Like the Commune Council, this parliament will have to assign *executive power* to one or more *committees* which by this act alone will be given an authoritarian character that the demands of the struggle will increasingly accentuate. We are thus confronted with a perfect reconstruction of all the elements of the "authoritarian State"; and the fact that we call this machine a "revolutionary Commune organised from bottom to top", makes little difference. The name changes nothing of the substance; organisation from bottom to top exists in any bourgeois republic and imperative mandates date from the middle ages. Indeed Bakunin himself admits as much when (in Article 8) he describes his organisation as a "new revolutionary State".

As for the practical value of this plan of revolution with its talking instead of fighting, we shall say nothing.

Now we shall reveal the secret of all the Alliance's double and triple-bottomed boxes. To make sure that the orthodox programme is adhered to and that anarchy behaves itself properly,

"it is necessary that in the midst of popular anarchy, which will make up the very life and all the energy of the revolution, *the unity of revolutionary thought and action should be embodied in a certain organ*. That organ must be the *secret and world-wide association of the international brothers*.

"This association arises from the conviction that revolutions are never made either by individuals or by secret societies. They come about, as it were, of their own accord, produced by the force of circumstances, by the course of events and facts. They slowly mature in the depths of the instinctive conscience of the popular masses, then they explode ... the only thing a well-organised secret society can do is first to assist the birth of revolution by spreading among the masses ideas that accord with the instinct of the masses, and to organise, not the army of the revolution—that army must always be the people," (cannon fodder) "but *a revolutionary General Staff* composed of devoted, energetic and intelligent individuals who are above all sincere—not vain or ambitious—friends of the people, capable of serving as intermediaries between the revolutionary idea" (monopolised by them) "and the popular instincts."

"The number of these individuals should not, therefore, be too large. For the international organisation throughout Europe *one hundred serious and firmly united revolutionaries would be sufficient*. Two or three hundred revolutionaries would be enough for the organisation of the largest country."

So everything changes. Anarchy, the "unleashing of popular life", of "evil passions" and all the rest is no longer enough. To assure the success of the revolution one must have "*unity of thought and action*". The members of the International are trying to create this unity by propaganda, by discussion and the public organisation of the proletariat. But all Bakunin needs is a secret organisation of one hundred people, the privileged representatives of the *revolutionary idea,* the general staff in the background, self-appointed and commanded by the permanent "Citizen B." Unity of thought and action means nothing but orthodoxy and blind obedience. *Perinde ac cadaver.** We are indeed confronted with a veritable Society of Jesus.

To say that the hundred international brothers must "serve as intermediaries between the revolutionary idea and the popular instincts," is to create an unbridgeable gulf between the Alliance's revolutionary idea and the proletarian masses; it means proclaiming that these hundred guardsmen cannot be recruited anywhere but from among the privileged classes.

VIII
ALLIANCE IN RUSSIA

In the student unrest[66] Bakunin discovers "an all-destroying spirit opposed to the State ... which has emerged from the very depths of the people's life"; he congratulates "our young brothers on their revolutionary tendencies.... This means that the end is in sight of this infamous Empire of all the Russias!"...

The Russian people, Bakunin continues, are at present living in conditions similar to those that forced them to rise under Tsar Alexei, father of Peter the Great. Then it was Stenka Razin, the Cossack brigand chief, who placed himself at their head and showed them "the road" to "freedom". In order to rise today the people are waiting only for a new Stenka Razin; but this time he

---

* "Be like unto a corpse." The phrase used by Loyola to formulate the Jesuit principle imposing unquestioning obedience on the junior members of the Society.—*Ed.*

"will be replaced by the legion of declassed youth who are already living the life of the people ... Stenka Razin, no longer an individual hero but a collective one" (!) "consequently they have an invincible hero behind them. Such a hero are all the magnificent young people over whom his spirit already soars."

To perform this role of a collective Stenka Razin, the young people must prepare themselves through ignorance:

"Therefore abandon with all speed this world doomed to destruction. Leave its universities, its academies, its schools and go among the people," to become "the midwife of the people's self-emancipation, the uniter and organiser of their forces and efforts. Do not bother at this moment with learning, in the name of which they would bind you, castrate you.... Such is the belief of the finest people in the West.... The workers' world of Europe and America calls you to join them in a fraternal alliance"....

Citizen B. ... acclaims here for the first time the Russian brigand as the type of true revolutionary and preaches the cult of ignorance to young Russians under the pretext that modern science is merely official science (can one imagine an official mathematics, physics or chemistry?), and that this is the opinion of the finest people in the West. Finally he ends his leaflet by letting it be understood that through his mediation the International is proposing an alliance to these young people, whom he forbids even the *learning* of the Ignorantines....[67]

By the law of anarchist assimilation Bakunin assimilates student youth:

"The government itself shows us the road *we* must follow to attain *our* goal, that is to say, the goal of the people. It drives *us* out of the universities, the academies, the schools. We are grateful to it for having thus put us on such glorious, such strong ground. Now we stand on firm ground, now we can do things. And what are we going to do? Teach the people? That would be stupid. The people know themselves, and better than we do, what they need" (compare the secret statutes which endow the masses with "popular instincts", and the initiates with "the revolutionary idea"). "Our task is not to teach the people but to rouse them." Up to now "they have always rebelled in vain because they have rebelled separately ... we can render them invaluable assistance, we can give them what they have always lacked, what has been the principal cause of all their defeats. We can give them the unity of a universal movement by rallying their own forces."[68]

This is where the doctrine of the Alliance, anarchy at the bottom and discipline at the top, emerges in all its purity. First by rioting comes the "unleashing of what are today called the evil passions" but "in the midst of the popular anarchy, which will constitute the very life and energy of the revolution, there must be an organ expressing unity of revolutionary idea and action." That organ will be the universal "Alliance", Russian section, the *Society of the People's Judgement.*

But Bakunin is not to be satisfied merely with youth. He calls all brigands to the banner of his Alliance, Russian section.

"Brigandage is one of the most honourable forms of the Russian people's life. The brigand is a hero, a protector, a people's avenger, the irreconcilable enemy of the State, and of all social and civil order established by the State, a fighter to the death against the whole civilisation of the civil servants, the nobles, the priests and the crown.... He who fails to understand brigandage understands nothing of Russian popular history. He who is not in sympathy with it, cannot be in sympathy with Russian popular life, and has no heart for the measureless, age-long sufferings of the people; he belongs to the enemy camp, among the supporters of the State.... Brigandage is the sole proof of the vitality, the passion and the strength of the people.... The brigand in Russia is the true and only revolutionary—the revolutionary without phrases, without rhetoric culled from books, an indefatigable revolutionary, irreconcilable and irresistible in action, a popular and social revolutionary, not a political or class revolutionary.... The brigands in the forests, in the towns and in the villages scattered all over Russia, and the brigands held in the countless gaols of the empire make up a single, indivisible, close-knit world—the world of the Russian revolution. It is here, and here alone, that the real revolutionary conspiracy has long existed. He who wants to undertake real conspiracy in Russia, who wants a people's revolution, must go into this world.... Following the road pointed out to us now by the government, which drives us from the academies, the universities and schools, let us throw ourselves, brothers, among the people, into the people's movement, into the brigand and peasant rebellion and, maintaining a true and firm friendship among ourselves, let us rally into a single mass all the scattered outbursts of the mujiks" (peasants). "*Let us turn* them into a people's revolution, meaningful but pitiless."[*]

In the second leaflet, *The Principles of Revolution*, we find a development of the order given in the secret statutes for "not leaving a stone standing". Everything must be des-

---

[*] To mystify his readers Bakunin confuses the leaders of the popular uprisings of the 17th and 18th centuries with the brigands and

troyed in order to produce "complete amorphism", for if even "one of the old forms" be preserved, it will become the "embryo" from which all the other old social forms will be regenerated. The leaflet accuses the political revolutionaries who do not take this amorphism seriously of deceiving the people. It accuses them of having erected

"new gallows and scaffolds where the surviving brother revolutionaries have been done to death.... So it is that the people have not yet known a real revolution.... A real revolution does not need individuals standing at the head of the crowd and commanding it, but men hidden invisibly among the crowd and forming an invisible link between one crowd and another, and thus invisibly giving one and the same direction, one spirit and character to the movement. This is the sole purpose of bringing in a secret preparatory organisation and only to this extent is it necessary."

Here, then, the existence of the *international brothers*, so carefully concealed in the West, is exposed before the Russian public and the Russian police. Further the leaflet goes on to preach systematic assassination and declares that for people engaged in practical revolutionary work all argument about the future is

"criminal because it hinders *pure destruction* and delays the march of revolution. We believe only in those who show their devotion to the cause of revolution by deeds, without fear of torture or imprisonment, because we renounce all words that are not immediately followed by deeds. We have no further use for aimless propaganda that does not set itself a definite time and place for realisation of the aims of revolution. What is more, it stands in our way and we shall make every effort to combat it.... We shall silence by force the chatterers who refuse to understand this."

These threats were addressed to the Russian émigrés who had not bowed to Bakunin's papal authority and whom he called doctrinaires.

---

thieves of the Russia of today. As regards the latter, the reading of Flerovsky's book *The Condition of the Working Class in Russia* would disillusion the most romantic souls concerning these poor creatures from whom Bakunin proposes to form the sacred phalanx of the Russian revolution. The sole brigandage—apart from the governmental sphere, of course—that is carried on still on a big scale in Russia is the stealing of horses, run as a commercial enterprise by the capitalists, of whom the "revolutionaries without phrases" are but the tools and victims.

"We break all ties with the political émigrés who refuse to return to their country to join our ranks, and, until these ranks become evident, with all those who refuse to work for their public emergence on the scene of Russian life. *We make exception for the émigrés who have already declared themselves workers of the European revolution.* From now on we shall make no further repetitions or appeals. ... He who has ears and eyes will hear and see the men of action, and if he does not join them his destruction will be no fault of ours, just as it will be no fault of ours if all who hide behind the scenes are cold-bloodedly and pitilessly destroyed, along with the scenery that hides them."

At this point we can see right through Bakunin. While enjoining the émigrés on pain of death to return to Russia as agents of his secret society—like the Russian police-spies who would offer them passports and money to go there and join in conspiracies—he grants himself a papal dispensation to remain peacefully in Switzerland as "a worker of the European revolution", and to occupy himself composing manifestos that compromise the unfortunate students whom the police hold in their prisons.

"While not recognising any other activity but that of destruction, we acknowledge that the forms in which it manifests itself may be extremely varied: poison, dagger, noose, etc. The revolution sanctifies all without distinction. The field lies open! ... Let all heads that are young and healthy undertake at once the sacred work of killing out evil, purging and enlightening the Russian land by fire and sword, joining fraternally with those who will do the same thing throughout Europe."

Let us add that in this lofty proclamation the inevitable brigand figures in the melodramatic person of Karl Moor (from Schiller's *Robbers*), and that No. 2 of *The People's Judgement*,[69] quoting a passage from this leaflet, calls it straight out "*a proclamation of Bakunin's*". . . .

No one will venture to doubt that these Russian pamphlets, the secret statutes, and all the works published by Bakunin since 1869 in French, come from one and the same source. On the contrary, all these three categories complement one another. They correspond to some extent to the three degrees of initiation into the famous organisation of universal destruction. The French brochures of Citizen B. are written for the rank and file of the Alliance, whose prejudices are taken into account. They are told of nothing but pure anar-

chy, of anti-authoritarianism, of a free federation of autonomous groups and other equally harmless things: a mere
jumble of words. The secret statutes are intended for the
international brothers of the West; there anarchy becomes
"the complete unleashing of popular life ... of evil passions",
but underneath this anarchy there lies the secret directing
element—the brothers themselves; they are given only a few
vague indications on the morality of the Alliance, stolen
from Loyola, and the necessity of leaving not a stone standing is mentioned only in passing, because these are West-
erners brought up on Philistine prejudices and some allowances have to be made for them. They are told that the truth,
too blinding for eyes not yet accustomed to true anarchism,
will be fully revealed in the programme of the Russian
section. Only to the born anarchists, to the people elect, to
his young people of Holy Russia does the prophet dare to
speak out openly. There anarchy means universal, pan destruction; the revolution, a series of assassinations, first individual and then *en masse*; the sole rule of action, the Jesuit
morality intensified; the revolutionary type, the brigand.
There, thought and learning are absolutely forbidden to the
young as mundane occupations that could lead them to doubt
the all-destructive orthodoxy. Those who persist in adhering
to these theoretical heresies or who apply their vulgar
criticism to the dogmas of universal amorphism are threatened with a holy inquisition. Before the youth of Russia the
Pope* need feel no restraint either in the form or substance
of his utterances. He gives his tongue free play and the
complete absence of ideas is expressed in such grandiloquent
verbiage that it cannot be reproduced in French without
weakening its comic effect. His language is not even real
Russian. It is Tatar, so a native Russian has stated. These
small men with atrophied minds puff themselves up with
horrific phrases in order to appear in their own eyes as
giants of revolution. It is the fable of the frog and the ox.
   What terrible revolutionaries! They want to annihilate
and amorphise everything, "absolutely everything". They
draw up lists of proscribed persons, doomed to die by their
daggers, their poison, their ropes, by the bullets from their

---

* Bakunin.—*Ed.*

revolvers; they "will tear out the tongues" of many, but they will bow before the majesty of the Tsar. Indeed, the Tsar, the officials, the nobility, the bourgeoisie may sleep in peace. The Alliance does not make war on the established states, but on the revolutionaries who do not stoop to the role of supernumeraries in this tragi-comedy. Peace to the palaces, war on the cottages! ...

The third article is entitled: *The Fundamental Principles of the Future Social Order*.[70] This article shows that if the ordinary mortal is punished like a criminal for even thinking about the social organisation of the future, this is because the leaders have arranged everything in advance.

"The ending of the present social order and the renewal of life with the aid of the new principles can be accomplished *only by concentrating all the means of social existence in the hands of* Our Committee, *and the proclamation of compulsory physical labour for everyone.*

"The Committee, as soon as the present institutions have been overthrown, proclaims that everything is common property, orders the setting up of workers' societies (*artels*) and at the same time publishes statistical tables compiled by experts and pointing out what branches of labour are most needed in a certain locality and what branches may run into difficulties there.

"For a certain number of days assigned for the revolutionary upheaval and the disorders that are bound to follow, each person must join one or another of these *artels* according to his own choice.... All those who remain isolated and unattached to workers' groups without sufficient reason will have no right of access either to the communal eating places or to the communal dormitories, or to any other buildings assigned to meet the various needs of the brother-workers or that contain the goods and materials, the victuals or tools reserved for all members of the established workers' society; in a word, he who without sufficient reason has not joined an *artel*, will be left without means of subsistence. All the roads, all the means of communication will be closed to him; he will have no other alternative but work or death."

Each *artel* will elect from its members an assessor *("otzienchtchik")*, who regulates the work, keeps the books on production and consumption and the productivity of every worker, and acts as go-between with the general office of the given locality. The office, consisting of members elected from among the artels of the locality, conducts exchange between these *artels*, administers all the communal establishments (dormitories, eating places, schools, hospitals) and directs all public works: "All general work is managed by the office, while all individual work requiring special skills and craftsmanship is performed by special *artels*." Then comes a long set of rules on education, hours of work, feeding of children, freeing of inventors from work and so on.

"With full publicity, knowledge and activity on the part of everyone all ambition, as we now know it, all deception will disappear without a trace, will vanish forever.... Everyone will endeavour to produce as much as possible for society and consume as little as possible; all the pride, all the ambition of the worker of those times will rest in the awareness of his usefulness to society."

What a beautiful model of barrack-room communism! Here you have it all: communal eating, communal sleeping, assessors and offices regulating education, production, consumption, in a word, all social activity, and to crown all, *Our Committee*, anonymous and unknown to anyone, as the supreme director. This is indeed the purest anti-authoritarianism....

Now that the common herd knows the role "our committee" is destined to perform, it is easy to understand this competitive hatred of the state and of any centralisation of the workers' forces. Assuredly, while the working class continues to have any representative bodies of its own, Messrs Bakunin and Nechayev, revolutionising under the incognito of "our committee", will not be able to put themselves in possession of the public wealth or reap the benefit of this sublime ambition which they so ardently desire to inspire in others—that of working much to consume little! ...

This same man who in 1870 preaches to the Russians passive, blind obedience to orders coming from above and from an anonymous committee; who declares that jesuitical discipline is the condition *sine qua non* of victory, the only thing capable of defeating the formidable centralisation of the State—not just the Russian State but any State; who proclaims a communism more authoritarian than the most primitive communism—this same man, in 1871, weaves a separatist and disorganising movement into the fabric of the International under the pretext of combating the authoritarianism and centralisation of the German Communists, of introducing autonomy of the sections, a free federation of autonomous groups, and of making the International what it should be: the image of the future society. If the society of the future were modelled on the Alliance, Russian section, it would far surpass the Paraguay of the Reverend Jesuit Fathers,[71] so dear to Bakunin's heart.

IX
CONCLUSION

While granting the fullest freedom to the movements and aspirations of the working class in various countries, the International had nevertheless succeeded in uniting it into a single whole and making the ruling classes and their governments feel for the first time the cosmopolitan power of the proletariat. The ruling classes and the governments recognised this fact by concentrating their attacks on the executive body of our whole organisation, the General Council. These attacks became increasingly intense after the fall of the Commune. And this was the moment that the Alliancists chose to declare open war on the General Council themselves! They claimed that its influence, a powerful weapon in the hands of the International, was but a weapon directed against the International itself. It had been won in a struggle not against the enemies of the proletariat but against the International. According to them, the General Council's domineering tendencies had prevailed over the autonomy of the sections and the national federations. The only way of saving autonomy was to decapitate the International.

Indeed the men of the Alliance realised that if they did not seize this decisive moment, it would be all up with their plans for the secret direction of the proletarian movement of which Bakunin's hundred international brothers had dreamed. Their invective wakened approving echoes in the police press of all countries.

Their resounding phrases about autonomy and free federation, in a word, war-cries against the General Council, were thus nothing but a manoeuvre to conceal their true purpose—to disorganise the International and by doing so subordinate it to the secret, hierarchic and autocratic rule of the Alliance.

Autonomy of the sections, free federation of the autonomous groups, anti-authoritarianism, anarchy—these were convenient phrases for a society of the "declassed", of "down-and-outs" "with no career or prospects", conspiring within the International to subject it to a secret dictatorship and impose upon it the programme of M. Bakunin!

Stripped of its melodramatic finery, this programme amounts to the following:

1. All the depravities in which the life of declassed persons ejected from the upper strata of society must inevitably become involved are proclaimed to be so many ultra-revolutionary virtues.

2. It is regarded as a matter of principle and necessity to debauch a small minority of carefully selected workers, who are enticed away from the masses by a mysterious initiation, by making them take part in the game of intrigues and deceit of the secret government, and by preaching to them that through giving free rein to their "evil passions" they can shake the old society to its foundations.

3. The chief means of propaganda is to attract young people by fantastic lies about the extent and power of the secret society, prophecies of the imminent revolution it has prepared and so on, and to compromise in government eyes the most progressive people from among the well-to-do classes with a view to exploiting them financially.

4. The economic and political struggle of the workers for their emancipation is replaced by the universal pan-destructive acts of heroes of the underworld—this latest incarnation of revolution. In a word, one must let loose the street hooligans suppressed by the workers themselves in "the revolutions on the Western classical model", and thus place gratuitously at the disposal of the reactionaries a well disciplined gang of *agents provocateurs*.

It is hard to say what predominates in the theoretical elucubrations and practical endeavours of the Alliance—clowning or infamy. Nevertheless, it has succeeded in provoking within the International a muffled conflict which for two years has hindered the actions of our Association and has culminated in the secession of some of the sections and federations. The resolutions adopted by the Hague Congress against the Alliance were therefore merely a matter of duty; the Congress could not allow the International, that great creation of the proletariat, to fall into nets spread by the riff-raff of the exploiting classes. As for those who wish to deprive the General Council of the prerogatives without which the International would be nothing but a confused, disjointed and, to use the language of the Alliance, "amorphous" mass, we cannot regard them otherwise than as traitors or dupes.

London, July 21, 1873

The Commission:

E. Dupont, F. Engels, Leó Frankel, A. Le Moussu, Karl Marx, Aug. Serraillier

Written by K. Marx and F. Engels in collaboration with P. Lafargue in April-July 1873

Published as a pamphlet in London and Hamburg in August 1873

Translated from the French

FROM THE INTERNATIONAL
(Excerpt)

...In Italy, where the anarchists of the secessionist variety are lording it for the present, one of them, Crescio of Piacenza, sent his new paper *L'Avvenire Sociale* (*The Social Future*) to Garibaldi, who, as these gentlemen constantly claim, is one of them. The paper was full of angry invective against what they call "the authoritarian principle", which in their view is at the root of all evil. Garibaldi replied:

> "Dear Crescio, many thanks, etc. In your paper you intend to wage a war against falsehood and slavery. That is quite a good programme. But I believe that the fight against the authoritarian principle is an error of the International, which hampers its advance. *The Paris Commune fell because there was no longer any authority in Paris but only anarchy.*"

This veteran fighter for freedom, who achieved more in one year—i.e. 1860—than all the anarchists will ever attempt in the course of their life, places a great value on discipline because he himself had to discipline his troops, and he did it not like the official soldiers, by drill and the threat of the firing-squad, but when facing the enemy.

Unfortunately we have not yet come to the end of the list of mishaps which the separatists had to endure. Only one thing was still missing and that too took place. The *Neue*,* whose police nose had long since caught the peculiar smell of these arch mischief-makers of the International, now supports

* *Neuer Social-Demokrat.*—Ed.

them whole-heartedly. In issue 68 the paper states that the rules drafted by the Belgians—who had in fact left the International—completely correspond to its views and holds out the prospect of its joining the separatists. Thus all our wishes have been fulfilled. When Hasselmann and Hasenclever appear at the separatist congress this separatist organisation will acquire its true character. On the right Bakunin, on the left Hasenclever and in the middle the hapless Belgians, who are led by the nose of their Proudhonist phrases.

Written June 19-20, 1873

Published in *Der Volksstaat*
No. 53, July 2, 1873

Translated from
the German

FREDERICK ENGELS

THE BAKUNINISTS AT WORK

From THE PREFACE TO THE BOOKLET— *INTERNATIONALES AUS DEM "VOLKSSTAAT"* *(1871-75)*

The second article, *The Bakuninists at Work*, which describes the activities of the anarchists in Spain during the July uprising of 1873, was previously published as a separate pamphlet. Although the anarchist caricature of the working-class movement has long since passed its zenith, the European and American governments are still so interested in its continued existence and are spending such large sums of money in its support, that we cannot entirely disregard the anarchists' heroic exploits. We are therefore reprinting the article here....

Written by F. Engels
January 3, 1894

Translated from
the German

Published in the booklet:
F. Engels, *Internationales aus dem "Volksstaat" (1871-75),*
Berlin, 1894

A few chronological data may help to make the following review more easily understood.

On February 9, 1873, King Amadeo, tired of his Spanish kingship, abdicated, thus becoming the first king to go on strike. On the 12th a republic was proclaimed[72] and immediately a new Carlist revolt broke out in the Basque provinces.

On April 10, a Constituent Assembly was elected, which met at the beginning of June and on June 8 proclaimed a Federal Republic. On the 11th, a new government under Pi y Margall was set up. At the same time a commission was elected to draw up a new constitution, but the radical republicans, known as the Intransigents, were excluded from it. When the new Constitution was announced on July 3, the Intransigents did not think it went far enough as regards the splitting up of Spain into "independent cantons"; they therefore immediately started uprisings in the provinces. Between July 5 and 11, the Intransigents were successful in Seville, Cordoba, Granada, Málaga, Cadiz, Alcoy, Murcia, Cartagena, Valencia, etc. and set up an independent cantonal government in each of these towns. On July 18, Pi y Margall resigned and was replaced by Salmeron, who promptly sent troops against the insurgents. After offering slight resistance the insurgents were defeated within a few days, and by July 26, with the fall of Cadiz government power was restored throughout Andalusia; at about the same time Murcia and

Valencia were subdued, and only Valencia fought with any energy.

Cartagena alone held out. This naval port, the largest in Spain, which had fallen to the insurgents together with the fleet, was protected on the landward side not only by a rampart but also by 13 separate forts, and was therefore difficult to take. Since the government did not like the idea of destroying its own naval base, the "sovereign canton of Cartagena" survived until January 11, 1874, when it finally capitulated, because there was nothing else left for it to do.

The only thing that concerns us here in this disgraceful insurrection is the even more disgraceful actions of the Bakuninist anarchists; only these are presented here in some detail as a warning example to our contemporaries.

Written at the beginning
of January 1894

Translated from
the German

Published in the booklet:
F. Engels, *Internationales aus dem "Volksstaat" (1871-75),*
Berlin. 1894

THE BAKUNINISTS AT WORK

AN ACCOUNT OF THE SPANISH REVOLT
IN THE SUMMER OF 1873

I

The report just published by the Hague Commission on
Mikhail Bakunin's secret Alliance* has revealed to the working class the underhand activities, the dirty tricks and phrase-
mongery by which the proletarian movement was to be placed
at the service of the inflated ambition and selfish ends of a
few misunderstood geniuses. Meanwhile these would-be great
men have given us the opportunity in Spain to see something
of their practical revolutionary activity. Let us see how they
put into practice their ultra-revolutionary phrases about
anarchy and autonomy, about the abolition of all authority,
especially that of the state, and the immediate and complete
emancipation of the workers.

We are at last able to do this, since, apart from the newspaper reports about the events in Spain, we now have the
report of the New Madrid Federation of the International[73]
presented to the Geneva Congress.[74]

As we know, at the time the split in the International occurred the odds were in favour of the members of the secret
Alliance[75] in Spain; the great majority of Spanish workers
followed their lead. When the Republic was proclaimed in
February 1873, the Spanish members of the Alliance found
themselves in a quandary. Spain is such a backward country

---

* *L'Alliance de la démocratie socialiste*, London 1873. The German
edition was published under the title: *Ein Komplott gegen die Internationale* (Buchhandlung des "Vorwärts"). (Note by F. Engels to the
1894 edition.—*Ed.*)

industrially that there can be no question there of *immediate* complete emancipation of the working class. Spain will first have to pass through various preliminary stages of development and remove quite a number of obstacles from its path. The Republic offered a chance of going through these stages in the shortest possible time and quickly surmounting the obstacles. But this chance could be taken only if the Spanish working class played an active *political* role. The labour masses felt this: they strove everywhere to participate in events, to take advantage of the opportunity for action, instead of leaving the propertied classes, as hitherto, a clear field for action and intrigues. The government announced that elections were to be held to the Constituent Cortes. What was the attitude of the International to be? The leaders of the Bakuninists were in a predicament. Continued political inaction became more ridiculous and impossible with every passing day; the workers wanted "to see things done". The members of the Alliance on the other hand had been preaching for years that no part should be taken in a revolution that did not have as its aim the immediate and complete emancipation of the working class, that political action of any kind implied recognition of the State, which was the root of all evil, and that therefore participation in any form of elections was a crime worthy of death. How they got out of this fix is recounted in the already mentioned Madrid report:

"The same people who rejected the Hague resolution on the political attitude of the working class and who trampled under foot the Rules of the [International Working Men's] Association, thus bringing division, conflict and confusion into the Spanish section of the International; the same people who had the effrontery to depict us to the workers as ambitious place-hunters, who, under the pretext of establishing the rule of the working class, sought to establish their own rule; the same people who call themselves autonomists, anarchist revolutionaries, etc., have on this occasion flung themselves into politics, bourgeois politics of the worst kind. They have worked, not to give political power to the working class—on the contrary this idea is repugnant to them—but to help to power a bourgeois faction of adventurers, ambitious men and place-hunters who call themselves Intransigent Republicans.

"On the eve of the general election to the Constituent Cortes the workers of Barcelona, Alcoy and other towns wanted to know what political line they should adopt in the parliamentary struggle and other campaigns. Two big meetings were therefore held, one in Barcelona, the other in Alcoy; at both meetings the Alliance members went out of their way to prevent any decision being reached as to what political line was to be taken by the International" (nota bene: by their own International). "It was therefore decided that the *International, as an association, should not engage in any political activity whatever, but that its members, as individuals, could act on their own as they thought fit and join any party they chose*, in accordance with their famous doctrine of autonomy! And what was the result of the application of this absurd doctrine? That most of the members of the International, including the anarchists, took part in the elections with no programme, no banner, and no candidates, thereby helping to bring about the election of almost exclusively bourgeois republicans. Only two or three workers got into the Chamber, and they represent absolutely nothing, their voice has not once been raised in defence of the interests of our class, and they cheerfully voted for all the reactionary motions tabled by the majority."

That is what Bakuninist "abstention from politics" leads to. At quiet times, when the workers know beforehand that at best they can return only a few representatives to parliament and have no chance whatever of winning a parliamentary majority, the workers may sometimes be made to believe that it is a great revolutionary action to sit out the elections at home, and in general, not to attack the State in which they live and which oppresses them, but to attack the State as such which exists nowhere and which accordingly cannot defend itself. This is a splendid way of behaving in a revolutionary manner, especially for people who lose heart easily; and the extent to which the leaders of the Spanish Alliance belong to this category of people is shown in some detail in the aforementioned publication.

As soon as events push the proletariat into the fore, however, abstention becomes a palpable absurdity and the active intervention of the working class an inevitable necessity. And this is what happened in Spain. The abdication of Amadeo ousted the radical monarchists[76] from power and deprived them of the possibility of recovering it in the near future; the Alfonsists[77] stood still less chance at the time; as for the Carlists,[78] they, as usual, preferred civil war to an election campaign. All these parties, according to Spanish custom, abstained. Only the federalist Republicans, split into two wings, and the bulk of the workers took part in the elections. Given the enormous attraction which the name of the International still enjoyed at that time among the Spanish workers and given the excellent organisation of the Spanish Section which, at least for practical purposes, still existed at the time, it was certain that any candidate nominated and supported by the International would be brilliantly successful in the industrial districts of Catalonia, in Valencia, in the Andalusian towns and so on, and that a minority would be elected to the Cortes large enough to decide the issue whenever it came to a vote between the two wings of the Republicans. The workers were aware of this; they felt that the time had come to bring their still powerful organisation into play. But their leaders of the Bakuninist school had been preaching the gospel of unqualified abstention too long to be able suddenly to reverse their line; and so they invented that deplorable way out—that of having the International abstain as a body, but allowing its members as individuals to vote *as they liked*. The result of this declaration of political bankruptcy was that the workers, as always in such cases, voted for those who made the most radical speeches, that is, for the Intransigents, and considering themselves therefore more or less responsible for subsequent steps taken by their deputies, became involved in them.

II

The members of the Alliance could not possibly persist in the ridiculous position into which their cunning electoral policy had landed them; it would have meant the end of their control over the International in Spain. They had to act, if only for the sake of appearances. Salvation for them lay in a *general strike*.

In the Bakuninist programme a general strike is the lever employed by which the social revolution is started. One fine morning all the workers in all the industries of a country, or even of the whole world, stop work, thus forcing the propertied classes either humbly to submit within four weeks at the most, or to attack the workers, who would then have the right to defend themselves and use this opportunity to pull down the entire old society. The idea is far from new; this horse was since 1848 hard ridden by French, and later Belgian socialists; it is originally, however, an English breed. During the rapid and vigorous growth of Chartism among the English workers following the crisis of 1837, the "holy month", a strike on a national scale was advocated as early as 1839 (see

Engels, *Die Lage der Arbeitenden Klasse*, zweite Auflage
p. 234, [The Condition of the Working Class in England][79])
and this had such a strong appeal that in July 1842 the industrial workers in northern England tried to put it into
practice. Great importance was also attached to the general
strike at the Geneva Congress of the Alliance held on
September 1, 1873,[80] although it was universally admitted
that this required a well-formed organisation of the working
class and plentiful funds. And there's the rub. On the one
hand the governments, especially if encouraged by political
abstention, will never allow the organisation or the funds of
the workers to reach such a level; on the other hand, political
events and oppressive acts by the ruling classes will lead to
the liberation of the workers long before the proletariat is
able to set up such an ideal organisation and this colossal
reserve fund. But if it had them, there would be no need to
use the roundabout way of a general strike to achieve its goal.

No one with any knowledge of the secret springs of the
Alliance can doubt that the idea of using this well-tried
method originated in the Swiss centre. Be that as it may,
the Spanish leaders saw in this a way of doing something
without actually delving in "politics" and they gladly took it.
The miraculous qualities of a general strike were everywhere
propounded and preparations were made to start it at
Barcelona and Alcoy.

Meanwhile the political situation was steadily heading for
a crisis. Castelar and his associates, the old federal republican
braggarts, were frightened by the movement, which had outgrown them. They were obliged to hand over the reigns of
government to Pi y Margall, who sought a compromise with
the Intransigents. Of all the official republicans, Pi was the
only Socialist, the only one who realised that the republic had
to depend on the support of the workers. He promptly produced a programme of social measures which could be carried
out immediately and would not only benefit the workers
directly but eventually lead to further steps, thus at least
giving the first impetus to the social revolution. But the
Bakuninist members of the International, who were obliged to
reject even the most revolutionary measures if they emanated
from the "State", preferred to support the most preposterous
swindlers among the Intransigents rather than a minister.

Pi's negotiations with the Intransigents dragged on. The Intransigents began to lose patience, and the most hot-headed of them started a cantonal uprising in Andalusia. The leaders of the Alliance now had to act too if they did not want to trail in the wake of the intransigent bourgeois. And so a general strike was ordered.

Presently, among other things, a poster was issued in Barcelona stating:

"Workers! We are calling a general strike to show the profound abhorrence we feel on seeing the government using the army fight our brother workers, while neglecting the struggle against the Carlists", etc.

The workers of Barcelona—Spain's largest industrial city, which has seen more barricade fighting than any other city in the world—were asked to oppose the armed government force not with arms in their hands, but with a general strike, that is, a measure directly involving only individual bourgeois, but not their collective representative—the State power. During the period of peacetime inaction, the workers of Barcelona had been able to listen to the inflammatory phrases of mild men like Alerini, Farga Pellicer and Viñas; but when the time came to act, when Alerini, Farga Pellicer and Viñas first announced their fine election programme, then proceeded to calm passions, and finally, instead of issuing a call to arms declared a general strike, the workers actually despised them. Even the weakest Intransigent showed more energy than the strongest member of the Alliance. The Alliance and the International which was hoodwinked by it lost all influence and when these gentlemen called for a general strike claiming that this would paralyse the government the workers simply ridiculed them. What the activities of the false International did achieve, however, was that Barcelona took no part in the cantonal uprising. Barcelona was the only town whose participation could have provided firm support for the working-class element, which was everywhere strongly represented in the movement, and thus hold out the prospect of the workers ultimately controlling the entire movement. Furthermore, with the participation of Barcelona, victory would have been as good as won. But Barcelona did not raise a finger; the workers of Barcelona, who had seen through the Intransigents and been cheated by the Alliance, remained inactive, thus allowing the Madrid government to secure the final victory. All of which did not prevent Alerini and Brousse, members of the Alliance (the report on the Alliance contained further details about them), from stating in their paper, the *Solidarité révolutionnaire*:[81]

"The revolutionary movement is spreading like wildfire throughout the peninsula ... *nothing has as yet happened* in Barcelona, *but the revolution is permanent in the market place!*"

But it was the revolution of the Alliance, which consists in beating the big drum and for this reason remains "permanently" in the same "place".

At the same time the general strike became the order of the day in Alcoy. Alcoy is a new industrial town of some 30,000 inhabitants, where the International, in its Bakuninist form, gained a foothold only a year ago and spread rapidly. Socialism, in any form, went down well with these workers, who until then had known nothing of the movement; the same thing happens in Germany where occasionally in some backward town the General Association of German Workers[82] suddenly gains a large temporary following. Alcoy was therefore chosen as the seat of the Bakuninist Federal Commission for Spain, and it is the work of this Federal Commission that we are going to see here.

On July 7, a workers' meeting voted for a general strike and on the following day sent a deputation to the alcalde (the mayor) asking him to summon the manufacturers within 24 hours and present to them the workers' demands. Albors, the alcalde, a bourgeois Republican, put off the workers, sent to Alicante for troops and advised the manufacturers not to yield but to barricade themselves in their houses. He himself would remain at his post. After a meeting with the manufacturers—we are here following the official report of the Bakuninist Federal Commission dated July 14, 1873[83]— Albors, who had originally promised the workers to remain neutral, issued a proclamation in which he "insulted and slandered the workers and sided with the manufacturers thus destroying the rights and the freedom of the strikers and challenging them to fight". How the pious wishes of a mayor can destroy the rights and the freedom of the strikers is not made clear. Anyway, the workers led by the Alliance notified the magistrate through a committee that if he did not intend to remain neutral during the strike as he promised, he had better resign in order to avoid a conflict. The committee was turned away and as it was leaving the town hall, the police opened fire on the peaceful and unarmed people standing in the square. This is how the fight started, according to the report of the Alliance. The people armed themselves, and a battle began which was said to have lasted "twenty hours". On one side, the workers, whose number is given by the *Solidarité révolutionnaire* as 5,000, on the other, 32 gendarmes in the town hall and a few armed men in four or five houses in the market place. These houses were burnt down by the people in the good Prussian manner. Eventually the gendarmes ran out of ammunition and had to surrender.

"There would have been less misfortunes to lament," says the report of the Commission, "if the Alcalde Albors had not deceived the people by pretending to surrender and then cowardly ordering the murder of those who entered the town hall relying on his word. And the Alcalde himself would not have been killed by the justly enraged population had he not fired his revolver point-blank at those who went to arrest him."

And what were the casualties in this battle?

"Although we cannot know exactly the number of dead and wounded" (on the people's side) "we can nevertheless say that they numbered *no less than ten.* On the side of provokers there were no less than *fifteen* dead and wounded."

This was the first street battle of the Alliance. For twenty hours 5,000 men fought against 32 gendarmes and a few armed bourgeois, and defeated them after they had run out of ammunition, losing ten men in all. The Alliance may well drum Falstaff's dictum into the heads of its adepts that "the better part of valour is discretion".[84]

Needless to say, all the horror stories carried by the bourgeois papers about factories senselessly burnt down, numerous gendarmes shot down, and of people having petrol poured over them and set on fire, are pure inventions. The victorious workers, even if led by members of the Alliance whose motto is, "high-handed behaviour everywhere", always treat their defeated adversaries far too generously, and so the latter accuse them of all the misdeeds which they themselves never fail to perpetrate when they are victorious.

And so victory had been won.

The *Solidarité révolutionnaire* writes jubilantly: "Our friends in Alcoy, numbering 5,000, are masters of the situation."

And what did these "masters" do with their situation?

Here the report of the Alliance and its newspaper leave us in the lurch and we have to rely on the ordinary newspaper reports. From these we learn that a "Committee of Public Safety", that is, a revolutionary government, was then set up in Alcoy. To be sure, at their Congress at Saint-Imier (Switzerland), on September 15, 1872, the members of the Alliance decided that "any organisation of political, so-called provisional or revolutionary authority, can be nothing but a new fraud and would be just as dangerous for the proletariat as any of the now existing governments". The members of the Spanish Federal Commission, meeting at Alcoy, had moreover done everything they could to get this resolution adopted also by the Congress of the Spanish Section of the International. And yet we find that Severino Albarracin, a member of this Commission, and, according to some reports, also Francisco Tomas, its secretary, became members of the Committee of Public Safety, that provisional and revolutionary government of Alcoy.

And what did this Committee of Public Safety do? What measures did it adopt to bring about "the immediate and complete emancipation of the workers"? It forbade any man to leave the city, although women were allowed to do so, provided they ... had a pass! The enemies of all authority re-introducing a pass! Everything else was utter confusion, inactivity and helplessness.

Meanwhile, General Velarde was coming up from Alicante with troops. The government had every reason for wishing to deal with the local insurrections in the provinces quietly. And the "masters of the situation" in Alcoy had every reason for wanting to extricate themselves from a situation which they did not know how to handle. Accordingly, Deputy Cervera, who acted as go-between, had an easy task. The Committee of Public Safety resigned, and on July 12 the troops entered the town without meeting any resistance, the only promise made to the Committee of Public Safety for this being ... a general amnesty. The "masters of the situation" had once again extricated themselves from a tight spot. And there the Alcoy adventure ended.

The Alliance report tells us that at Sanlucar de Barrameda, near Cadiz,

"the Alcalde closed down the premises of the International and his threats and his incessant attacks on the personal rights of the citizens incensed the workers. A commission demanded of the minister observance of the law and the reopening of the premises which had been arbitrarily closed down. Mr Pi agreed to this in principle... but refused to comply in practice. It became clear to the workers that the Government was determined to outlaw their Association; they dismissed the local authorities and appointed others in their place, who reopened the premises of the Association."

"In Sanlucar ... the people are masters of the situation", the *Solidarité révolutionnaire* writes triumphantly. The members of the Alliance who here too, contrary to their anarchist principles, formed a revolutionary government, did not know what to do with their power. They wasted time in futile debates and paper resolutions, and when General Pavía, on August 5, after taking Seville and Cadiz, sent a few companies of the Soria brigade to Sanlucar he encountered no resistance.

Such were the heroic deeds performed by the Alliance where it had no competition.

III

The street fighting in Alcoy was immediately followed by a revolt of the Intransigents in Andalusia. Pi y Margall was still at the helm, engaged in continuous negotiation with the leaders of this party with the object of forming a ministry with them; why then did they begin an uprising before the negotiations had failed? The reason for this rash action has never been properly explained, it is however certain, that the main concern of the Intransigents was the actual establishment of a federal republic as quickly as possible in order to seize power and the many new administrative posts that were to be created in the various cantons. The splitting up of Spain had been deferred too long by the Cortes in Madrid, and so they had to tackle the job themselves and proclaim

sovereign cantons everywhere. The attitude hitherto maintained by the (Bakuninist) International, which since the elections was deeply involved in the actions of the Intransigents,
gave grounds for counting on the Bakuninists' support: indeed, had not the Bakuninists just seized Alcoy by force and
were thus in open conflict with the government? The
Bakuninists moreover had for years been preaching that all
revolutionary action from above was an evil, and everything
should be organised and carried through from below. And
now here was an opportunity to apply the famous principle
of autonomy from below, at least in a few towns. The
Bakuninist workers were bound to fall into the trap and pull
the chestnuts out of the fire for the Intransigents, only to be
rewarded later by their allies with the usual kicks and bullets.

What was the position of the Bakuninist members of the
International in all this movement? They helped to evolve
its federalist particularism; they put into practice as far as
possible their anarchist ideal. The same Bakuninists who
in Cordoba a few months earlier had declared that to
establish a revolutionary government was to betray and cheat
the workers, the same Bakuninists now sat in all the revolutionary municipal governments of Andalusia, but always in a
minority, so that the Intransigents could do whatever they
wished. While the latter retained the political and military
leadership, the workers were put off with pompous phrases or
resolutions purporting to introduce social reforms of the
crudest and most meaningless sort, which moreover existed
only on paper. As soon as the Bakuninist leaders demanded
real concessions, they were scornfully repulsed. When talking
to English newspaper correspondents, the Intransigent leaders
of the movement hastened to dissociate themselves from these
so-called "members of the International" and to reject all
responsibility for them, declaring that their leaders and all
fugitives from the Paris Commune were being kept under
strict police supervision. Finally, as we shall see, the Intransigents in Seville, during the battle with the government
troops, fired also on their Bakuninist allies.*

Thus it happened that within a few days the whole of

---

* *Der Volksstaat* (No. 106, November 2, 1873) printed the following
three paragraphs at the end of Section III.—*Ed.*

Andalusia was in the hands of the armed Intransigents. Seville, Malaga, Granada, Cadiz, etc. were taken almost without resistance. Each town proclaimed itself a sovereign canton and set up a revolutionary committee (junta). Murcia, Cartagena, and Valencia followed suit. A similar attempt, but of a more peaceful nature, was made in Salamanca. Thus, nearly all the large Spanish cities were held by the insurgents, with the exception of Madrid, the capital, which is purely a luxury city and hardly ever plays a decisive role, and of Barcelona. If Barcelona had risen success would have been almost assured, and in addition it would have provided powerful support for the working-class element of the movement. But, as we have seen, the Intransigents in Barcelona were comparatively powerless, whereas the Bakuninists, who were still very strong there at the time, used the general strike only for appeasement purposes. Thus, Barcelona this time was not at its post.

Nevertheless, the uprising, though started in a senseless way, had a fair chance of success if conducted with some intelligence, even if in the manner of the Spanish military revolts, in which the garrison of one town rises, marches to the next town and wins over the garrison there which had been propagandised in advance, and, growing like an avalanche, advances on the capital, until a successful engagement or the desertion to its side of the troops sent out against it, decides the victory. This method was eminently suited to the occasion. The insurgents had long been organised everywhere into volunteer battalions, whose discipline, it is true, was poor, but certainly no worse than that of the remnants of the old Spanish army, which for the most part had been disbanded. The only reliable troops the government had were the gendarmes (*guardias civiles*), and these were scattered all over the country. The thing was to prevent the gendarmes from mustering, and this could only be done by boldly giving battle in the open field. No great risk was involved in this since the government could send against the volunteers only troops that were just as undisciplined as they themselves. And if they wanted to win, this was the only way to go about it.

But no. The federalism of the Intransigents and their Bakuninist tail consisted precisely in the fact that each town acted on its own, declaring that the important thing was not co-operation with other towns but separation from them, thus precluding any possibility of a combined attack. What was an unavoidable evil during the German Peasants' War[85] and the German insurrections of May 1849, namely, the fragmentation and isolation of the revolutionary forces which enabled the government troops to smash one revolt after the other,[86] was here proclaimed a principle of supreme revolutionary wisdom. Bakunin had that satisfaction. As early as September 1870 (in his *Lettres à un français*[87]) he had declared that the only way to drive the Prussians out of France by a revolutionary struggle was to do away with all forms of centralised leadership and leave each town, each village, each parish to wage war on its own.

If one thus opposed the Prussian army under its centralised command with unfettered revolutionary passion victory would be ensured. Confronted with the collective mind of the French people, thrown at last on its own resources, the individual mind of Moltke would obviously sink into insignificance. The French then refused to see this, but in Spain Bakunin had won a brilliant victory, as we have already seen and shall yet see.

Meanwhile, this uprising, launched without reason like a bolt from the blue, had made it impossible for Pi y Margall to continue his negotiations with the Intransigents. He was compelled to resign and was replaced by pure republicans like Castelar, undisguised bourgeois, whose primary aim was to crush the working-class movement, which they had previously used but which had now become a hindrance to them. One division under General Pavía was sent against Andalusia, another under General Campos against Valencia and Cartagena. The main body consisted of gendarmes drawn from all over Spain, all of them old soldiers whose discipline was still unshaken. Here too, as during the attacks of the Versailles army on Paris, the gendarmes were to bolster up the demoralised regulars and to form the spearhead of the attacking columns, a task which in both cases they fulfilled to the best of their abilities. Besides the gendarmes, the divisions contained a few rather diminished line regiments, so that each of them numbered some 3,000 men. This was all the Government was able to raise against the insurgents.

General Pavía took the field round about July 20. A detachment of gendarmes and line troops under Ripoll occupied Cordoba on the 24th. On the 29th Pavía attacked the barricaded Seville, which fell to him on the 30th or 31st, the dates are often not clearly stated in these telegrams. Leaving behind a flying column to put down the surrounding country, he marched against Cadiz, whose defenders only fought on the approaches to the city, and with little spirit at that, and then, on August 4, they allowed themselves to be disarmed without resistance. In the days that followed, Pavía disarmed, also without resistance, Sanlucar de Barrameda, San Roque, Tarifa, Algeciras, and a great many other small towns, each of which had set itself up as a sovereign canton. At the same time he sent detachments against Málaga, which surrendered on August 3rd, and Granada, which surrendered on August 8, without offering any resistance. Thus by August 10, in less than a fortnight and almost without a struggle, the whole of Andalusia had been subdued.

On July 26 Martinez Campos began the attack on Valencia. The revolt there had been raised by the workers. When the split in the Spanish International occurred, the real International had the majority in Valencia, and the new Spanish Federal Council was transferred there. Soon after the proclamation of the Republic, when revolutionary battles lay ahead, the Bakuninist workers of Valencia, mistrusting the Barcelona leaders who cloaked their appeasement policy with ultra-revolutionary phrases, offered the members of the real International their co-operation in all local movements. When the cantonal movement started, both groups, making use of the Intransigents, immediately attacked and ejected the troops. Who formed the Valencia Junta remains unknown, but from the reports of the English newspaper correspondents it appears that workers definitely predominated in the Junta, just as they did among the Valencia Volunteers. The same correspondents spoke of the Valencia insurgents with a respect which they were far from showing towards the other rebels, who were mostly Intransigents; they praised their discipline and the order which prevailed in the city, and predicted a long resistance and a hard struggle. They were not mistaken. Valencia, an open city, withstood the attacks of

Campos' division from July 26 to August 8, longer than the whole of Andalusia.

In the province of Murcia, the capital of the same name was occupied without a fight; after the fall of Valencia Campos moved against Cartagena, one of the strongest fortresses in Spain, protected on the landward side by a rampart and advanced forts on the commanding heights. The 3,000 government troops, who had no siege artillery, and whose light field guns were of course powerless against the heavy artillery of the forts, had to confine themselves to laying siege to the city from the landward side. This was of little avail, however, as long as the Cartagenians dominated the sea with the naval vessels they had captured in the harbour. The insurgents, who, while the fight had been going on in Valencia and Andalusia, were wholly preoccupied with their own affairs, began to think of the outside world after the other revolts had been quelled, when they themselves began to run short of money and provisions. Only then did they make an attempt to march on Madrid, which was at least 60 miles away, more than twice as far as, for instance, Valencia or Granada! The expedition ended in disaster not far from Cartagena. The siege precluded any possibility of further land sorties, so they attempted sorties with the aid of the fleet. And what sorties! There could be no question of raising revolts again with the aid of Cartagenan warships in the coastal towns which had recently been subdued. The fleet of the Sovereign Canton of Cartagena therefore confined itself to threatening to shell the other coastal towns from Valencia to Málaga, which, according to the theory of the Cartagenans, were likewise sovereign—and if need be to shell them in actual fact if they failed to deliver on board the required provisions and war contribution in hard cash. While these cities, as sovereign cantons, had been fighting the government, Cartagena adhered to the principle of "every man for himself". Now when they had been defeated the principle which was held to be valid was—"everyone for Cartagena". That was how the Intransigents of Cartagena and their Bakuninist supporters interpreted the federalism of the sovereign cantons.

In order to reinforce the ranks of the fighters for liberty, the government of Cartagena released from the local jail

about 1,800 convicts—Spain's worst robbers and murderers.
After the disclosures made in the report on the Alliance
there can no longer be any room for doubt that this revolutionary step was suggested to it by the Bakuninists. The
report shows Bakunin enthusiastically advocating the
"unleashing of all evil passions" and holding up the Russian
robber as a model for all true revolutionaries.* What is fair
for the Russian is fair for the Spaniard. When the local
government of Cartagena released the "evil passions" of the
1,800 jailed cutthroats, thereby carrying demoralisation
among its troops to the extreme limit, it acted wholly in the
spirit of Bakunin. And when, instead of battering down its
own fortifications, the Spanish Government awaited the fall
of Cartagena through the internal disorganisation of its defenders, it was pursuing an entirely correct policy.

IV

Now let us hear what the report of the New Madrid
Federation has to say about the whole movement.

"On the second Sunday in August a Congress was to be held in
Valencia, which, among other things, was to determine the attitude
the Spanish International Federation was to adopt towards the important political events taking place in Spain since February 11, the day
the Republic was proclaimed. But this nonsensical" (descabellada,
literally—dishevelled) "cantonal uprising, which was such an abject
failure and in which members of the International eagerly took part
in almost all the insurgent provinces, has not only brought the work
of the Federal Council to a standstill by dispersing most of its members,
but has almost completely disorganised the local federations and, what
is worse, exposed their members to the full measure of hatred and
persecution that an ignominiously started and defeated popular insurrection always entails. . . .

"When the cantonal uprising started, when the juntas, i.e., the
cantonal governments, were formed, these people" (the Bakuninists)
"who had spoken so violently against political power, and accused us
of authoritarianism, lost no time in joining those governments. And in
important cities such as Seville, Cadiz, Sanlucar de Barrameda, Granada and Valencia, many members of the International who call themselves anti-authoritarians sat on the cantonal juntas with no programme
other than that of autonomy for the provinces or cantons. This is
officially established by the proclamations and other documents issued

* See pp. 113-14 of this volume.—Ed.

by those juntas over the signatures of well-known members of this
International.

"Such a flagrant contradiction between theory and practice, between
propaganda and action, would be of small account if our Association
could have derived any benefit from it, or if it could have advanced the
organisation of our forces, or in any way furthered the attainment of
our main goal—the emancipation of the working class. Just the opposite
took place, as it was bound to in the absence of the primary condition,
namely, the active collaboration of the Spanish proletariat, which
could have been so easily achieved by acting in the name of the
International. There was no agreement between the local federations;
the movement was abandoned to individual or local initiative without
leadership (apart from that which *the mysterious Alliance was able to
force upon it, and that Alliance to our shame still dominates the
Spanish International*) and without any programme other than that of
our natural enemies, the bourgeois republicans. Thus, the cantonal
movement suffered the most ignominious defeat without offering hardly
any resistance, and dragging down with it also the prestige and organisation of the International in Spain. For every excess, every crime,
every outrage that takes place the Republicans today blame the
members of the International. We are even assured, that at Seville
during the fighting the Intransigents fired at their own allies, the"
(Bakuninist) "members of the International. Taking clever advantage
of our follies, the reactionaries are inciting the Republicans to perse-
cute us and vilify us in the eyes of the indifferent masses; it seems
that what they were unable to achieve in the days of Sagasta, i.e., to
give the International a bad name among the great mass of Spanish
workers, they may be able to achieve now.

"A number of workers' sections in Barcelona dissociated themselves
from the International and publicly protested against the people of the
newspaper *La Federación*" (the main organ of the Bakuninists) "and
their inexplicable attitude. In Jérez, Puerto de Santa Maria and other
towns the federations have decided to dissolve themselves. The few
members of the International who lived in Loja (Granada province)
were expelled by the population. In Madrid, where people still enjoy
the greatest freedom, the old" (Bakuninist) "Federation shows no sign
of life, while ours is compelled to remain inactive and silent if it does
not want to take the blame for other people's sins. In the northern
cities the Carlist war, which is becoming more bitter day by day,
precludes any activity on our part. Finally, in Valencia, where the
government won the day after a struggle lasting a fortnight, the
members of the International who have not fled are forced to remain
in hiding, and the Federal Council has been dissolved."

So much for the Madrid report. As we see, it agrees in all
particulars with the above historical account.

What then is the result of our whole investigation?

1. As soon as they were faced with a serious revolutionary
situation, the Bakuninists had to throw the whole of their old
programme overboard. First they sacrificed their doctrine of

absolute abstention from political and especially electoral, activities. Then anarchy, the abolition of the State, shared the same fate. Instead of abolishing the State they tried, on the contrary, to set up a number of new, small states. They then dropped the principle that the workers must not take part in any revolution that did not have as its aim the immediate and complete emancipation of the proletariat, and they themselves took part in a movement that was notoriously bourgeois. Finally they went against the dogma they had only just proclaimed—that the establishment of a revolutionary government is but another fraud, another betrayal of the working class—for they sat quite comfortably in the juntas of the various towns, and moreover almost everywhere as an impotent minority outvoted and politically exploited by the bourgeoisie.

2. This renunciation of the principles they had always been preaching was made moreover in the most cowardly and deceitful manner and was prompted by a guilty conscience, so that neither the Bakuninists themselves nor the masses they led had any programme or knew what they wanted when they joined the movement. The natural consequence of this was that the Bakuninists either prevented any action from being taken, as in Barcelona, or drifted into sporadic, desultory and senseless uprisings, as in Alcoy and Sanlucar de Barrameda; or that the leadership of the uprising was taken over by the intransigent bourgeois, as was the case in most of the revolts. Thus, when it came to doing things, the ultra-revolutionary rantings of the Bakuninists either turned into appeasement or into uprisings that were doomed to failure, or, led to their joining a bourgeois party which exploited the workers politically in the most disgraceful manner and treated them to kicks into the bargain.

3. Nothing remains of the so-called principles of anarchy, free federation of independent groups, etc., but the boundless, and senseless fragmentation of the revolutionary resources, which enabled the government to conquer one city after another with a handful of soldiers, practically unresisted.

4. The outcome of all this is that not only have the once so well organised and numerous Spanish sections of the International—both the false and the true ones—found themselves involved in the downfall of the Intransigents and are now

actually dissolved, but are also having ascribed to them innumerable atrocities, without which the Philistines of all nationalities cannot imagine a workers' uprising, and this may make impossible, perhaps for years to come, the reorganisation of the Spanish proletariat in the International.

5. In short, the Bakuninists in Spain have given us an unparalleled example of how a revolution should *not* be made.

Written in September and October 1873

Translated from the German

Published in the newspaper
Der Volksstaat, Nos. 105, 106 and 107,
October 31, November 2 and 5, 1873;
and as a pamphlet in Leipzig in 1874.
Reprinted in the booklet:
F. Engels, *Internationales aus dem "Volksstaat" (1871-75)*, Berlin, 1894

KARL MARX

From THE CONSPECTUS OF BAKUNIN'S BOOK
STATE AND ANARCHY[88]

"We have already expressed our profound aversion to the theory
of Lassalle and Marx which advises the workers *to establish* ⟨*a
people's State*⟩*—at least as an immediate principal goal if not as an
ultimate ideal—which, they explain, will be simply 'the proletariat
⟨*transformed into the ruling class*⟩'. If the proletariat will be the ruling
class, the question arises, whom will it rule? ⟨This means⟩ that another
proletariat will still remain which will be subject to this new rule, this
new ⟨State⟩"

It means that as long as other classes, and the capitalist
class in particular, still exist, and as long as the proletariat
fights against them (for its enemies and the old organisation
of society do not vanish as a result of its coming to power)
it must employ *coercive* measures, that is, government
measures; so long it is still a class itself, and the economic
conditions which give rise to the class struggle and the
existence of classes have not yet disappeared and must be
forcibly removed or transformed, and the process of their
transformation accelerated by the use of force.

"For example, the common peasant, ⟨the peasant rabble⟩, who, as
we know, [are not regarded] with favour by the Marxists, and are at
the lowest stage of civilisation, will probably be governed by the urban
and industrial proletariat."

That is to say, wherever large numbers of peasants exist
as private proprietors, and where they even constitute a more
or less considerable majority, as in all countries of the West

---

* The words in ⟨   ⟩ were written by Marx in Russian.—*Ed.*

European continent where they have not disappeared and
been supplanted by agricultural day-labourers as in England,
the following alternatives exist: either the peasants prevent
and doom to failure every workers' revolution, as they have
done in France up to now, or the proletariat (for the peasant
proprietor does not belong to the proletariat; even where he
does belong to it by reason of his position, he does not consider himself as belonging to it) functioning as the government must take steps that will directly improve his position
and thus win him over to the revolution; these steps moreover
further the transition from private to communal ownership of
land in such a way, that the peasant comes to it of his own
accord on economic grounds. But one must not affront the
peasant, for instance by proclaiming the abolition of the right
of inheritance or the abolition of his property—the latter can
only be done where the peasant has been ousted by the
capitalist tenant farmers, so that the real cultivator is as much
a proletarian, a wage-worker, as the urban worker, and consequently shares with him, not indirectly, but *directly*, the
same interests; still less should parcelled property be rein-
forced by enlarging the parcel simply by allowing the
peasants to annex the larger estates, as Bakunin advocated in
his revolutionary campaign.

"Or if the matter is regarded from a national standpoint, one has
to assume that as regards the Germans the Slavs will for that very
reason be placed in the same servile subordination to the victorious
German proletariat in which the latter now stands in relation to its
bourgeoisie" (p. 278).

Schoolboy nonsense! A radical social revolution depends
on particular historical conditions of economic development;
they are its prerequisites. Thus a revolution is possible only
where, together with capitalist production, the industrial proletariat occupies at least an important place within the
population. And to have any chance of success it must
mutatis mutandis be able immediately to do at least as much
for the peasants as the French bourgeoisie during its revolution did for the French peasants of the time. A fine idea to
assume that the rule of the workers stands for the subjuga-
tion of agricultural workers. This is where the inmost
thoughts of Mr Bakunin are revealed. He understands

nothing whatever about social revolution; all he knows about it is political phrases; its economic prerequisites do not exist for him. Since all the economic forms, developed or undeveloped, that have existed till now included the enslavement of the worker (whether in the shape of the wage-worker or the peasant, etc.) he presumes that a *radical revolution* is equally possible in all of them. What is more, he wants the European social revolution, which is based on the economic foundation of capitalist production, to be carried out on the level of the Russian or Slav agricultural or pastoral nations, and not to overstep this level, although he perceives that navigation creates distinctions among brethren, but only *navigation*, since these distinctions are known to all politicians! The basis of Bakunin's social revolution is the *will*, and not the economic conditions.

"Where there is ⟨State⟩ there is bound to be ⟨domination⟩, consequently slavery too; domination without slavery, whether open or disguised, is inconceivable, and that is why we are enemies of the State" (p. 278).
"What is meant by the proletariat transformed into the ruling class?"

It means that the proletariat, instead of fighting individually against the economically privileged classes, has gained sufficient strength and is sufficiently well organised to employ general means of compulsion in its struggle against these classes. It can, however, use only economic means designed to abolish its own distinctive trait as a wage-earner, and hence to abolish itself as a class. Its complete victory is consequently also the end of its domination, since its class character has disappeared.

"Will perhaps the proletariat as a whole head the government?"

Does in a trade union, for instance, the whole union constitute the executive committee? Will all division of labour in a factory disappear and also the various functions arising from it? And will everybody be at the top in Bakunin's construction built from the bottom upwards? There will in fact be no below then. Will all members of the commune also administer the common affairs of the region? In that case there will be no difference between commune and region.

"The Germans number nearly 40 million. Will, for example, all 40 million be members of the government?"

Certainly, for the thing begins with the self-government of the commune.

"The whole people will govern and no one will be governed."

If a man has self-control, then, according to this principle, he has no self-control, for he is only himself and nobody else.

"Then there will be no government and no state, but if there should be a state then there will also be rulers and slaves" (p. 279).

That is simply to say, when class rule has disappeared a state in the now accepted political sense of the word no longer exists.

"This dilemma contained in the theory of the Marxists is easily solved. By people's government they" (i.e., Bakunin) "understand governing the people by means of a small number of representatives elected by the people."

This democratic drivel, political claptrap is asinine. Elections are a political form which exists in the smallest Russian commune and artel. The nature of the elections is determined not by the name, but by the economic basis, the economic interrelations of the voters, and from the moment when the functions have ceased to be political ones (1) government functions no longer exist; (2) the distribution of general functions becomes a routine matter and does not entail any domination; (3) elections completely lose their present political character.

"The universal right of election of representatives and rulers of the state by the whole people"—

(such a thing as the whole people in the present sense of the word is a phantasm)—

"this last word of the Marxists as well as of the democratic school— is a lie, which conceals the despotism of the *ruling minority*, and is all the more dangerous for appearing as the expression of a would-be popular will."

Under collective property the so-called popular will disappears to be replaced by the genuine will of the co-operative.

"Hence the result is that the vast majority of the people is governed by a privileged minority. But this minority will consist of workmen say the Marxists."

Where?

"Yes it may perhaps consist of former workmen, but as soon as they become representatives or rulers of the people they *cease to be workmen*"

—no more than does a manufacturer today cease to be a capitalist on becoming a town-councillor—

"and view all ordinary workers from the eminence of state; they will then no longer represent the people, but only themselves and their pretensions to govern the people. Anyone who doubts this does not understand human nature" (p. 279).

If Mr Bakunin understood at least the position of a manager in a co-operative factory, all his illusions about domination would go to the devil. He ought to have asked himself what form the functions of management could assume in such a workers' state, if he chooses to call it thus.

On p. 279 he writes: "But these elected men will become fervently convinced and also learned socialists. The words which the Lassalleans and Marxists constantly use in their writings and speeches—

the words "*learned socialism*" have never been used "and *scientific socialism*" used only in contradistinction to utopian socialism which seeks to foist new fantasies upon the people instead of confining its field of investigation to the social movement created by the people; see my book against Proudhon—

"only go to prove that the so-called people's state will be nothing but a rather despotic rule over the masses of the people exercised by a very small aristocracy of genuine or spurious scholars. The people is not scientifically trained, it will accordingly be completely relieved of all the cares of government and wholly included in the herd that has to be governed. A fine liberation!" (pp. 279-80).

"The Marxists are aware of this" (!) "contradiction and realising that the government of scholars" (what a fantastic notion!) "will be the world's most oppressive, resented and despicable government and that despite its democratic forms it will in fact be a dictatorship, they seek consolation in the thought that this dictatorship will be a provisional and shortlived measure."

Non, mon cher! [in the thought] that the *class rule* of the workers over the resisting strata of the old world can only continue until the economic basis that makes the existence of classes possible has been destroyed.

"They say that their only concern and aim will be to educate and raise the people" (arm-chair politician!) "both economically and politically to such a level that any sort of government will soon become superfluous, that the state will completely lose its political, i.e., authoritarian, nature, and that it will automatically become a free organisation of economic interests and communes. This is an obvious contradiction. If their state is really a people's state, then why should it be abolished and if its abolition is essential to the real liberation of the people, how dare they call it a people's state?" (p. 280).

Leaving aside this harping on Liebknecht's *people's state*,[89] which is nonsense directed against the Communist Manifesto, etc., this means simply that since the proletariat, during the period of struggle to overthrow the old society, still acts on the basis of the old society and consequently within political forms which more or less belong to that society, it has, during this period of struggle, not yet attained its ultimate structure, and to achieve its liberation it employs means which will be discarded after the liberation; hence Mr B. concludes that the proletariat should rather do nothing at all and wait for the *day of universal liquidation*—the Last Judgement.

"*By our polemic*" (which was, of course, published before my book against Proudhon, before the Communist Manifesto, and even before Saint-Simon) "against them" (a wonderful hysteron proteron) "*we* have made them *admit* that freedom, or anarchy" (Mr Bakunin has merely translated Proudhon's and Stirner's anarchy into the crude language of the Tartars),

"that is, the free organisation of the working masses from below upwards" (nonsense) "is the ultimate goal of social development, and that every state, including the people's state, is a yoke that creates despotism on the one hand, and slavery on the other" (p. 280)....

Written in 1874 and the   Translated from
beginning of 1875   the German

First published
in *Letopisi marksizma* No. 11,
1926

FREDERICK ENGELS

A LETTER TO A. BEBEL

London, March 18-28, 1875

The free people's state is transformed into the free state. Taken in its grammatical sense, a free state is one where the state is free in relation to its citizens, hence a state with a despotic government. The whole talk about the state should be dropped, especially since the Commune,* which was no longer a state in the proper sense of the word. The "people's state" has been thrown in our faces by the Anarchists to the point of disgust, although already Marx's book against Proudhon[90] and later the *Communist Manifesto*[91] directly declare that with the introduction of the socialist order of society the state will dissolve of itself and disappear. As, therefore, the state is only a transitional institution which is used in the struggle, in the revolution, to hold down one's adversaries by force, it is pure nonsense to talk of a free people's state: so long as the proletariat still *uses* the state, it does not use it in the interests of freedom but in order to hold down its adversaries, and as soon as it becomes possible to speak of freedom the state as such ceases to exist. We would therefore propose to replace *state* everywhere by *Gemeinwesen*, a good old German word which can very well convey the meaning of the French word "*commune*".

Written March 18-28, 1875

First published in the book:
A. Bebel, *Aus meinem Leben*,
T. II, Stuttgart, 1911

Translated from
the German

---

* Paris Commune.—*Ed.*

FREDERICK ENGELS

IN ITALY

The socialist movement in Italy has at last been placed on a firm foundation and a rapid and successful development can be expected there. But to enable the reader to fully grasp the changes that have taken place, we have to retrace the history of the origin of Italian socialism.

The origin of the Italian movement can be traced back to Bakuninist influences. While a passionate but extremely confused class hatred against their exploiters prevailed among the masses of workers, a group of young lawyers, physicians, writers, clerks, etc., under the command of Bakunin himself, seized the leadership in all towns where the revolutionary workers were active. All of them, albeit in varied degrees of initiation, were members of the secret Bakuninist Alliance, whose aim was to impose its leadership on the European labour movement as a whole, and thus enable the Bakuninist sect surreptitiously to gain control of the future social revolution. A detailed account of this can be found in the pamphlet *Ein Complot gegen die Internationale* (A Conspiracy Against the International) (published by Bracke in Brunswick).[92]

This worked satisfactorily while the workers' movement itself was still in the process of formation. Bakunin's extravagant revolutionary phrases called forth the desired applause everywhere; even elements stemming from earlier political revolutionary movements were swept along in this current, and together with Spain, Italy became in Bakunin's own words, "the most revolutionary country in Europe".[93]

Revolutionary in the sense of there being much cry and little wool. Unlike the essentially political struggle by means of which the English labour movement, followed by the French and finally the German movement, became great and powerful, here all political activity was rejected since it implied recognition of "the State", and "the State" was the epitome of all evil. Hence, the ban on the formation of a workers' *party*, the ban on the fight for safeguards against exploitation, e.g., a normal working day, limitation of female and child labour; and above all a ban on all participation in *elections*. On the other hand, we have the command to agitate, organise and conspire for the coming revolution, which, when it drops from the skies, should be carried through solely by the initiative of the working masses (secretly directed by the Alliance) without any provisional government and in the total absence of any state or state-like institutions, which are to be destroyed—"But do not ask me how!"[94]

As we have already said, so long as the movement was in its infancy this was very effective. The vast majority of Italian towns exist largely outside the framework of world traffic, which they know only in the shape of tourist traffic. These towns supply the local peasants with handicraft products and facilitate the sale of agricultural produce in a wider territory; moreover, the landowning aristocrats live in these towns and spend their revenue there; and, finally, a multitude of tourists spend their money there. The proletarian strata in these towns are not very numerous, still less advanced, and in addition comprise a strong admixture of people who have no regular or steady jobs, a circumstance which is favoured by the tourist traffic and the mild climate. These were the first places where ultra-revolutionary phrases, which tacitly implied dagger and poison, fell upon fertile soil. But there are also industrial towns in Italy, especially in the north, and as soon as the movement gained a foothold among the truly proletarian masses of *these* towns such hazy food could no longer suffice, nor could *these* workers allow those frustrated young bourgeois—who had thrown themselves into socialism because, to use Bakunin's words, their "career had reached a deadlock"—to act for long as their guardians.

That is exactly what happened. The resentment of the

North Italian workers against the ban on all political action, i.e., on all *real* action which went further than idle talk and conspiratorial humbug, steadily hardened. The German electoral victories of 1874 and their consequences which brought about the unification of the German Socialists were noticed in Italy as well. The elements which stemmed from the old republican movement and had only reluctantly submitted to the "anarchistic" clamour began more and more often to stress the necessity of political struggle and to voice the growing opposition in *La Plebe*.[95] This weekly, which was republican during the first years of its existence, soon joined the socialist movement and kept aloof as long as possible from all "anarchical" sectionalism. When, finally, the labour masses in Northern Italy outgrew their officious leaders and created a real movement in place of the fantastic one, they found in *La Plebe* a willing organ prepared from time to time to publish heretical hints about the necessity of waging a political struggle.

Had Bakunin been alive he would have fought this heresy in his usual manner. He would have imputed "authoritarianism", despotic leanings, ambition, etc., to the people connected with *La Plebe*; he would have made various petty personal complaints against them and would have caused this to be constantly reiterated in all the organs of the Alliance in Switzerland, Italy and Spain. Only afterwards would he have demonstrated that all these crimes were simply the inevitable outcome of that original deadly sin—that of the heresy of recognising political action; for political action implied recognition of the state, and since the state was the embodiment of authoritarianism, of domination, it followed that everybody who stood for working-class political action must logically stand for political domination for himself, and hence be an enemy of the working class—lynch him! Bakunin used this method, which he borrowed from the late Maximilien Robespierre, with great skill, but applied it far too often and too monotonously. This was nevertheless the only method which promised at least temporary success.

But Bakunin died and the secret world government passed into the hands of Mr James Guillaume of Neuchâtel in Switzerland. The cunning man of the world was superseded by a strait-laced pedant who applied the fanaticism of the

Swiss Calvinists to the anarchist doctrine. The true faith had to be asserted at all costs and the narrow-minded school-master of Neuchâtel had in any case to be recognised as the Pope of this true faith. The *Bulletin de la Federation Jurassienne*[96]—a Federation with a membership of no more than 200 as against the 5,000 of the Swiss Workers Association—was designated as the official gazette of the sect and began bluntly to revile those whose faith had been shaken. But the workers of Lombardy who had formed the North Italian Federation were no longer willing to put up with these exhortations. When last autumn the Jurassic *Bulletin* even presumed to order the *Plebe* to get rid of its Paris correspondent who had incurred Mr Guillaume's displeasure, the friendship came to an end. The *Bulletin* continued to accuse the *Plebe* and the North Italians of heresy, but these now knew what was what; they knew that the preaching of anarchy and autonomy served to conceal the claim of a few plotters to dictate their orders to the whole working class movement.

"A remark of four short and very calm lines has strongly irritated the Jura *Bulletin*, and it tries to make out that we were enraged by it, whereas we were merely *amused*. Indeed, one would have to be very childish to swallow the bait of people who, ill with envy, knock at all doors and by means of vilification seek to solicit some malicious expressions against us and our friends. The hand which has long been sowing the seeds of *discord and strife* is too well known for anyone to be still deceived by its Jesuitical (Loyolian) machinations." (*Plebe*, January 21, 1877.)

And in the issue of February 26 these same people are called "a few narrow-minded *anarchistic* and—what a monstrous contradiction!—at the same time *dictatorial* minds"; this is the best proof that the minds of these gentlemen have been fully understood in Milan and that they can cause no more mischief there.

The finishing touches were put by the German elections of January 10 and the change which they brought about in the Belgian movement, i.e., the abandonment of the old policy of political abstention and its replacement by agitation for universal suffrage and factory legislation. The North Italian Federation held a Congress in Milan on February 17 and 18. In its resolutions the Congress refrains from all unnecessary

and misplaced hostility towards the Bakuninist groups of the
Italian section of the International. They also expressed will-
ingness to send delegates to the Congress which is to meet in
Brussels and which will attempt to unite the various factions
of the European labour movement. But at the same time they
very clearly formulate three points which are of decisive
importance for the Italian movement, namely:

1. that *all* available means—hence also political means—
must be used to promote the movement;

2. that the socialist workers must set up a socialist *party*,
which is to be independent of any other political or religious
party;

3. that the North Italian Federation considers itself a
member of this great association, without prejudice to the
Federation's autonomy and on the basis of the *original* Rules
of the International, and moreover *independent* of all its
other Italian connections, which however will continue to
receive proofs of its solidarity.

And so—political struggle, organisation of a political party
and separation from the anarchists. These resolutions show
that the North Italian Federation has definitely broken with
the Bakuninist sect and taken its stand on the common ground
of the great European labour movement. And since it
embraces the industrially advanced regions of Italy—
Lombardy, Piedmont and Venetia—it is bound to be successful. In face of the rational means of agitation which
experience has shown to be effective in all other countries,
the cliquishness of the Bakuninist quacks will quickly reveal
its impotence, and in the South of the country too the Italian
proletariat will throw off the yoke imposed by people whose
mission to lead the workers' movement derives from the fact
that they are down-and-out bourgeois.

Written between March 6   Translated from
and 14, 1877   the German

Published in the *Vorwärts* No. 32,
March 16, 1877

From THE WORKINGMEN
OF EUROPE IN 1877

II

Great as was the effect of the German elections in the country itself, it was far greater abroad.[97] And in the first instance, it restored that harmony to the European working-class movement which had been disturbed, for the last six years, by the pretensions of a small but extremely busy sect.

Those of our readers who have followed the history of the International Workingmen's Association, will recollect, that, immediately after the fall of the Paris Commune, there arose dissensions in the midst of the great labor organisation, which led to an open split, at the Hague Congress 1872 and to consequent disintegration. These dissensions were caused by a Russian, Bakounine and his followers, pretending to supremacy, by fair means or by foul, over a body of which they formed but a small minority. Their chief nostrum was an objection, on principle, to All political action on the part of the working class; so much so, that in their eyes, to vote at an election, was to commit an act of treason against the interests of the proletariat. Nothing, but downright, violent revolution would they admit as means of action. From Switzerland, where these "anarchists" as they called themselves, had first taken root, they spread to Italy and Spain, where, for a time, they actually dominated the working-class movement. They were more or less supported, within the "International", by the Belgians, who, though from different motives, also declared in favor of political abstention. After the split they kept up a show of organisation and held congresses, in which a couple of dozen men, always the same, pretending to represent the working class of all Europe, proclaimed their dogmas in its name. But already the German elections of 1874, and the great advantage which the German movement experienced from the presence of nine of its most active members in Parliament, had thrown elements of doubt in the midst of the "anarchists". Political events had repressed the movement in Spain, which disappeared without leaving scarcely a trace; in Switzerland the party in favor of political action, which worked hand in hand with the Germans, became stronger every day and soon outnumbered the few anarchists at the rate of 300 to 1; in Italy, after a childish attempt at "social revolution" (Bologna, 1874[98]) at which neither the sense nor the pluck of the "anarchists" showed to advantage, the real working-class element began to look out, for more rational means of action. In Belgium, the movement, thanks to the abstentionist policy of the leaders, which left the working class without any field for real action, had come to a dead stand. In fact, while the political action of the Germans led them from success to success, the working class of those countries, where abstention was the order of the day, suffered defeat after defeat, and got tired of a movement barren of results; their organisations dropped into oblivion, their press organs disappeared one after the other. The more sensible portion of these workmen could not but be struck by this contrast; rebellion against the "anarchist" and abstentionist doctrine broke out in Italy as well as in Belgium, and people begun to ask themselves and each other, why for the sake of a stupid dogmatism they should be deprived of applying the very means of action which had proved itself the most efficacious of all. This was the state of things when the grand electoral victory of the Germans settled all doubts, overcame all hesitation. No resistance was possible against such a stubborn fact. Italy and Belgium declared for political action; the remnants of the Italian abstentionists, driven to despair, attempted another insurrection near Naples;[99] some thirty anarchists proclaimed the "social revolution", but were speedily taken care of by the police. All they attained was the complete breakdown of their own sectarian movement in Italy. Thus the anarchist organisation, which had pretended to rule the working class movement from one end of Europe to the other, was again reduced to its original nucleus, some two hundred men in the Jura district of Switzerland, where from the isolation of their mountain recesses, they continue to protest against the victorious heresy of the rest of the world, and to uphold the true orthodoxy as laid down by the Emperor Bakounine, now defunct. And when in September last the Universal Socialist Congress met at Ghent,[100] in Belgium—a congress which they themselves had convoked—they found themselves an insignificant minority, face to face with the delegates of the united and unanimous great working class organisations of Europe. The Congress, while energetically repudiating their ridiculous doctrines and their arrogant pretentions, and establishing the fact that they repudiated merely a small sect, extended to them, in the end, a generous toleration.

Thus, after a four years' intestine struggle, complete harmony was restored to the action of the working class of Europe, and the policy proclaimed by the majority of the last Congress of the International was thoroughly vindicated by events. A basis was now recovered upon which the workingmen of the different European countries could again act firmly together, and give each other that mutual support which constitutes the principal strength of the movement. The International Workingmen's Association had been rendered an impossi* many, which forbade the workmen of these countries to enter into any such international bond. The Governments might have spared themselves all this trouble. The working class movement had outgrown not only the necessity but even the possibility of any such formal bond; but not only has the work of the great proletarian organisation been fully accomplished, it continues to live itself, more powerful than ever, in the far stronger bond of union and solidarity, in the community of action and policy which now animates the working class of all Europe, and which is emphatically its own and its grandest work. There is plenty of variety of views amongst the workmen of the different countries, and even of those of each country taken by itself; but there are no longer any sects, no more pretensions to

---

* Here one or two lines of type were missing in the newspaper column.—*Ed.*

dogmatic orthodoxy and supremacy of doctrine, and there is a common plan of action originally traced by the International but now universally adopted because everywhere it has grown consciously or unconsciously out of the struggle of the necessities of the movement; a plan which, while adapting itself freely to the varying conditions of each nation and each locality, is nevertheless the same everywhere in its fundamental traits, and thus secures unity of purpose and general congruence of the means applied to obtain the common end, the emancipation of the working class through the working class itself.

III

In the preceding article, we have already foreshadowed the principal facts of interest connected with the history of the working class movement in Italy, Spain, Switzerland and Belgium. Still, something remains to be told.

In Spain, the movement had rapidly extended between 1868 and 1872, when the International boasted of more than 30,000 paying members. But all this was more apparent than real, the result more of momentary excitement, brought on by the unsettled political state of the country than by real intellectual progress. Involved in the Cantonalist, (federalist-republican) rising of 1873,* the Spanish International was crushed along with it. For a time it continued in the shape of a secret society, of which no doubt, a nucleus is still in existence. But as it has never given any sign of life save sending three delegates to the Ghent Congress, we are driven to the conclusion that these three delegates represent the Spanish working class much in the same way as whilome the three tailors of Tooley-street represented the People of England. And whenever a political revulsion will give the workingmen of Spain the possibility of again playing an active part, we may safely predict that the new departure will not come from these "anarchist" spouters, but from the small body of intelligent and energetic workmen who, in 1872, remained true to the International[101] and who now bide their time instead of playing at secret conspiracy.

---

* See pp. 123-46 of this volume—*Ed.*

In Portugal the movement remained always free from the "anarchist" taint, and proceeded upon the same rational basis as in most other countries. The Portuguese workmen had numerous International sections and trades' Unions; they held a very successful Congress in January 1877, and had an excellent weekly: "O Protesto" (The Protest).[102] Still, they too were hampered by adverse laws, restrictive of the press and of the right of association and public meeting. They keep struggling on for all that, and are now holding another Congress at Oporto, which will afford them an opportunity of showing to the world that the working class of Portugal takes its proper share in the great and universal struggle for the emancipation of labor.

The workmen of Italy too, are much obstructed in their action by middle class legislation. A number of special laws enacted under the pretext of suppressing brigandage and wide spread secret brigand organisations, laws which give the government immense arbitrary powers are unscrupulously applied to workmen's association; their more prominent members equally with brigands are subjected to police supervision and banishment without judge or jury. Still the movement proceeds, and, best sign of life, its centre of gravity has been shifted from the venerable, but half dead cities of Romagna to the busy industrial and manufacturing towns of the North, a change which secured the predominance of the real working class element over the host of "anarchist" interlopers of middle class origin who previously had taken the lead. The workmen's clubs and trades' Unions, ever broken up and dissolved by the government, are ever reformed under new names. The Proletarian Press, though many of its organs are but shortlived in consequence of the prosecutions, fines and sentences of imprisonment against the editors, springs up afresh after every defeat, and, in spite of all obstacles, counts several papers of comparatively old standing. Some of these organs, mostly ephemeral ones, still profess "anarchist" doctrines, but, that fraction has given up all pretensions to rule the movement and is gradually dying out, along with the Mazzinian or middle class Republican party, and every inch of ground lost by these two factions is so much ground won by the real and intelligent working class movement.

In Belgium, too, the centre of gravity of working class

6*

action has been shifted, and this action itself has undergone an important change in consequence. Up to 1875, this centre lay in the French-speaking part of the country, including Brussels, which is half French and half Flemish; the movement was, during this period, strongly influenced by Proudhonist doctrines, which also enjoin abstention from political interference, especially from elections. There remained, then, nothing but strikes, generally repressed by bloody intervention of the military, and meetings in which the old stock phrases were constantly repeated. The work-people got sick of this and the whole movement gradually fell asleep. But since 1875 the manufacturing towns of the Flemish speaking portion entered into the struggle with a greater and as was soon to be proved, a new spirit. In Belgium there are no factory laws whatever to limit the hours of labor of women or children; and the first cry of the factory voters of Ghent and neighbourhood was for protection for their wives and children, who were made to slave fifteen and more hours a day in the Cotton Mills. The opposition of the Proudhonist doctrinaires who considered such trifles as far beneath the attention of men occupied with transcendent revolutionism, was of no avail, and was gradually overcome. The demand of legal protection for factory-children became one of the points of the Belgian working class platform, and with it was broken the spell which hitherto had tabooed political action. The example of the Germans did the rest, and now the Belgian workmen, like those of Germany, Switzerland, Denmark, Portugal, Hungary, Austria and part of Italy, are forming themselves into a political party, distinct from, and opposed to, all other political parties, and aiming at the conquest of their emancipation by whatever political action the situation may require.

The great mass of the Swiss workmen—the German speaking portion of them—had for some years been formed into a "Workmen's Confederation" which at the end of 1876 counted above 5,000 paying members. There was, alongside of them another organisation, the "Grutli Society", originally formed by the middle class radicals for the spread of Radicalism amongst workmen and peasants; but gradually social democraticideas penetrated into this widely-spread association and finally conquered it. In 1877, both these societies entered into an alliance, almost a fusion, for the purpose of organising a Swiss political labor party; and with such vigor did they act that they carried, at the national vote, the new Swiss Factory Law, of all existing factory acts the one which is most favorable to the work-people. They are now organising a vigilant supervision to secure its due execution against the loudly proclaimed ill-will of the mill owners. The "anarchists", from their superior revolutionary standpoint as a matter of course violently opposed all this action, denouncing it as a piece of arrant treason against what they call "the Revolution"; but as they number 200 at the outside and here as elsewhere, are but a general staff of officers without an army, this made no difference.

The programme of the Swiss working men's Party is almost identical with that of the Germans, only too identical, having adopted even some of its more imperfect and confused passages. But the mere wording of the programme matters little, so long as the spirit which dominates the movement, is of the right sort.

The Danish workingmen entered the lists about 1870 and at first made very rapid progress. By an alliance with the small peasant proprietors' party, amongst which they succeeded in spreading their views, they attained considerable political influence, so much so, that the "United Left", of which the peasant party formed the nucleus, for a number of years had the majority in parliament. But there was more show than solidity in this rapid growth of the movement. One day it was found out that two of the leaders had disappeared after squandering the money collected for party purposes from the workingmen. The scandal caused by this was extreme, and the Danish movement has not yet recovered from the discouragement consequent upon it. Anyhow, if the Danish workingmen's party is now proceeding in a more unobtrusive way than before, there is every reason to believe that it is gradually replacing the ephemeral and apparent domination over the masses, which it has now lost, by a more real and more lasting influence.

In Austria and Hungary the working class has the greatest difficulties to contend with. Political liberty, as far as the press, meetings and associations are concerned, is there reduced to the lowest level consistent with a sham constitu-

tional monarchy. A code of laws of unheard-of elasticity
enables the Government to obtain convictions against even
the mildest expression of the demands and interests of the
working class. And yet the movement there, as well as elsewhere, goes on irrepressibly. The principal centres are the
manufacturing districts of Bohemia, Vienna, and Pesth.
Workingmens' periodicals are published in the German, the
Bohemian and the Hungarian languages. From Hungary the
movement has spread to Servia, where, before the war, a
weekly newspaper[103] was published in the Servian language,
but when the war broke out the paper was simply suppressed.

Thus, wherever we look in Europe, the working class movement is progressing, not only favourably but rapidly, and
what is more, everywhere in the same spirit. Complete
harmony is restored, and with it constant and regular intercourse, in one way or another, between the workmen of the
different countries. The men who founded, in 1864, the
International Workingmen's Association, who held high its
banner during years of strife, first against external, then
against internal foes, until political necessities even more than
intestine feuds brought on disruption and seeming retire-
ment—these men can now proudly exclaim: "The International has done its work; it has fully attained its grand
aim—the union of the Proletariat of the whole world in the
struggle against their oppressors."

Written in English,
February-March 1878

Printed according to the
newspaper text

Published in *The Labor
Standard* (New York),
March 3, 10, 17, 24 and 31,
1878

FREDERICK ENGELS

From SOCIALISM:
UTOPIAN AND SCIENTIFIC

III

Whilst the capitalist mode of production more and more completely transforms the great majority of the population into proletarians, it creates the power which, under penalty of its own destruction, is forced to accomplish this revolution. Whilst it forces on more and more the transformation of the vast means of production, already socialised, into state property, it shows itself the way to accomplishing this revolution. *The proletariat seizes political power and turns the means of production into state property.*

But, in doing this, it abolishes itself as proletariat, abolishes all class distinctions and class antagonisms, abolishes also the state as state. Society thus far, based upon class antagonisms, had need of the state. That is, of an organisation of the particular class which was *pro tempore* the exploiting class, an organisation for the purpose of preventing any interference from without with the existing conditions of production, and, therefore, especially, for the purpose of forcibly keeping the exploited classes in the condition of oppression corresponding with the given mode of production (slavery, serfdom, wage-labour). The state was the official representative of society as a whole; the gathering of it together into a visible embodiment. But it was this only in so far as it was the state of that class which itself represented, for the time being, society as a whole: in ancient times, the state of slave-owning citizens; in the Middle Ages, the feudal lords; in our own time, the bourgeoisie. When at last it becomes the real representative of the whole of society, it renders itself unnecessary. As soon as there is no longer any social class to be held in subjection; as soon as class rule, and the individual struggle for existence based upon our present anarchy in production, with the collisions and excesses arising from these, are removed, nothing more remains to be repressed, and a special repressive force, a state, is no longer necessary. The first act by virtue of which the state realy constitutes itself the representative of the whole of society—the taking possession of the means of production in the name of society—this is, at the same time, its last independent act as a state. State interference in social relations becomes, in one domain after another, superfluous, and then dies out of itself; the government of persons is replaced by the administration of things, and by the conduct of processes of production. The state is not "abolished". *It dies out.* This gives the measure of the value of the phrase "*a free state*", both as to its justifiable use at times by agitators, and as to its ultimate scientific insufficiency; and also of the demands of the so-called anarchists for the abolition of the state out of hand....

III. *Proletarian Revolution*—Solution of the contradictions. The proletariat seizes the public power, and by means of this transforms the socialised means of production, slipping from the hands of the bourgeoisie, into public property. By this act, the proletariat frees the means of production from the character of capital they have thus far borne, and gives their socialised character complete freedom to work itself out. Socialised production upon a predetermined plan becomes henceforth possible. The development of production makes the existence of different classes of society thenceforth an anachronism. In proportion as anarchy in social production vanishes, the political authority of the state dies out. Man, at last the master of his own form of social organisation, becomes at the same time the lord over Nature, his own master—free.

To accomplish this act of universal emancipation is the historical mission of the modern proletariat. To thoroughly comprehend the historical conditions and thus the very nature of this act, to impart to the now oppressed proletarian class a full knowledge of the conditions and of the meaning of the momentous act it is called upon to accomplish, this is the task of the theoretical expression of the proletarian movement, scientific socialism.

Written in the first half
of March, 1880

Translated from
the German

Published in the journal
La Revue socialiste Nos. 3, 4, 5,
March 20, April 20 and May 5, 1880,
and as a separate pamphlet in French:
F. Engels, *Socialisme utopique et
socialisme scientifique*, Paris, 1880

ENGELS TO J. BECKER
IN GENEVA

London, December 16, 1882

...The anarchists commit suicide every year and arise anew from the ashes every year; this will continue until anarchism is persecuted in earnest. It is the only socialist sect which can really be destroyed by persecution. For its perpetual resurrection is due to the fact that there are always would-be great men who would like on the cheap to play an important rôle. It seems as if anarchism were specially made for this purpose. But to run a risk—that is no go! The present persecutions of anarchists in France, therefore, will harm these people only if they are not just pretence and police humbug. Those who are bound to suffer are those poor fellows—the miners of Montceau.[104] Incidentally, I have got so used to these anarchist buffoons that it seems quite natural to me to see alongside the real movement this clownish caricature. The anarchists are dangerous only in countries like Austria and Spain, and even there only temporarily. The Jura too with its watchmaking, which is always carried on in scattered cottages seems to have been destined to become a focus of this nonsense, and your blows will probably do them good.

First published in the book:
F. Engels, *Vergessene Briefe (Briefe Friedrich Engels' an Johann Philipp Becker)*, Berlin 1920

Translated from the German

FREDERICK ENGELS

ON THE OCCASION OF KARL MARX'S DEATH

II

The death of a great man is an excellent opportunity for little men to make political and literary capital and ready money. I quote here only a few examples which took place in public; many others which occur in the sphere of private correspondence are not worth mentioning.

Philipp Van Patten, Secretary of the Central Labor Union in New York,[105] wrote to me on April 2:

"In connection with the recent demonstration in honor of the memory of Karl Marx, all factions united in testifying their regard for the deceased philosopher, there were very loud statements made by *John Most* and his friends to the effect that *he*, Most, was upon intimate terms with Karl Marx, had made his work *Das Kapital* popular in Germany and that Marx was in accord with the propaganda conducted by him.

"We have a high appreciation of the talents and the achievements of Marx but cannot believe that he was in sympathy with the anarchistic disorganising methods of Most and I would like to obtain from you an expression of opinion as to Karl Marx's position upon the question of Anarchy versus Social-Democracy. Too much mischief has already been done here by the untimely and imprudent talk of Most and it is rather disagreeable for us to learn that so high an authority as Marx endorsed such tactics."

My reply to this of April 18 follows here in a German translation.[106]

"My statement in reply to your inquiry of the 2nd April as to Karl Marx's position with regard to the Anarchists in general and Johann Most in particular shall be short and clear.

"Marx and I, ever since 1845,[107] have held the view that *one* of the final results of the future proletarian revolution will be the gradual dissolution and ultimate disappearance of that political organisation called *the State*; an organisation the main object of which has ever been to secure, by armed force, the economical subjection of the working majority to the wealthy minority. With the disappearance of a wealthy minority the necessity for an armed repressive State-force disappears also. At the same time we have always held, that in order to arrive at this and the other, far more important ends of the social revolution of the future, the proletarian class will first have to possess itself of the organised political force of the State and with this aid stamp out the resistance of the Capitalist class and re-organise society. This is stated already in the Communist Manifesto of 1847, end of Chapter II.

"The Anarchists reverse the matter. They say, that the Proletarian revolution has to *begin* by abolishing the political organisation of the State. But after the victory of the Proletariat, the only organisation the victorious working class finds ready-made for use is that of the State. It may require adaptation to the new functions. But to destroy that at such a moment, would be to destroy the only organism by means of which the victorious working class can exert its newly conquered power, keep down its capitalist enemies and carry out that economic revolution of society without which the whole victory must end in a defeat and in a massacre of the working class like that after the Paris Commune.

"Does it require my express assertion that Marx opposed these anarchist absurdities from the very first day that they were started in their present form by Bakunin? The whole internal history of the International Working Men's Association is there to prove it. The Anarchists tried to obtain the lead of the International, by the foulest means, ever since 1867 and the chief obstacle in their way was Marx. The result of the five years' struggle was the expulsion, at the Hague Congress, Sept. 1872, of the Anarchists from the International, and the man who did most to procure that expulsion was Marx. Our old friend *F. A. Sorge* of Hoboken, who was present as a delegate, can give you further particulars if you desire.

"Now as to Johann Most. If any man asserts that Most, since he turned anarchist, has had any relations with, or support from Marx, he is either a dupe or a deliberate liar. After the first No. of the London *Freiheit*[108] had been published, Most did not call upon Marx and myself more than once, at most twice. Nor did we call on him or even meet him accidentally anywhere or at any time since his new-fangled anarchism had burst forth in that paper. Indeed, we at last ceased to take it in as there was absolutely "nothing in it". We had for his anarchism and anarchist tactics the same contempt as for those people from whom he had learnt it.". . .

Written May 12, 1883
Published in *Der Sozialdemokrat*
No. 21 of May 17, 1883

Translated from
the German

FREDERICK ENGELS

From LUDWIG FEUERBACH AND THE END OF CLASSICAL GERMAN PHILOSOPHY

...Finally came Stirner, the prophet of contemporary anarchism—Bakunin has taken a great deal from him....

Stirner remained a curiosity, even after Bakunin blended him with Proudhon and labelled the blend "anarchism"....

Written early in 1886

Published in the journal
Die Neue Zeit Nos. 4 and 5,
1886 and as a separate
publication in Stuttgart
in 1888

Translated from
the German

FREDERICK ENGELS

From THE PREFACE TO THE SECOND EDITION OF THE BOOK:
*THE HOUSING QUESTION**

I have revised the text for this new edition, inserted a few additions and notes, and have corrected a small economic error in the first part, as my opponent, Dr. Mülberger, unfortunately failed to discover it. During this revision it was borne in on me what gigantic progress the international working-class movement has made during the past fourteen years. At that time it was still a fact that "for twenty years the workers speaking Romance languages have had no other mental pabulum than the works of Proudhon," and, in a pinch, the still more one-sided version of Proudhonism presented by the father of "anarchism," Bakunin, who regarded Proudhon as "the schoolmaster of us all," *notre maitre à nous tous*. Although the Proudhonists in France were only a small sect among the workers, they were still the only ones who had a definitely formulated programme and who were able in the Commune to take over the leadership in the economic field. In Belgium, Proudhonism reigned unchallenged among the Walloon workers, and in Spain and Italy, with a few isolated exceptions, everything in the working-class movement which was not anarchist was decidedly Proudhonist. And today? In France, Proudhon has been completely disposed of among the workers and retains supporters only among the radical bourgeois and petty bourgeois, who as Proudhonists also call themselves "Socialists", but against whom the most energetic

* See pp. 88-93 of this volume. —*Ed.*

fight is carried on by the socialist workers. In Belgium, the Flemings have ousted the Walloons from the leadership of the movement, deposed Proudhonism and greatly raised the level of the movement. In Spain, as in Italy, the anarchist high tide of the seventies has receded and swept away with it the remnants of Proudhonism. While in Italy the new party is still in process of clarification and formation, in Spain the small nucleus, which as the *Nueva Federación Madrilena* remained loyal to the General Council of the International, has developed into a strong party,[109] which—as can be seen from the republican press itself—is destroying the influence of the bourgeois republicans on the workers far more effectively than its noisy anarchist predecessors were ever able to do. Among Latin workers the forgotten works of Proudhon have been replaced by *Capital*, the *Communist Manifesto* and a number of other works of the Marxist school, and the main demand of Marx—the seizure of all the means of production in the name of society by a proletariat risen to sole political power—is now the demand of the whole revolutionary working class in the Latin countries also.

If therefore Proudhonism has been finally supplanted among the workers of the Latin countries also, if it—in accordance with its real destination—only serves French, Spanish, Italian and Belgian bourgeois radicals as an expression of their bourgeois and petty-bourgeois desires, why revert to it today? Why combat anew a dead opponent by reprinting these articles?

First of all, because these articles do not confine themselves to a mere polemic against Proudhon and his German representative. As a consequence of the division of labour that existed between Marx and myself, it fell to me to present our opinions in the periodical press, and, therefore, particularly in the fight against opposing views, in order that Marx should have time for the elaboration of his great basic work. This made it necessary for me to present our views for the most part in a polemical form, in opposition to other kinds of views. So also here. Parts One and Three contain not only a criticism of the Proudhonist conception of the question, but also a presentation of our own conception.

Secondly, Proudhon played much too significant a role in the history of the European working-class movement for

him to fall into oblivion without more ado. Refuted theoretically and discarded practically, he still retains his historical
interest. Whoever occupies himself in any detail with modern
socialism must also acquaint himself with the "surmounted
standpoints" of the movement. Marx's *Poverty of Philosophy*
appeared several years before Proudhon put forward his
practical proposals for social reform. Here Marx could only
discover in embryo and criticise Proudhon's exchange bank.
From this angle, therefore, this work of mine supplements,
unfortunately imperfectly enough, Marx's work. Marx would
have accomplished all this much better and more convincingly.

And finally, bourgeois and petty-bourgeois socialism is
strongly represented in Germany down to this very hour. On
the one hand, by Katheder-Socialists[110] and philanthropists of
all sorts, with whom the wish to turn the workers into owners
of their dwellings still plays a great role and against whom,
therefore, my work is still appropriate. On the other hand,
a certain petty-bourgeois socialism finds representation in
the Social-Democratic Party itself, and even in the ranks of
the Reichstag group. This is done in the following way: while
the fundamental views of modern socialism and the demand
for the transformation of all the means of production into
social property are recognised as justified, the realisation of
this is declared possible only in the distant future, a future
which for all practical purposes is quite out of sight. Thus, for
the present one has to have recourse to mere social patch-
work, and sympathy can be shown, according to circumstances, even with the most reactionary efforts for so-called
"up-lifting of the labouring class." The existence of such a
tendency is quite inevitable in Germany, the land of philistinism *par excellence*, particularly at a time when industrial
development is violently and on a mass scale uprooting this
old and deeply-rooted philistinism. The tendency is quite
harmless to the movement, in view of the wonderful common
sense of our workers, which has been demonstrated so magni-
ficently precisely during the last eight years of the struggle
against the Anti-Socialist Law,[111] the police and the courts.
But it is necessary clearly to realise that such a tendency
exists. And if later on this tendency takes on a firmer shape
and more clearly defined contours, as is necessary and even

desirable, it will have to go back to its predecessors for the formulation of its programme, and in doing so it will hardly be able to avoid Proudhon.

Written January 10, 1887

Published in the newspaper   Translated from
Der Sozialdemokrat Nos. 3 and 4,   the German
January 15 and 22, 1887 and in the
book: F. Engels, *Zur Wohnungsfrage,*
Nottingen-Zürich, 1887

ENGELS TO M. HILDEBRAND
IN BERLIN

London, October 22, 1889

...During the latter part of my stay in Berlin I saw less of Stirner, probably because he had already begun to develop the train of thoughts which led later to his main work. Our views had already widely diverged when the book was published;[112] the two years that I had spent in Manchester had had their effect upon me.[113] Later on, in Brussels, when Marx and I felt the need to analyse the ramifications of the Hegelian school, we criticised among others Stirner, too; the criticism is as bulky as the book itself. The manuscript,[114] which was never published, is still in my possession, in so far as it has not been eaten by mice.

Stirner was resurrected by Bakunin, who, incidentally was also in Berlin at the time, and at Werder's lectures on logic he, together with four or five other Russians, occupied the row of seats in front of mine (1841-42). Proudhon's innocuous, merely etymological anarchy (i.e., absence of political authority) would have never led to the present anarchistic doctrines, if Bakunin had not added a good deal of Stirnerian "rebellion"[115] to it. Consequently the anarchists have all become "unique ones", so unique that no two of them can agree with each other....

First published in Russian
in the magazine *Pod znamenem
marxizma*, No. 6, 1927

Translated from
the German

FREDERICK ENGELS

THE BRUSSELS CONGRESS AND THE SITUATION IN EUROPE
(FROM A LETTER TO P. LAFARGUE)

London, September 2, 1891

THE BRUSSELS CONGRESS

We have every reason to be satisfied with the Brussels Congress.[116]

They did well to vote for the exclusion of the anarchists: with this the old International came to an end, with this the new one begins again. It is purely and simply the ratification, nineteen years later, of the Hague Congress resolutions.

No less important was the move to leave the door wide open to the British *Trade-Unions*. It shows how well the situation has been understood. And the resolutions which pledged the *Trade-Unions* to the "class struggle and the abolition of wages" means that this was not a concession on our part.

The Domela Nieuwenhuis incident has shown that the European workmen have definitely outgrown the stage of being swayed by the high-sounding phrase and that they are conscious of the responsibilities which fall on them: it means a class organised in a "fighting" party, a party which reckons with "deeds". And the deeds take a more and more revolutionary turn....

Published in the newspaper
Le Socialiste, No. 51,
September 12, 1891

Translated from
the French

ENGELS TO P. INGLESIAS
IN MADRID
(Draft)

London, March 26, 1894

... As for the anarchists, they are perhaps on the point of committing suicide. This violent fever, this salvo of insane outrages, ultimately paid for and provoked by the police, cannot fail to open the eyes even of the bourgeoisie to the nature of this propaganda by madmen and provocateurs.[117] Even the bourgeoisie will realise in the long run that it is absurd to pay the police and, through the police, the anarchists, to blow up the very bourgeois who pay them. And even if we ourselves are now liable to suffer from the bourgeois reaction against the anarchists, we shall gain in the long run because this time we shall succeed in establishing in the eyes of the world that there is a great gulf between us and the anarchists.

First published in Russian
in K. Marx and F. Engels,
Works, 1st Ed., Vol. XXIX, 1946

Translated from
the French and Spanish

V. I. Lenin

ANARCHISM AND SOCIALISM

Theses:

1. Anarchism, in the course of the 35 to 40 years (Bakunin and the *International*, 1866—) of its existence (and with Stirner included, in the course of many more years), has produced nothing but general platitudes against *exploitation*.

These phrases have been current for more than 2,000 years. What is missing is (α) an understanding of the causes of exploitation; ( ) an understanding of the *development* of society, which leads to socialism; (γ) an understanding of the *class struggle* as the creative force for the realisation of socialism.

2. An understanding of the *causes* of exploitation. *Private* property as the basis of *commodity* economy. Social property in the means of production. In anarchism—nil.

Anarchism is bourgeois *individualism* in reverse. Individualism as the basis of the entire anarchist world outlook.

Defence of petty property and *petty economy* on the land. *Keine Majorität.** Negation of the unifying and organising power of authority.

3. Failure to understand the development of society—the role of large-scale production—the development of capitalism into socialism.

(Anarchism is a product of *despair*. The psychology of the

---

* No majority (i.e., the anarchists' non-acceptance of the submission by the minority to the majority).—*Ed.*

unsettled intellectual or the vagabond and not of the proletarian.)

4. Failure to understand the *class* struggle of the proletariat.

Absurd negation of politics in bourgeois society.

Failure to understand the role of the organisation and the education of the workers.

Panaceas consisting of one-sided, disconnected means.

5. What has anarchism, at one time dominant in the Romance countries, contributed in recent European history?

—No doctrine, revolutionary teaching, or theory.

—Fragmentation of the working-class movement.

—Complete fiasco in the experiments of the revolutionary movement (Proudhonism*, 1871; Bakuninism**, 1873).

—Subordination of the working class to *bourgeois* politics in the guise of negation of politics.

Written in 1901

First published in 1936 in
the magazine *Proletarskaya
Revolutsia*, No. 7

V. I. Lenin,
Collected Works,
Vol. 5, pp. 327-28

---

* See pp. 89-90 of this volume. —*Ed.*
** See p. 188 of this volume. —*Ed.*

From REPORT ON THE QUESTION
OF THE PARTICIPATION
OF THE SOCIAL-DEMOCRATS
IN A PROVISIONAL REVOLUTIONARY
GOVERNMENT AT THE THIRD CONGRESS
OF THE R.S.D.L.P.,
April 18 (May 1), 1905

...Perhaps we might find in Marx and Engels an answer which, though not applying to the concrete situation in Russia, would apply to the general principles of the revolutionary struggle of the proletariat? *Iskra*[118] at any rate raises one such general question.

It states in issue No. 93: "The best way to organise the proletariat into a party in opposition to the bourgeois-Democratic state is to develop the bourgeois revolution *from below* through the pressure of the proletariat on the democrats in power." *Iskra* goes on: "*Uperyod* wants the pressure of the proletariat on the revolution [?] to be exerted not only from below, not only from the street, but also from above, from the marble halls of the provisional government." This formulation is correct; *Uperyod*[119] does want this. We have here a really general question of principle: is revolutionary action permissible only from below, or also from above? To this general question we can find an answer in Marx and Engels.

I have in mind Engels' interesting article "The Bakuninists at Work"* (1873). Engels describes briefly the Spanish Revolution of 1873, when the country was swept by a revolution of the Intransigentes, i.e., the extreme republicans. Engels stresses the fact that the immediate emancipation of the working class was out of the question at that time. The task was to accelerate for the proletariat the transition

---

* See pp. 128-46 of this volume. —*Ed.*

through the preliminary stages that prepare the social revolution and to clear the obstacles in its way. The republic gave the opportunity to achieve this goal. The working class of Spain could utilise this opportunity only by taking an active part in the revolution. In this it was hindered by the influence of the Bakuninists and, among other things, by their idea of the general strike, which Engels criticised so effectively. Engels describes, in passing, the events in Alcoy, a city with 30,000 factory workers, where the proletariat found itself master of the situation. How did the proletariat act? Despite the principles of Bakuninism, they were obligated to participate in the provisional revolutionary government. "The Bakuninists," says Engels, "had for years been propagating the idea that all revolutionary action from above downward was pernicious, and that everything must be organised and carried out from below upward."

This, then, is Engels' answer to the general question of "from above or from below" raised by *Iskra. The "Iskra" principle of "only from below and never from above" is an anarchist principle*. Drawing his conclusion from the events of the Spanish revolution, Engels says: "The Bakuninists repudiated the credo which they had just proclaimed: that the establishment of a revolutionary government was only a new deception and a new betrayal of the working class [as Plekhanov is trying to persuade us now], by figuring quite complacently on the government committees of the various cities, and at that almost everywhere as an impotent minority outvoted and exploited politically by the bourgeoisie." *Thus, what displeases Engels is the fact that the Bakuninists were in the minority, and not the fact that they sat there on these committees*. At the conclusion of his pamphlet, Engels declares that the example of the Bakuninists is "an example of how *not* to make a revolution".

Published in 1905 in the book:
*The Third Congress of the
R.S.D.L.P. Minutes*, Geneva,
by the C.C., R.S.D.L.P.

V. I. Lenin,
Collected Works,
Vol. 8, pp. 390-92

From ON THE PROVISIONAL
REVOLUTIONARY GOVERNMENT

Article Two
ONLY FROM BELOW OR FROM ABOVE AS WELL AS
FROM BELOW?

In our previous article analysing Plekhanov's reference to history we showed that he draws unwarranted general conclusions on points of principle from statements by Marx, which apply wholly and exclusively to the concrete situation in Germany in 1850. That concrete situation fully explains why Marx did not raise, and at that time could not have raised, the question of the Communist League's participation in a provisional revolutionary government. We shall now proceed to examine the general, fundamental question of the admissibility of such participation.

In the first place, the question at issue must be accurately presented. In this respect, fortunately, we are able to use a formulation given by our opponents and thus avoid arguments on the essence of the dispute. *Iskra*, No. 93, says: "The best way towards achieving such organisation [the organisation of the proletariat into a party in opposition to the bourgeois-democratic state] is to develop the bourgeois revolution *from below* [*Iskra*'s italics] through the pressure of the proletariat on the democrats in power." *Iskra* goes on to say that *Uperyod* "wants this pressure of the proletariat on the revolution to proceed not only 'from below', not only from the street, but also from above, from the marble halls of the provisional government".

The issue is thus clearly stated, *Iskra* wants pressure from below, *Uperyod* wants it "from above as well as from below". Pressure from below is pressure by the citizens on the revolutionary government. Pressure from above is pressure by the revolutionary government on the citizens. Some *limit* their activity to pressure from below; others do not agree with such a limitation and demand that pressure from below be *supplemented* by pressure from above. The issue, consequently, reduces itself to the question contained in our subtitle: only from below, or from above as well as from below? Some consider it wrong in principle for the proletariat, in the epoch of the democratic revolution, to exert pressure from above, "from the marble halls of the provisional government". Others consider it wrong in principle for the proletariat, in the epoch of the democratic revolution, to reject entirely pressure from above, to renounce participation in the provisional revolutionary government. Thus, the question is not whether pressure from above is probable in a given situation, or whether it is practicable under a given alignment of forces. We are for the moment not considering any concrete situation, and in view of the numerous attempts to substitute one question at issue for another, we urgently ask the readers to bear this in mind. We are dealing with the general question of principle, whether in the epoch of the democratic revolution it is *admissible* to pass from pressure from below to pressure from above.

To elucidate this question, let us first refer to the history of the tactical views of the founders of scientific socialism. Were there no disputes in this history over the general question of the admissibility of pressure from above? There was such a dispute. It was caused by the Spanish insurrection of the summer of 1873. Engels assessed the lessons which the socialist proletariat should learn from that insurrection in an article entitled "The Bakuninists at Work",* printed in the German Social-Democratic newspaper *Volksstaat* in 1873 and reprinted in the pamphlet *Internationales aus dem Volksstaat* in 1894. Let us see what general conclusions Engels drew.

On February 9, 1873, King Amadeo of Spain abdicated the throne—"the first king to go on strike", as Engels facetiously remarks. On February 12 the republic was proclaimed, soon to be followed by a Carlist revolt in the Basque provinces.

---

* See pp. 128-46 of this volume. —*Ed.*

April 10 saw the election of a Constituent Assembly which, on June 8, proclaimed the federal republic. On June 11 ...ew Cabinet was formed by Pi y Margall. In the commission charged with drafting the constitution the extreme republicans, known as the "Intransigentes", were not represented. And when, on July 3, the new constitution was proclaimed the Intransigentes rose in revolt. Between July 5 and 11 they gained the upper hand in the Seville, Granada, Alcoy, Valencia, and several other provinces. The government of Salmeron, who succeeded Pi y Margall when the latter resigned, sent troops against the rebel provinces. The revolt was suppressed after a more or less stiff resistance. Cádiz fell on July 26, 1873, and Cartagena on January 11, 1874. Such are the brief chronological facts with which Engels introduces his subject.

In evaluating the lessons to be drawn from these events, Engels stresses, first, that the struggle for the republic in Spain was not and could not have been a struggle for the socialist revolution. "Spain," he says, "is such an industrially backward country that there can be no thought of an *immediate* complete emancipation there of the working class of that country. Before it comes to that, Spain will have to pass through various preliminary stages of development and remove a considerable number of obstacles from its path. The republic offered that country the chance of going through those preliminary stages in the shortest possible time and of quickly surmounting the obstacles. But that chance could be utilised only through the active *political* intervention of the Spanish working class. The mass of the workers felt this. They strove everywhere to have a part in the events, to take advantage of the opportunity for action, instead of leaving the owning classes, as heretofore, a clear field for action and intrigues."

It was thus a question of struggle for the republic, a question of the democratic, not of the socialist, revolution. The question of the workers' taking a hand in the events presented itself in a twofold aspect at the time. On the one hand, the Bakuninists (or "Alliancists"—the founders of the "Alliance" for struggle against the Marxist "International") negated political activity, participation in elections, etc. On the other hand, they were against participation in a revolution which

did not aim at the immediate and complete emancipation of
the working class; they were against participation of whatever kind in a revolutionary government. It is this second
aspect of the question that holds special interest for us in
the light of our dispute. It was this aspect, incidentally, which
gave rise to the formulation of the difference *in principle* between the two tactical slogans.

"The Bakuninists," says Engels, "had for years been propagating the idea that *all revolutionary action from above
was pernicious*, and that *everything must be organised* and
carried out from below upward."

Hence, the principle, "only from below" is an *anarchist*
principle.

Engels demonstrates the utter absurdity of this principle
in the epoch of the democratic revolution. It naturally and
inevitably leads to the practical conclusion that the establishment of revolutionary governments is a betrayal of the working class. The Bakuninists drew this very conclusion, which
they elevated into a principle, namely, that "*the establishment
of a revolutionary government is but a new deception and a
new betrayal of the working class.*"

We have here, as the reader will see, the same two
"principles" which the new *Iskra* has arrived at, namely:
(1) that only revolutionary action from below is admissible,
as opposed to the tactics of "from above as well as from
below"; (2) that participation in a provisional revolutionary
government is a betrayal of the working class. Both these
new-*Iskra* principles are anarchist principles. The actual
course of the struggle for the republic in Spain revealed the
utter preposterousness and the utterly reactionary essence of
both these principles.

Engels brings this truth home with several episodes from
the Spanish revolution. The revolution, for example, breaks
out in Alcoy, a manufacturing town of comparatively recent
origin with a population of 30,000. The workers' insurrection
is victorious despite its leadership by the Bakuninists, who
will, in principle, have nothing to do with the idea of organising the revolution. After the event the Bakuninists began to
boast that they had become "masters of the situation". And
how did these "masters" deal with their "situation", asks
Engels. First of all, they established in Alcoy a "Welfare

Committee", that is, a revolutionary government. Mind you, it was these selfsame Alliancists (Bakuninists), who, only ten months before the revolution, had resolved at their Congress, on September 15, 1872, that "every organisation of a political, so-called provisional or revolutionary power can only be a new fraud and would be as dangerous to the proletariat as all existing governments". Rather than refute this anarchist phrase-mongering, Engels confines himself to the sarcastic remark that it was the supporters of this resolution who found themselves "members of this provisional and revolutionary governmental power" in Alcoy. Engels treats these gentlemen with the scorn they deserve for the "utter helplessness, confusion, and passivity" which they revealed when in power. With equal contempt Engels would have answered the charges of "Jacobinism", so dear to the Girondists of Social-Democracy. He shows that in a number of other towns, e.g., in Sanlúcar de Barrameda (a port of 26,000 inhabitants near Cádiz) "the Alliancists ... here too, in opposition to their anarchist principles, formed a revolutionary government". He reproves them for "not having known what to do with their power". Knowing well that the Bakuninist labour leaders participated in provisional governments *together with the Intransigentes*, i.e., together with the republicans, the representatives of the petty bourgeoisie, Engels reproves the Bakuninists, not for their participation in the government (as he should have done according to the "principles" of the new *Iskra*), but for their *poor organisation, the feebleness of their participation*, their subordination to the leadership of the bourgeois republican gentry. With what withering sarcasm Engels would have flayed those people who, in the epoch of the revolution, try to minimise the importance of "technical" and military leadership, may incidentally be seen from the fact that he reproved the Bakuninist labour leaders for having, as members of the revolutionary government, left the "political and *military* leadership" to the bourgeois republican gentry, while they fed the workers with bombastic phrases and paper schemes of "social" reforms.

A true Jacobin of Social-Democracy, Engels not only appreciated the importance of action from above, he not only viewed participation in a revolutionary government together with the republican bourgeoisie as perfectly legitimate, but he *demanded* such participation, as well as energetic military initiative on the part of the revolutionary power, considering it his duty to give *practical* and guiding *military* advice.

"Nevertheless," he says, "the uprising, even if begun in a brainless way, would have had a good chance to succeed, *had it been conducted with some intelligence,** if only in the manner of the Spanish military revolts, in which the garrison of one town rises, marches on to the next, sweeping along with it the town's garrison previously worked on by propaganda, and, growing into an avalanche, the insurgents press on to the capital, until a fortunate engagement, or the crossing over to their side of the troops sent against them, decides the victory. This method was especially applicable in the given situation. The insurgents had long been organised everywhere into volunteer battalions, whose discipline, true, was pitiable, yet assuredly not more pitiable than that of the remnants of the old, largely demoralised Spanish army. The government's only dependable troops were the gendarmes, and these were scattered all over the country. The thing was, above all, to prevent these gendarmes from being drawn together, which could be done only by a bold assumption of the offensive in the open field. Such a course of action would not have involved much danger, since the government could only put up against the volunteers equally undisciplined troops. For anyone bent on winning there was no other way."

That is how a founder of scientific socialism reasoned when faced with the problems of an uprising and direct action in the epoch of a revolutionary upheaval! Although the uprising was begun by the petty-bourgeois republicans and although confronting the proletariat was neither the question of the socialist revolution nor that of elementary political freedom, Engels set very great store on the highly active participation of the workers in the struggle for the republic; he demanded of the proletariat's leaders that they should

---

* *Wäre er nur mit einigem Verstand geleitet worden.* Poor Engels! A pity he was not acquainted with the new *Iskra*! He would have known then how disastrous, noxious, utopian, bourgeois, technically one-sided, and conspiratorially narrow is the "Jacobin" idea that an insurrection can be *conducted* (*geleitet werden*)!

subordinate their entire activity to the need for achieving victory in the struggle, which had begun. Engels himself, as a leader of the proletariat, even went into the details of military organisation; he was not averse to using the old-fashioned methods of struggle by military revolts when victory demanded it; he attached paramount importance to offensive action and the centralisation of the revolutionary forces. He bitterly reproved the Bakuninists for having made a principle of "what in the German Peasant War and in the German uprisings of May 1849 was an unavoidable evil, namely, *the state of disunion and isolation of the revolutionary forces*, which enabled the same government troops to put down one uprising after another." Engels' views on the conduct of the uprising, on the organisation of the revolution, and on the utilisation of the revolutionary governmental power are as far removed from the tail-ist views of the new *Iskra* as heaven is from earth.

Summarising the lessons of the Spanish revolution, Engels established in the first place that "the Bakuninists, as soon as they were confronted with a serious revolutionary situation, were compelled to give up their whole former programme". To begin with, they had to scrap the principle of abstention from political activity and from elections, the principle of the "abolition of the state". Secondly, "they gave up the principle that the workers must not participate in any revolution that did not aim at the immediate and complete emancipation of the proletariat, and they themselves participated in an avowedly purely bourgeois movement". Thirdly, and this conclusion answers precisely the point in dispute, "they trampled under foot the article of faith they had only just proclaimed—that the establishment of a revolutionary government is but a new deception and a new betrayal of the working class; they did this, sitting coolly in the government committees of the various towns, almost everywhere as an impotent minority outvoted and politically exploited by the bourgeois". By their inability to lead the uprising, by splitting the revolutionary forces instead of centralising them, by leaving the leadership of the revolution to the bourgeois, and by dissolving the solid and strong organisation of the International, "the Bakuninists in Spain gave us an unsurpassable example of how *not* to make a revolution".

7*

* * *

Summing up the foregoing, we arrive at the following conclusions:

1) Limitation, in principle, of revolutionary action to
pressure from below and renunciation of pressure also from
above is *anarchism*.

2) He who does not understand the new tasks in the epoch
of revolution, the tasks of action from above, he who is unable
to determine the conditions and the programme for such
action, has no idea whatever of the tasks of the proletariat in
every democratic revolution.

3) The principle that for Social-Democracy participation
in a provisional revolutionary government with the bourgeoisie is inadmissible, that every such participation is a betrayal of the working class, is a principle of *anarchism*.

4) Every "serious revolutionary situation" confronts the
party of the proletariat with the task of giving purposive
leadership of the uprising, of organising the revolution, of
centralising all the revolutionary forces, of boldly launching
a military offensive, and of making the most energetic use of
the revolutionary governmental power.*

5) Marx and Engels could not have approved, and never
would have approved, the tactics of the new *Iskra* at the
present revolutionary moment; for these tactics are nothing
short of a repetition of all the errors enumerated above. Marx
and Engels would have called the new *Iskra*'s doctrinal position a contemplation of the "posterior" of the proletariat, a
rehash of anarchist errors.**

Published on June 3 and 9,   V. I. Lenin,
(May 21 and 27), 1905   *Collected Works*,
in *Proletary*, Nos. 2 and 3   Vol. 8, pp. 474-81

---

* In the manuscript after the word "power" follows: "The leaders
of the working class who do not understand these tasks and systematically underestimate them must be ruthlessly thrown overboard by
the proletariat."—*Ed*.
** In the manuscript "anarchist platitudes". —*Ed*.

From TWO TACTICS OF SOCIAL-DEMOCRACY IN THE DEMOCRATIC REVOLUTION

2. WHAT CAN WE LEARN FROM THE RESOLUTION OF THE THIRD CONGRESS OF THE R.S.D.L.P. ON A PROVISIONAL GOVERNMENT?

The next question is that of the proletariat's attitude in general towards a provisional revolutionary government. The Congress resolution answers this first of all by directly advising the Party to spread among the working class the conviction that a provisional revolutionary government is necessary. The working class must be made aware of this necessity. Whereas the "democratic" bourgeoisie keeps in the background the question of the overthrow of the tsarist government, we must bring it to the fore and insist on the need for a provisional revolutionary government. Moreover, we must outline for such a government a programme of action that will conform with the objective conditions of the present period and with the aims of proletarian democracy. This programme is the *entire* minimum programme of our Party, the programme of the immediate political and economic reforms which, on the one hand, can be fully realised on the basis of the existing social and economic relationships, and, on the other hand, are requisite for the next step forward, for the achievement of socialism.

Thus, the resolution clearly defines the nature and the purpose of a provisional revolutionary government. In origin and basic character such a government must be the organ of a popular uprising. Its formal purpose must be to serve as an instrument for convening a national constituent assembly. The content of its activities must be the implementation of the minimum programme of proletarian democracy, the only programme capable of safeguarding the interests of a people that has risen in revolt against the autocracy.

It might be argued that a provisional government, being only provisional, cannot carry out a constructive programme that has not yet received the approval of the entire people. Such an argument would merely be the sophistry of reactionaries and "absolutists". To refrain from carrying out a constructive programme means tolerating the existence of the feudal regime of a corrupt autocracy. Such a regime could be tolerated only by a government of traitors to the cause of the revolution, but not by a government that is the organ of a popular insurrection. It would be mockery for anyone to propose that we should refrain from exercising freedom of assembly pending the confirmation of such freedom by a constituent assembly, on the plea that the constituent assembly might not confirm freedom of assembly. It is equal mockery to object to the immediate execution of the minimum programme by a provisional revolutionary government.

Finally, we will note that the resolution, by making implementation of the minimum programme the provisional revolutionary government's task, eliminates the absurd and semi-anarchist ideas of giving immediate effect to the maximum programme, and the conquest of power for a socialist revolution. The degree of Russia's economic development (an objective condition), and the degree of class-consciousness and organisation of the broad masses of the proletariat (a subjective condition inseparably bound up with the objective condition) make the immediate and complete emancipation of the working class impossible. Only the most ignorant people can close their eyes to the bourgeois nature of the democratic revolution which is now taking place; only the most naive optimists can forget how little as yet the masses of the workers are informed about the aims of socialism and the methods of achieving it. We are all convinced that the emancipation of the working classes must be won by the working classes themselves; a socialist revolution is out of the question unless the masses become class-conscious and organised, trained, and educated in an open class struggle against the entire bourgeoisie. Replying to the anarchists' objections that we are putting off the socialist revolution, we say: we are not putting it off, but are taking the first step towards it in the only possible way, along the only correct path, namely, the path of a democratic republic. Whoever wants to reach socialism by any other path than that of political democracy, will inevitably arrive at conclusions that are absurd and reactionary both in the economic and the political sense. If any workers ask us at the appropriate moment why we should not go ahead and carry out our maximum programme we shall answer by pointing out how far from socialism the masses of the democratically-minded people still are, how undeveloped class antagonisms still are, and how unorganised the proletarians still are. Organise hundreds of thousands of workers all over Russia; get the millions to sympathise with our programme! Try to do this without confining yourselves to high-sounding but hollow anarchist phrases—and you will see at once that achievement of this organisation and the spread of this socialist enlightenment depend on the fullest possible achievement of democratic transformations.

Let us continue. Once the significance of a provisional revolutionary government and the attitude of the proletariat toward it have been made clear, the following question arises: is it permissible for us to participate in such a government (action from above) and, if so, under what conditions? What should be our action from below? The resolution supplies precise answers to both these questions. It emphatically declares that it is *permissible* in principle for Social-Democrats to participate in a provisional revolutionary government (during the period of a democratic revolution, the period of struggle for a republic). By this declaration we once and for all dissociate ourselves both from the anarchists, who answer this question in the negative in principle, and from the tailenders in Social-Democracy (like Martynov and the new-*Iskra* supporters), who have *tried to frighten* us with the prospect of a situation in which it might prove necessary for us to participate in such a government. By this declaration the Third Congress of the Russian Social-Democratic Labour Party irrevocably rejected the new-*Iskra* idea that the participation of Social-Democrats in a provisional revolutionary government would be a variety of Millerandism,[120] that it is impermissible in principle, as sanctifying the bourgeois order, etc.

It stands to reason, however, that the question of permissibility in principle does not solve the question of practical expediency. Under what conditions is this new form of struggle—the struggle "from above", recognised by the Party Congress—expedient? It goes without saying that it is impossible at present to speak of concrete conditions, such as the relation of forces, etc., and the resolution, naturally, refrains from defining these conditions in advance. No intelligent person would venture at present to predict anything on this subject. What we can and must do is to determine the nature and aim of our participation. That is what is done in the resolution, which points to the two purposes for which we participate: 1) a relentless struggle against counter-revolutionary attempts, and 2) the defence of the independent interests of the working class. . . .

6. WHENCE IS THE PROLETARIAT THREATENED WITH THE DANGER OF FINDING ITSELF WITH THE HANDS TIED IN THE STRUGGLE AGAINST THE INCONSISTENT BOURGEOISIE?

Marxists are absolutely convinced of the bourgeois character of the Russian revolution. What does that mean? It means that the democratic reforms in the political system, and the social and economic reforms that have become a necessity for Russia, do not in themselves imply the undermining of capitalism, the undermining of bourgeois rule; on the contrary, they will, for the first time, really clear the ground for a wide and rapid, European, and not Asiatic, development of capitalism; they will, for the first time, make it possible for the bourgeoisie to rule as a class. The Socialist-Revolutionaries[121] cannot grasp this idea, for they do not know the ABC of the laws of development of commodity and capitalist production; they fail to see that even the complete success of a peasant insurrection, even the redistribution of the whole of the land in favour of the peasants and in accordance with their desires ("general redistribution" or something of the kind) will not destroy capitalism at all, but will, on the contrary, give an impetus to its development and hasten the class disintegration of the peasantry itself. Failure to grasp this truth makes the Socialist-Revolutionaries unconscious ideologists of the petty bourgeoisie. Insistence on this truth is of enormous importance for Social-Democracy not only from the standpoint of theory but also from that of practical politics, for it follows therefrom that complete class independence of the party of the proletariat in the present "general democratic" movement is an indispensable condition.

But it does not by any means follow that a *democratic* revolution (bourgeois in its social and economic essence) would not be of *enormous* interest to the proletariat. It does not follow that the democratic revolution could not take place both in a form advantageous mainly to the big capitalist, the financial magnate, and the "enlightened" landlord, and in a form advantageous to the peasant and the worker.

The new-*Iskra* group completely misunderstands the meaning and significance of bourgeois revolution as a category. The idea that is constantly running through their arguments is that a bourgeois revolution is one that can be advantageous only to the bourgeoisie. And yet nothing can be more erroneous than such an idea. A bourgeois revolution is a revolution which does not depart from the framework of the bourgeois, i.e., capitalist, socio-economic system. A bourgeois revolution expresses the needs of capitalist development, and, far from destroying the foundations of capitalism, it effects the contrary—it broadens and deepens them. This revolution, therefore, expresses the interests not only of the working class but of the entire bourgeoisie as well. Since the rule of the bourgeoisie over the working class is inevitable under capitalism, it can well be said that a bourgeois revolution expresses the interests not so much of the proletariat as of the bourgeoisie. But it is quite absurd to think that a bourgeois revolution does not at all express proletarian interests. This absurd idea boils down either to the hoary Narodnik theory that a bourgeois revolution runs counter to the interests of the proletariat, and that, therefore, we do not need bourgeois political liberty; or to anarchism which denies any participation of the proletariat in bourgeois politics, in a bourgeois revolution and in bourgeois parliamentarism. From the standpoint of theory this idea disregards the elementary propositions of Marxism concerning the inevitability of capitalist development on the basis of commodity production. Marxism teaches us that at a certain stage of its development a society which is based on commodity production and has commercial intercourse with civilised capitalist nations must inevitably take the road of capitalism. Marxism has irrevocably broken with the Narodnik[122] and anarchist gibberish that Russia, for instance, can bypass capitalist development, escape from capitalism, or skip it in some way other than that of the class struggle, on the basis and within the framework of this same capitalism.

Written in June-July 1905

Published as a book
in July 1905 in Geneva
by the C.C. R.S.D.L.P.

V. I. Lenin,
Collected Works,
Vol. 9, pp. 27-30, 32-33

SOCIALISM AND ANARCHISM

The Executive Committee of the Soviet of Workers' Deputies decided yesterday, November 23, to reject the application of the anarchists for representation on the Executive Committee and on the Soviet of Workers' Deputies.[123] The Executive Committee itself has given the following reasons for this decision: "(1) In the whole of international practice, congresses and socialist conferences have never included representatives of the anarchists, since they do not recognise the political struggle as a means for the achievement of their ideals; (2) only parties can be represented, and the anarchists are not a party."

We consider the decision of the Executive Committee to be in the highest degree correct, and of enormous importance from the point of view both of principle and of practical politics. If we were to regard the Soviet of Workers' Deputies as a workers' parliament or as an organ of proletarian self-government, then of course it would have been wrong to reject the application of the anarchists. However insignificant (fortunately) the influence of the anarchists among our workers may be, nevertheless, a certain number of workers undoubtedly support them. The question whether the anarchists constitute a party, an organisation, a group, or a voluntary association of like-minded people, is a formal question, and not of major importance in terms of principle. Lastly, if the anarchists, while rejecting the political struggle, apply for representation in an institution which is conducting such a

struggle, this crying inconsistency merely goes to show once
again how utterly unstable are the philosophy and tactics of
the anarchists. But, of course, instability is no reason for ex-
cluding anyone from a "parliament", or an "organ of self-
government".

We regard the decision of the Executive Committee as
absolutely correct and in no way contradicting the functions,
the character and the composition of this body. The Soviet of
Workers' Deputies is not a labour parliament and not an
organ of proletarian self-government, nor an organ of self-
government at all, but a fighting organisation for the achievement of definite aims.

This fighting organisation includes, on the basis of a
temporary, unwritten fighting agreement, representatives of
the Russian Social-Democratic Labour Party (the party of
proletarian socialism), of the "Socialist-Revolutionary" Party
(the representatives of petty-bourgeois socialism, or the
extreme Left wing of revolutionary bourgeois democrats), and
finally many "non-party" workers. The latter, however, are
not non-party in general, but are non-party revolutionaries,
their sympathies being entirely on the side of the revolution,
for the victory of which they are fighting with boundless
enthusiasm, energy and self-sacrifice. For that reason it will
be quite natural to include representatives of the revolutionary peasantry in the Executive Committee.

For all practice purposes, the Soviet of Workers' Deputies
is an inchoate, broad fighting alliance of socialists and revolutionary democrats, the term "non-party revolutionary", of
course, representing a series of transitional stages between the
former and the latter. Such an alliance is obviously necessary
for the purpose of conducting political strikes and other, more
active forms of struggle, for the urgent democratic demands
which have been accepted and approved by the overwhelming
majority of the population. In an alliance of this sort, the
anarchists will not be an asset, but a liability; they will merely
bring disorganisation and thus weaken the force of the joint
assault; to them it is still "debatable" whether political reform is urgent and important. The exclusion of anarchists
from the fighting alliance which is carrying out, as it were,
our democratic revolution, is quite necessary from the point of
view of this revolution and is in its interests. There can be a

place in a fighting alliance only for those who fight for the aim of that alliance. If, for example, the "Cadets"[124] or the "Party of Law and Order"[125] had managed to recruit at least several hundred workers into their St. Petersburg branches, the Executive Committee of the Soviet of Workers' Deputies would hardly have opened its doors to the representatives of such organisations.

In explaining its decision, the Executive Committee refers to the practice of international socialist congresses. We warmly welcome this statement, this recognition by the executive body of the St. Petersburg Soviet of Workers' Deputies of the ideological leadership of the international Social-Democratic movement. The Russian revolution has already acquired international significance. The enemies of the revolution in Russia are already conspiring with Wilhelm II and with all sorts of reactionaries, tyrants, militarists and exploiters in Europe against free Russia. Neither shall we forget that the complete victory of our revolution demands an alliance of the revolutionary proletariat of Russia with the socialist workers of all countries.

It is not for nothing that international socialist congresses adopted the decision not to admit the anarchists. A wide gulf separates socialism from anarchism, and it is in vain that the *agents-provocateurs* of the secret police and the newspaper lackeys of reactionary governments pretend that this gulf does not exist. The philosophy of the anarchists is bourgeois philosophy turned inside out. Their individualistic theories and their individualistic ideal are the very opposite of socialism. Their views express, not the future of bourgeois society, which is striding with irresistible force towards the socialisation of labour, but the present and even the past of that society, the domination of blind chance over the scattered and isolated small producer. Their tactics, which amount to a repudiation of the political struggle, disunite the proletarians and convert them in fact into passive participators in one bourgeois policy or another, since it is impossible and unrealisable for the workers really to dissociate themselves from politics.

In the present Russian revolution, the task of rallying the forces of the proletariat, of organising it, of politically educating and training the working class, is more imperative than ever. The more outrageous the conduct of the Black-Hundred government, the more zealously its *agents-provocateurs* strive to fan base passions among the ignorant masses and the more desperately the defenders of the autocracy, which is rotting alive, clutch at every opportunity to discredit the revolution by organising hold-ups, pogroms and assassinations, and by fuddling lumpen proletarians with drink, the more important is the task of organisation that falls primarily to the party of the socialist proletariat. And we shall therefore resort to every means of ideological struggle to keep the influence of the anarchists over the Russian workers just as negligible as it has been so far.

Written on November 24
(December 7), 1905

Published in *Novaya Zhizn*, No. 21
November 25, 1905
Signed: *N. Lenin*

V. I. Lenin,
Collected Works,
Vol. 10, pp. 71-74

From THE SOCIAL-DEMOCRATS
AND ELECTORAL AGREEMENTS

I

Social-Democrats regard parliamentarism (participation in representative assemblies) as one of the means of enlightening and educating the proletariat and organising it in an independent class party; as one of the methods of the political struggle for the emancipation of the workers. This Marxist standpoint radically distinguishes Social-Democracy from bourgeois democracy, on the one hand, and from anarchism on the other. Bourgeois liberals and radicals regard parliamentarism as the "natural" and the only normal and legitimate method of conducting state affairs in general, and they repudiate the class struggle and the class character of modern parliamentarism. The bourgeoisie exerts every effort, by every possible means and on every possible occasion, to put blinkers on the eyes of the workers to prevent them from seeing that parliamentarism is an instrument of bourgeois oppression, to prevent them from realising the historically limited importance of parliamentarism. The anarchists are also unable to appreciate the historically defined importance of parliamentarism and entirely renounce this method of struggle. That is why the Social-Democrats in Russia strenuously combat both anarchism and the efforts of the bourgeoisie to *stop* the revolution as soon as possible by coming to terms with the old regime on a parliamentary basis. They subordinate their parliamentary activities entirely and

absolutely to the general interests of the working-class movement and to the special tasks of the proletariat in the present
bourgeois-democratic revolution.

Written towards the end
of October 1906

Published as a pamphlet
in November 1906,
by *Uperyod* Publishers,
in Petersburg

V. I. Lenin,
Collected Works,
Vol. 11, pp. 277-78

DRAFT RESOLUTION FOR THE FIFTH CONGRESS OF THE R.S.D.L.P. ON "NON-PARTY WORKERS' ORGANISATIONS AND THE ANARCHO-SYNDICALIST TREND AMONG THE PROLETARIAT"

Whereas:

1. in connection with Comrade Axelrod's agitation for a non-Party labour congress,[126] a trend (represented by Larin, Shcheglo, El, Ivanovsky, Mirov, and the Odessa publication *Osvobozhdeniye Truda*[127]) has appeared in the ranks of the R.S.D.L.P., the aim of which is to destroy the Social-Democratic Labour Party and to set up in its place a non-party political organisation of the proletariat;

2. besides this, outside of and actually against the Party, anarcho-syndicalist agitation is being carried on among the proletariat, using this same slogan of a non-party labour congress and non-party organisations (*Soyuznoye Dyelo* and its group in Moscow, the anarchist press in Odessa, etc.);

3. notwithstanding the resolution passed by the November All-Russian Conference of the R.S.D.L.P.,[128] a series of disruptive actions has been observed in our Party, with the object of setting up non-party organisations;

4. on the other hand, the R.S.D.L.P. has never renounced its intention of utilising certain non-party organisations, such as the Soviets of Workers' Deputies, in periods of more or less intense revolutionary upheaval, to extend Social-Democratic influence among the working class and to strengthen the Social-Democratic labour movement (see the September resolutions of the St. Petersburg Committee and the Moscow

Committee on the labour congress, in *Proletary*, Nos. 3 and 4);[129]

5. the incipient revival creates the opportunity to organise or utilise non-party representative working-class institutions, such as Soviets of Workers' Deputies, Soviets of Workers' Delegates, etc., for the purpose of developing the Social-Democratic movement; at the same time the Social-Democratic Party organisations must bear in mind that if Social-Democratic activities among the proletarian masses are properly, effectively and widely organised, such institutions may actually become superfluous;

This conference declares:

1. that a most determined ideological struggle must be waged against the anarcho-syndicalist movement among the proletariat and against Axelrod's and Larin's ideas in the Social-Democratic Party;

2. that a most determined struggle must be waged against all disruptive and demagogic attempts to weaken the R.S.D.L.P. from within or to utilise it for the purpose of substituting non-party political, proletarian organisations for the Social-Democratic Party;

3. that Social-Democratic Party organisations may, in case of necessity, participate in inter-party Soviets of Workers' Delegates, Soviets of Workers' Deputies, and in congresses of representatives of these organisations, and may organise such institutions, provided this is done on strict Party lines for the purpose of developing and strengthening the Social-Democratic Labour Party;

4. that for the purpose of extending and strengthening the influence of the Social-Democratic party among the broad masses of the proletariat, it is essential, on the one hand, to increase efforts to organise trade unions and conduct Social-Democratic propaganda and agitation within them, and, on the other hand, to draw still larger sections of the working class into the activities of all types of Party organisations.

Written on February 15-18
(February 28-March 3), 1907

Published in *Proletary* No. 14,
March 4, 1907

V. I. Lenin,
Collected Works,
Vol. 12, pp. 142-44

A LETTER TO A. V. LUNACHARSKY

Between November 2 and 11, 1907

Dear An. Vas.,

I have received your pamphlet at last—the first part arrived quite a long time ago.[130] I kept waiting for the end so as to read it as a whole, but I waited in vain. So far the third supplement is still missing ("How Marx Regarded", etc.). This is most unfortunate for, not having the complete manuscript, one is afraid of giving it to the press to be set up. If this third supplement has not been sent yet, please try to send it as quickly as possible. The money (200 rubles) has been sent to you; did you receive it?

As regards the content of your pamphlet, I liked it very much, as did all our people here. A most interesting pamphlet and excellently written. The only thing is, there are many unguarded statements, so to speak—I mean the kind of things which various S.R.s, Mensheviks,[131] syndicalists, etc., will *pick on*. We discussed collectively whether we should touch it up or give an explanation in the preface. We decided on the latter course, as it would be a pity to touch it up; it would impair the integral character of the exposition.

The conscientious and attentive reader will be able to understand you correctly, of course; nevertheless, you should *specially guard yourself* against false interpreters, whose name is legion. For example, we must of course criticise Bebel, and I do not approve of Trotsky, who recently sent us a hymn of praise to Essen and German Social-Democracy in general. You are right in pointing out that in Essen Bebel was wrong both on the question of militarism and on the question of colonial policy (or rather on the character of the radicals' fight at Stuttgart on this subject).[132] But it should be mentioned in this connection that these are the mistakes of a person with whom we are going the same way, and which can only be rectified in this, Marxist, Social-Democratic way. For there are many people among us (you probably do not see their press) who maliciously chuckle over Bebel *for the sake of glorifying* Socialist-Revolutionarism, syndicalism (*à la* Yezersky, Kozlovsky, Krichevsky— see *Obrazovaniye*,[133] etc.) and anarchism.

In my opinion, *all* your ideas can and should always be set forth in such a way that criticism will be aimed not at orthodoxy, not at the Germans in general, but at *opportunism*. Then it will be *impossible* to misinterpret you. Then the conclusion will be clear, namely, that Bolshevism, taking a lesson from the Germans and profiting by their experience (this demand of yours is a thousand times correct!), will take *all that is vital* from syndicalism *in order to kill Russian syndicalism and opportunism*. To do this is easier and more natural for us Bolsheviks than for anyone else, for in the revolution we have always fought against parliamentary cretinism and Plekhanovite opportunism. And it is we alone who, from the revolutionary and not from the pedantic Cadet standpoint of Plekhanov and Co., can refute syndicalism, which produces no end of confusion (particularly dangerous confusion in the case of Russia).

Proletary No. 17 has come out and has been sent to you, and so has *Zarnitsy*.[134] Have you received them? Do you read *Tovarishch*?[135] How do you like it now? What about your remembering old times and poking fun at them in verse? Write please.

All the very best.

                                                            Yours,
                                                                Lenin

Written between   V. I. Lenin,
November 2 and 11, 1907   *Collected Works*,
Sent from Kuokkala (Finland) to Italy   Vol. 34, pp. 370-71

First published in 1934
in *Lenin Miscellany XXVI*

Now, on the question of the trade unions, equally strong emphasis should be placed on the fact that Bolshevism applies the tactics of revolutionary Social-Democracy in all fields of struggle, in all spheres of activity. What distinguishes Bolshevism from Menshevism is not that the former "repudiates" work in the trade unions or the co-operative societies, etc., but that the former *takes a different line* in the work of propaganda, agitation, and organisation of the working class. Today activity in the trade unions undoubtedly assumes tremendous importance. In contrast to the neutralism of the Mensheviks we must conduct this activity on the lines of closer alignment of the unions with the Party, of the development of socialist consciousness and an understanding of the revolutionary tasks of the proletariat. In Western Europe revolutionary syndicalism in many countries was a direct and inevitable result of opportunism, reformism, and parliamentary cretinism. In our country, too, the first steps of "Duma activity" increased opportunism to a tremendous extent and reduced the Mensheviks to servility before the Cadets. Plekhanov, for example, in his everyday political work, virtually *merged* with the Prokopovich and Kuskova gentry. In 1900, he denounced them for Bernsteinism,[136] for contemplating only the "posterior" of the Russian proletariat (*Vademecum* for the editorial staff of *Rabocheye Dyelo*,[137] Geneva, 1900). In 1906-07, the first ballot papers threw Plekhanov into the arms of these

gentlemen, who are now contemplating the "posterior" of
Russian liberalism. Syndicalism cannot help developing on
Russian soil as a reaction against this shameful conduct of
"distinguished" Social-Democrats.

Comrade Voinov, therefore, is quite correct in taking the
line of calling upon the Russian Social-Democrats to learn
from the example of opportunism and *from* the example of
syndicalism. Revolutionary work in the trade unions, shifting the emphasis from parliamentary trickery to the education of the proletariat, to rallying the purely class organisations, to the struggle outside parliament, to ability to use
(and to prepare the masses for the possibility of successfully
using) the general strike, as well as the "December forms
of struggle", in the Russian revolution[138]—all this comes
very strongly into prominence as the task of the Bolshevik
trend. And the experience of the Russian revolution immense-
ly facilitates this task for us, provides a wealth of practical guidance and historical data making it possible to
appraise in the most concrete way the new methods of
struggle, the mass strike, and the use of direct force. These
methods of struggle are least of all "new" to the Russian
Bolsheviks, the Russian proletariat. They are "new" to the
opportunists, who are doing their utmost to erase from the
minds of the workers in the West the memory of the Commune, and from the minds of the workers in Russia the
memory of December 1905. To strengthen these memories,
to make a scientific study of that great experience*, to spread
its lessons among the masses and the realisation of its
inevitable repetition on a new scale—this task of the revolutionary Social-Democrats in Russia opens up before us
prospects infinitely richer than the one-sided "anti-opportun-
ism" and "anti-parliamentarism" of the syndicalists.

---

* It is natural that the Cadets should be eagerly studying the
history of the two Dumas.[139] It is natural that they should regard the
platitudes and betrayals of Rodichev-Kutlerov liberalism as gems of
creation. It is natural that they should falsify history by drawing a veil
of silence over their negotiations with the reaction, etc. It is unnatural
for the Social-Democrats not to eagerly study October-December 1905,
if only because each day of that period meant a hundred times more to
the destinies of all the peoples of Russia and the working class in particular than Rodichev's "loyal" phrases in the Duma.

Against syndicalism, as a special trend, Comrade Voinov levels four accusations (p. 19 onwards of his pamphlet), which show up its falsity with striking clearness: (1) the "anarchistic looseness of the organisation"; (2) keeping the workers keyed up instead of creating a firm "stronghold of class organisation"; (3) the petty-bourgeois-individual-istic features of its ideal and of the Proudhon theory; (4) a stupid "aversion to politics".

There are here not a few points of resemblance to the old "Economism"[140] among the Russian Social-Democrats. Hence I am not so optimistic as Comrade Voinov in regard to a "reconciliation" with revolutionary Social-Democracy on the part of those Economists who have gone over to syndi-calism. I also think that Comrade Voinov's proposals for a "General Labour Council' as a superarbiter, with the parti-cipation in it of Socialist-Revolutionaries, are quite unpract-ical. This is mixing up the "music of the future" with the organisational forms of the present. But I am not in the least afraid of Comrade Voinov's perspective, namely: "subordination of political organisations to a class social organisation" ... "*only when* [I am still quoting Comrade Voinov, stressing the important words] ... *all trade-union-ists will have become socialists*". The class instinct of the proletarian mass has *already* begun to be manifested in Russia with full force. This class instinct already provides tremendous guarantees both against the petty-bourgeois woolliness of the Socialist-Revolutionaries and against the Mensheviks' servility to the Cadets. We can already boldly assert that the mass *workers'* organisation in Russia (if it were to be created and in so far as it is for a minute created, if only by elections, strikes, demonstrations, etc.) is *sure* to be closer to Bolshevism, to revolutionary Social-Democracy.

Written in November 1907

First published in 1933
in *Lenin Miscellany XXV*

V. I. Lenin,
Collected Works,
Vol. 13, pp. 166-68

From MARXISM AND REVISIONISM

The inevitability of revisionism is determined by its class roots in modern society. Revisionism is an international phenomenon. No thinking socialist who is in the least informed can have the slightest doubt that the relation between the orthodox[141] and the Bernsteinians in Germany, the Guesdists[142] and the Jauresists[143] (and now particularly the Broussists[144]) in France, the Social Democratic Federation[145] and the Independent Labour Party in Great Britain,[146] Brouckère and Vandervelde in Belgium, the Integralists[147] and the Reformists in Italy, the Bolsheviks and the Mensheviks in Russia, is everywhere essentially similar, notwithstanding the immense variety of national conditions and historical factors in the present state of all these countries. In reality, the "division" within the present international socialist movement is now proceeding along the *same* lines in all the various countries of the world, which testifies to a tremendous advance compared with thirty or forty years ago, when heterogeneous trends in the various countries were struggling within the one international socialist movement. And that "revisionism from the left" which has taken shape in the Latin countries as "revolutionary syndicalism", is also adapting itself to Marxism, "amending" it: Labriola in Italy and Lagardelle in France frequently appeal from Marx who is understood wrongly to Marx who is understood rightly.

We cannot stop here to analyse the ideological content of *this* revisionism, which as yet is far from having developed to the same extent as opportunist revisionism: it has not yet become international, has not yet stood the test of a single big practical battle with a socialist party in any single country. We confine ourselves therefore to that "revisionism from the right" which was described above.

Written in the second half
of March, not later than
April 3 (16), 1906

Published between September 25
and October 2 (October 8 and 15),
1908 in the symposium:
Karl Marx (1818-1883),
St. Petersburg, O. and M. Kedrovs
Publishers
Signed: *Ul. Ilyin*

V. I. Lenin,
Collected Works
Vol. 15, p. 38

If Marx, who had said six months before the Commune
that an insurrection would be madness, nevertheless was
able to sum up that "madness" as the greatest mass movement of the proletariat in the nineteenth century, then with
a thousand times more justification must the Russian Social-
Democrats inspire the masses with the conviction that the
December struggle was the most essential, the most legitimate, the greatest proletarian movement since the Commune.
And the working class of Russia will be trained up in such
views, whatever individual intellectuals in the ranks of
Social-Democracy may say, and however loudly they may
lament.

Here perhaps one remark is necessary, bearing in mind
that this article is being written for the Polish comrades.
Not being familiar, to my regret, with the Polish language,
I know Polish conditions only by hearsay. And it may be
easy to retort that it is precisely in Poland that a whole
party strangled itself by impotent guerrilla warfare, terrorism and fireworky outbreaks, and those precisely in the
name of rebel traditions and a joint struggle of the proletariat and the peasantry (the so-called Right wing in the
Polish Socialist Party).[148] It may very well be that from
this standpoint Polish conditions do in fact radically differ
from conditions in the rest of the Russian Empire. I cannot
judge of this. I must say, however, that nowhere except
in Poland have we seen such a senseless departure from

revolutionary tactics, one that has aroused justified resistance and opposition. And here the thought arises unbidden: why, it was precisely in Poland that there was no mass armed struggle in December 1905! And is it not for this very reason that in Poland, and only in Poland, the distorted and senseless tactics of revolution-"making" anarchism have found their home, and that conditions did not permit of the development there of mass armed struggle, were it only for a short time? Is it not the tradition of just *such* a struggle, the tradition of the December armed uprising, that is at times the only serious means of overcoming anarchist tendencies within the workers' party—not by means of hackneyed, philistine, petty-bourgeois moralising, but by turning from aimless, senseless, sporadic acts of violence to purposeful, mass violence, linked with the broad movement and the sharpening of the direct proletarian struggle?

Published in April 1908
in the journal *Przegląd
Socjaldemokratyczny* No. 2
Signed: N. Lenin

Published in Russian
in May 10 (23), 1908
in *Proletary* No. 30

V. I. Lenin,
Collected Works,
Vol. 15, pp. 60-61

From BELLICOSE MILITARISM
AND THE ANTI-MILITARIST TACTICS
OF SOCIAL-DEMOCRACY

II

Thus the principle which connects militarism and capitalism is firmly established among socialists, and on this point there are no differences. But the recognition of this link does not of itself concretely determine the anti-militarist *tactics* of the socialists: it does not solve the practical problem of how to fight the burden of militarism and how to prevent wars. And it is in the answers to these questions that a considerable divergence of views is to be found among socialists. At the Stuttgart Congress[149] these differences were very marked.

At one pole are German Social-Democrats like Vollmar. Since militarism is the offspring of capitalism, they argue, since wars are a necessary concomitant of capitalist development, there is no need for any special anti-militarist activity. That exactly is what Vollmar declared at the Essen Party Congress. On the question of how Social-Democrats should behave if war is declared, the majority of the German Social-Democrats, headed by Bebel and Vollmar, hold rigidly to the view that the Social-Democrats must defend their country against aggression, and that they are bound to take part in a "defensive" war. This proposition led Vollmar at Stuttgart to declare that "all our love for humanity cannot prevent us being good Germans", while the Social-Democratic deputy Noske proclaimed in the Reichstag that, in the event of war against Germany, "the Social-Democrats will not lag behind the bourgeois parties and will shoulder their rifles". From this Noske had to make only one more step to declare that "we want Germany to be armed as much as possible".

At the other pole is the small group of supporters of Hervé. The proletariat has no fatherland, they argue. Hence all wars are in the interests of the capitalists. Hence the proletariat must combat every war. The proletariat must meet every declaration of war with a military strike and an uprising. This must be the main purpose of anti-militarist propaganda. At Stuttgart Hervé therefore proposed the following draft resolution: "The Congress calls for *every declaration of war, whencesoever it may come*, being met with a military strike and an uprising."

Such are the two "extreme" positions on this question in the ranks of the Western socialists. "Like the sun in a drop of water", there are reflected in them the two diseases which still cause harm to the activity of the socialist proletariat in the West—opportunist tendencies on the one hand and anarchist phrase-mongering on the other.

First of all, a few remarks about patriotism. That "working men have no country" was really said in the *Communist Manifesto*.[150] That the attitude of Vollmar, Noske and Co. strikes at this basic principle of *international* socialism is also true. But it does not follow from this that Hervé and his followers are right in asserting that it is of no concern to the proletariat in what country it lives—in monarchical Germany, republican France or despotic Turkey. The fatherland, i.e., the given political, cultural and social environment, is a most powerful factor in the class struggle of the proletariat: and if Vollmar is wrong when he lays down some kind of "truly German" attitude of the proletariat to "the fatherland", Hervé is just as wrong when he takes up an unforgivably uncritical attitude on such an important factor in the struggle of the proletariat for emancipation. The proletariat cannot be indifferent to the political, social and cultural conditions of its struggle; consequently it cannot be indifferent to the destinies of its country. But the destinies of the country interest it only *to the extent* that they affect its class struggle, and not in virtue of some bourgeois "patriotism", quite indecent on the lips of a Social-Democrat.

More complicated is the other question, namely, the

attitude to militarism and war. At the very first glance it is obvious that Hervé is unforgivably confusing these two questions, and forgetting the causal connection between war and capitalism. By adopting Hervé's tactics, the proletariat would condemn itself to fruitless activity: it would use up all its fighting preparedness (the reference is to insurrection) in the struggle against the effect (war) and allow the cause (capitalism) to remain.

The anarchist mode of thought is displayed in full measure here. Blind faith in the miracle-working power of all direct action*; the wrenching of this "direct action" out of its general social and political context, without the slightest analysis of the latter: in short the "arbitrarily mechanical interpretation of social phenomena" (as Karl Liebknecht put it) is obvious.

Hervé's plan is "very simple": on the day war is declared the socialist soldiers desert, while the reservists declare a strike and stay in their homes. But "the strike of the reservists is not passive resistance: the working class would soon go over to open resistance, to insurrection, and the latter would have all the greater chance of ending in triumph because the army on active service would be at the frontiers" (G. Hervé, *Leur patrie*).

Such is this "effective, direct and practical plan"; and Hervé, confident in its success, proposes that a military strike and insurrection should be the reply to every declaration of war.

It will be clear from this that the question here is not whether the proletariat is able, when it finds such a course desirable, to reply with a strike and insurrection to a declaration of war. The point at issue is whether the proletariat should be bound by an obligation to reply by an insurrection to *every* war. To decide the question in the latter sense means to take away from the proletariat the choice of the moment for a decisive battle, and to hand it over to its enemies. It is not the proletariat which chooses the moment of struggle in accordance with its own interests, when its general socialist consciousness stands at a high level, when its organisation is strong, when the occasion is appropriate,

---

* These words are in French in the original: *action directe.—Ed.*

etc. No, the bourgeois governments would be able to provoke it to an insurrection even when the conditions for it were unfavourable, for example, by declaring a war specially calculated to arouse patriotic and chauvinist feelings among wide sections of the population and thus isolate the insurgent proletariat. It should be borne in mind, moreover, that the bourgeoisie which, from monarchist Germany to republican France and democratic Switzerland, persecutes anti-militarist activity with such ruthlessness in peace-time, would descend with the utmost fury on any attempt at a military strike in the event of war, when war-time laws, declarations of martial law, courts martial, etc., are in force.

Kautsky was right when he said of Hervé's idea: "The idea of a military strike sprang from 'good' motives, it is noble and full of heroism, but it is heroic folly."

The proletariat, if it finds it expedient and suitable, may reply with a military strike to a declaration of war. It may, among other means of achieving a social revolution, also have recourse to a military strike. But to commit itself to this "tactical recipe" is not in the interests of the proletariat.

And that precisely was the reply given to this debatable question by the Stuttgart International Congress.

Proletary No. 33,
July 23 (August 5), 1908

V. I. Lenin,
Collected Works,
Vol. 15, pp. 193-96

From A CARICATURE OF BOLSHEVISM[151]

Point (a) "The Duma being ... a deal ... and a weapon of the counter-revolution".... Quite right! ... "only serves to bolster up the autocracy".... This "only" is wrong. The autocracy has staved off its downfall by organising such a Duma in time: but it has not been strengthened thereby, rather on the contrary, advanced in its *decay*. The Duma, as a "screen", is more effective than many an "exposure", because for the first time, on a thousand and one issues, it reveals tsarism's dependence on the counter-revolutionary sections of society: it is for the first time demonstrating *en grand* how close is the alliance between Romanov and Purishkevich, between tsarism and the "Union of the Russian People",[152] between the autocracy and the Dubrovins, the Iliodors and the Polovnyovs.[153]

That the Duma sanctions the crimes of tsarism is beyond doubt; but it is the sanction of particular classes, on behalf of particular class interests, and it is the duty of the Social-Democrats precisely to use the Duma rostrum to reveal these instructive truths of the class struggle.

..."The eight months' proceedings of the Third Duma have shown that the Social-Democrats cannot make use of it.."...

Here is the very essence of otzovism, the error of which our "ultimatumists" are only covering up, confusing the issue by their ridiculous equivocation—that since we have spent so much energy on creating a Duma group, we must not recall it lightly!

There is a straightforward question, and evasions won't do: have these eight months' proceedings proved that it is possible to make use of the rostrum of the Duma, or not? The otzovists' reply is wrong. In spite of the immense difficulties involved in Party *guidance* of the Duma group, it has beyond question *proved the possibility* of making use of the Duma as a platform. To be daunted by difficulties and mistakes is timidity; it is intellectual "yelping", whereas what we want is patient, consistent and persistent proletarian effort. Other socialist parties in Europe encountered even greater difficulties at the beginning of their parliamentary activity, and made many more mistakes, but they did not shirk their duty. They succeeded in overcoming the difficulties and in correcting their mistakes.

(b) "Our Duma group ... persistently pursuing opportunist tactics, could not and cannot be a staunch and consistent representative of the revolutionary proletariat."

The grandest truths can be vulgarised, otzovist comrades, the noblest aims can be reduced to mere *phrase-mongering* —and that is what you are doing. You have degraded the fight against opportunism into mere phrase-mongering, and are thereby only playing into the hands of the opportunists. Our Duma group has made and is making mistakes, but by its very work it has proved that it "could and can" staunchly and consistently represent the proletariat—*could and can*, when we, the Party, guide it, help it, appoint our best men to lead it, draw up directives, and draft speeches, and explain the harmful and fatal effects of taking advice from the petty-bourgeois intelligentsia who, not only in Russia but *all over the world, always* gain easy access to all kinds of institutions on the parliamentary fringe.

Have the courage to admit, comrades, that we have as yet done far too little to provide this *real* guidance of the work of the Duma group, to help it with *deeds*. Have the courage to admit that we *can* do ten times as much in this direction, if we succeed in strengthening our organisations, consolidating our Party, bringing it closer to the masses, creating Party media exercising a constant influence on large sections of the proletarians. That is what we are working for, that is what everybody must work for who wants to fight opportunism in deeds and not in words.

The otzovists have reduced the struggle against opportunism in the Duma group to a mere phrase. They have learned words by rote without understanding the difference between anarchist and Social-Democratic criticism of opportunism. Take the anarchists. They all pounce on every mistake every Social-Democratic member of parliament makes. They all shout that *even* Bebel once made a speech in an almost patriotic spirit, once took up a wrong stand on the agrarian programme, and so on and so forth. True, even Bebel made opportunist mistakes in his parliamentary career. But what does this prove? The anarchists say that it proves that all the workers' M.P.s should be recalled. The anarchists rail at the Social-Democratic members of parliament and refuse to have anything to do with them, refuse to do anything to develop a proletarian party, a proletarian policy and proletarian members of parliament. And in practice the anarchists' phrase-mongering converts them into the truest accomplices of opportunism, into the reverse side of opportunism.

Social-Democrats draw quite a different conclusion from their mistakes—the conclusion that *even* Bebel could not become Bebel without prolonged Party work in training up real Social-Democratic representatives. They need not tell us, "We have no Bebels in our group". Bebels are not born. They have to be made. Bebels don't spring fully formed like Minerva from the head of Jupiter, but are created by the Party and the working class. Those who say we have no Bebels don't know the history of the German Party: they don't know that there was a time, under the Anti-Socialist Law, when August Bebel made opportunist blunders and that the Party corrected him, the Party guided Bebel.*

(c) "The continued presence of the Social-Democratic group in the Duma ... can only do harm to the interests of the proletariat ... lower the dignity and influence of the Social-Democrats." To show how "quantity passes into quality" in these preposterous exaggerations, and how

---

* We hope to deal with this illuminating history and with *its* condemnation of German trends akin to our otzovists in a separate article.

anarchist phrases *grow out* of them (irrespective of whether our otzovist comrades desire it or not), we need only refer to Belousov's speech during the 1909 budget debate. If *such* speeches are considered as "harmful", and not as proof that the rostrum of the Duma can and must be utilised, then our disagreement ceases to be a mere difference of opinion about the character of a speech, and becomes a disagreement concerning the fundamental principles of Social-Democratic tactics.

(I) "Launch a wide campaign ... for the slogan: 'Down with the Third Duma' "....

We have already said in *Proletary*, No. 39, that this slogan, which for a time appealed to some anti-otzovist workers, is *wrong*.[154] It is either a Cadet slogan, calling for franchise reform under the autocracy, or a repetition of words learned by rote from the period when liberal Dumas were a screen for counter-revolutionary tsarism, designed to prevent the people from seeing clearly who their real enemy was.

(II) "Recall ... the Duma group; this will emphasise both ... the character of the Duma and the revolutionary tactics of the Social-Democrats."

This is a paraphrase of the proposition advanced by the Moscow otzovists, that the recall of the Duma group will emphasise that the revolution is not dead and buried. Such a conclusion—we repeat the words of *Proletary*, No. 39, "emphasises" only the *burial* of those Social-Democrats who are capable of arguing in this way. They *bury* themselves thereby as Social-Democrats; they lose all feeling for genuine proletarian revolutionary work; and for that reason they are so painfully contorting themselves to "emphasise" their revolutionary phrases.

(III) "Devote all efforts to organisation and preparation ... for open ... struggle [and therefore renounce open agitation from the rostrum of the Duma!] ... and to propaganda", etc., etc.

The otzovists have forgotten that it is unseemly for Social-Democrats to refuse to conduct *propaganda* from the rostrum of the Duma.

At this point they give us the argument repeated by some ultimatumists, that "there is no sense in wasting energy on hopeless work in the Duma, let us use *all our forces* more productively". This is not reasoning, but sophistry, which—again irrespective of whether the authors desire it or not—leads to anarchist conclusions. For in *all* countries the anarchists, pointing to the mistakes committed by Social-Democratic members of parliament, argue that it is "a waste of time to bother with bourgeois parliamentarism" and call for the concentration of "all these forces" on organising "direct action". But this leads to disorganisation and to the shouting of "slogans" which are futile because they are isolated, instead of conducting work in every field on the widest possible scale. It only seems to the otzovists and ultimatumists that their argument is new, and applies *only* to the Third Duma. But they are wrong. It is a common argument heard all over Europe, and it is *not* a Social-Democratic argument.

Supplement to *Proletary*
No. 44, April 4 (17), 1909

V. I. Lenin,
Collected Works,
Vol. 15, pp. 389-93

Marxism is materialism. As such, it is as relentlessly hostile to religion as was the materialism of the eighteenth-century Encyclopaedists or the materialism of Feuerbach. This is beyond doubt. But the dialectical materialism of Marx and Engels goes further than the Encyclopaedists and Feuerbach, for it applies the materialist philosophy to the domain of history, to the domain of the social sciences. We must combat religion—that is the ABC of *all* materialism, and consequently of Marxism. But Marxism is not a materialism which has stopped at the ABC. Marxism goes further. It says: We must *know how* to combat religion, and in order to do so we must explain the source of faith and religion among the masses *in a materialist way*. The combating of religion cannot be confined to abstract ideological preaching, and it must not be reduced to such preaching. It must be linked up with the concrete practice of the class movement, which aims at eliminating the social roots of religion. Why does religion retain its hold on the backward sections of the town proletariat, on broad sections of the semi-proletariat, and on the mass of the peasantry? Because of the ignorance of the people, replies the bourgeois progressist, the radical or the bourgeois materialist. And so: "Down with religion and long live atheism; the dissemination of atheist views is our chief task!" The Marxist says that this is not true, that it is a superficial view, the view of narrow bourgeois uplifters. It does not explain the roots of religion profoundly enough; it explains them, not in a materialist but in an idealist way. In modern capitalist countries these roots are mainly *social*. The deepest root of religion today is the socially downtrodden condition of the working masses and their apparently complete helplessness in face of the blind forces of capitalism, which every day and every hour inflicts upon ordinary working people the most horrible suffering and the most savage torment, a thousand times more severe than those inflicted by extraordinary events, such as wars, earthquakes, etc. "Fear made the gods." Fear of the blind force of capital—blind because it cannot be foreseen by the masses of the people—a force which at every step in the life of the proletarian and small proprietor threatens to inflict, and does inflict "sudden", "unexpected", "accidental" ruin, destruction, pauperism, prostitution, death from starvation—such is *the root* of modern religion which the materialist must bear in mind first and foremost, if he does not want to remain an infant-school materialist. No educational book can eradicate religion from the minds of masses who are crushed by capitalist hard labour, and who are at the mercy of the blind destructive forces of capitalism, until those masses themselves learn to fight this *root* of religion, fight *the rule of capital* in all its forms, in a united, organised, planned and conscious way.

Does this mean that educational books against religion are harmful or unnecessary? No, nothing of the kind. It means that Social-Democracy's atheist propaganda must be *subordinated* to its basic task—the development of the class struggle of the exploited *masses* against the exploiters.

This proposition may not be understood (or at least not immediately understood) by one who has not pondered over the principles of dialectical materialism, i.e., the philosophy of Marx and Engels. How is that?—he will say. Is ideological propaganda, the preaching of definite ideas, the struggle against that enemy of culture and progress which has persisted for thousands of years (i.e., religion) to be subordinated to the class struggle, i.e., the struggle for definite practical aims in the economic and political field?

This is one of those current objections to Marxism which testify to a complete misunderstanding of Marxian dialectics. The contradiction which perplexes these objectors is a real contradiction in real life, i.e., a dialectical contradiction, and not a verbal or invented one. To draw a hard-and-fast line between the theoretical propaganda of atheism, i.e., the destruction of religious beliefs among certain sections of the proletariat, and the success, the progress and the conditions of the class struggle of these sections, is to reason undialectically, to transform a shifting and relative boundary into an absolute boundary; it is forcibly to disconnect what is indissolubly connected in real life. Let us take an example. The proletariat in a particular region and in a particular industry is divided, let us assume, into an advanced section of fairly class-conscious Social-Democrats, who are of course atheists, and rather backward workers who are still connected with the countryside and with the peasantry, and who believe in God, go to church, or are even under the direct influence of the local priest—who, let us suppose, is organising a Christian labour union. Let us assume furthermore that the economic struggle in this locality has resulted in a strike. It is the duty of a Marxist to place the success of the strike movement above everything else, vigorously to counteract the division of the workers in this struggle into atheists and Christians, vigorously to oppose any such division. Atheist propaganda in such circumstances may be both unnecessary and harmful—not from the philistine fear of scaring away the backward sections, of losing a seat in the elections, and so on, but out of consideration for the real progress of the class struggle, which in the conditions of modern capitalist society will convert Christian workers to Social-Democracy and to atheism a hundred times better than bald atheist propaganda. To preach atheism at such a moment and in such circumstances would only be playing *into the hands* of the priest and the priests, who desire nothing better than that the division of the workers according to their participation in the strike movement should be replaced by their division according to their belief in God. An anarchist who preached war against God at all costs would in effect be helping the priests and the bourgeoisie (as the anarchists always do help the bourgeoisie *in practice*). A Marxist must be a materialist, i.e., an enemy of religion, but a dialectical materialist, i.e., one who treats the struggle against religion not in an abstract way, not on the basis of remote, purely theoretical, never varying preaching, but in a concrete way, on the basis of the class struggle which is going on *in practice* and is educating the masses more and better than anything else could. A Marxist must be able to view the concrete situation as a whole, he must always be able to find the boundary between anarchism and opportunism (this boundary is relative, shifting and changeable, but it exists). And he must not succumb either to the abstract, verbal, but in reality empty "revolutionism" of the anarchist, or to the philistinism and opportunism of the petty bourgeois or liberal intellectual, who boggles at the struggle against religion, forgets that this is his duty, reconciles himself to belief in God, and is guided not by the interests of the class struggle but by the petty and mean consideration of offending nobody, repelling nobody and scaring nobody—by the sage rule: "live and let live", etc., etc.

Let us now pass to the conditions which in the West gave rise to the opportunist interpretation of the thesis: "religion is a private matter". Of course, a contributing influence are those general factors which give rise to opportunism as a whole, like sacrificing the fundamental interests of the working-class movement for the sake of momentary advantages. The party of the proletariat demands that *the state* should declare religion a private matter, but does not regard the fight against the opium of the people, the fight against religious superstitions, etc., as a "private matter". The opportunists distort the question to mean that the *Social-Democratic* Party *regards* religion as a private matter!

But in addition to the usual opportunist distortion (which was not made clear at all in the discussion within our Duma group when it was considering the speech on religion), there are special historical conditions which have given rise to the present-day, and, if one may so express it, excessive, indifference on the part of the European Social-Democrats to the question of religion. These conditions are of a twofold nature. First, the task of combating religion is historically the task of the revolutionary bourgeoisie, and in the West this task was to a large extent performed (or tackled) by bourgeois democracy, in the epoch of *its* revolutions or its

assaults upon feudalism and medievalism. Both in France
and in Germany there is a tradition of bourgeois war on
religion, and it began long before socialism (the Encyclopaedists, Feuerbach). In Russia, because of the conditions of
our bourgeois-democratic revolution, this task too falls
almost entirely on the shoulders of the working class. Petty-
bourgeois (Narodnik) democracy in our country has not
done too much in this respect (as the new-fledged Black-
Hundred Cadets, or Cadet Black Hundreds, of Vekhi[155]
think), but rather *too little*, in comparison with what has
been done in Europe.

On the other hand, the tradition of bourgeois war on
religion has given rise in Europe to a specifically bourgeois
distortion of this war by anarchism—which, as the Marxists
have long explained time and again, takes its stand on the
bourgeois world-outlook, in spite of all the "fury" of its
attacks on the bourgeoisie. The anarchists and Blanquists
in the Latin countries, Most (who, incidentally, was a
pupil of Dühring) and his ilk in Germany, the anarchists
in Austria in the eighties, all carried revolutionary phrase-
mongering in the struggle against religion to a *nec plus
ultra*. It is not surprising that, compared with the anarchists,
the European Social-Democrats now *go to the other extreme*.
This is quite understandable and to a certain extent legitimate, but it would be wrong for us Russian Social-
Democrats to forget the special historical conditions of the
West.

Secondly, in the West, *after* the national bourgeois revolutions were over, *after* more or less complete religious
liberty had been introduced, the problem of the democratic
struggle against religion had been pushed, historically, so
far into the background by the struggle of bourgeois
democracy against socialism that the bourgeois governments
deliberately tried to draw the attention of the masses away
from socialism by organising a quasi-liberal "offensive"
against clericalism. Such was the character of the *Kultur-
kampf* in Germany and of the struggle of the bourgeois-
republicans against clericalism in France. Bourgeois anti-
clericalism, as a means of drawing the attention of the
working-class masses away from socialism—this is what
preceded the spread of the modern spirit of "indifference"

to the struggle against religion among the Social-Democrats in the West. And this again is quite understandable and legitimate, because Social-Democrats had to counteract bourgeois and Bismarckian anti-clericalism by *subordinating* the struggle against religion to the struggle for socialism.

Proletary No. 45,   V. I. Lenin,
May 13 (26), 1909   *Collected Works*,
                                     Vol. 15, pp. 405-08, 409-11

From THE FACTION OF SUPPORTERS OF OTZOVISM AND GOD-BUILDING[156]

II

For any Marxist who has at all pondered over the philosophy of Marx and Engels, for any Social-Democrat who is at all acquainted with the history of the international socialist movement, this conversion of one of the lowest forms of struggle into the specific weapon of struggle of a special historic moment contains nothing surprising. The anarchists have absolutely never been able to understand this simple thing. Now our otzovists and their removed echoers are trying to introduce anarchist modes of thought among Russian Social-Democrats, crying out (like Maximov and Co.) that *Proletary* is dominated by the theory of "*parliamentarism at any price*".

To show how stupid and un-Social-Democratic these outcries of Maximov and Co. are, we shall once more have to begin with the ABC. Just reflect, O unjustly removed ones, what is the specific difference between the policy and tactics of the German Social-Democrats and those of the socialist workers' parties in other countries? The utilisation of parliamentarism; the conversion of bourgeois Junker (approximate Russian equivalent: Octobrist-Black-Hundred)[157] parliamentarism into an instrument for the socialist education and organisation of the mass of the workers. Does this mean that parliamentarism is the highest form of struggle of the socialist proletariat? Anarchists the world over think it does mean that. Does it mean that the German Social-Democrats stand for parliamentarism at any price? Anarchists the world over think it does mean that, and hence there is no enemy more hateful to them than German Social-Democracy, there is no target they love to aim at more than the German Social-Democrats. And in Russia, when our Socialist-Revolutionaries begin to flirt with the anarchists and advertise their own "revolutionary militancy" they never fail to drag in real or imaginary errors of the German Social-Democrats, and draw conclusions from them to the detriment of Social-Democracy.

Now let us go further. In what lies the fallacy of the anarchists' argument? It lies in the fact that, owing to their radically incorrect ideas of the course of social development, they are unable to take into account those peculiarities of the concrete political (and economic) situation in different countries which determine the specific significance of one or another means of struggle *for a given period of time*. In point of fact the German Social-Democrats, far from standing for parliamentarism at any price, not only do not subordinate everything to parliamentarism, but, on the contrary, in the international army of the proletariat they best of all have developed such extra-parliamentary means of struggle as the socialist press, the trade unions, the systematic use of popular assemblies, the socialist education of youth, and so on and so forth.

What is the point then? The point is that a combination of a number of historic conditions has made parliamentarism *a specific* weapon of struggle for Germany over a *given period*, not the chief one, not the highest, not of prime and essential importance in comparison with other forms, but merely specific, the most characteristic in comparison with other countries. Hence, the ability to use parliamentarism *has proved to be a symptom* (not a condition but a symptom) of exemplary organisation of the *entire* socialist movement, in *all* its branches, which we have enumerated above.

Let us turn from Germany to Russia. Anyone who presumed to draw an exact parallel between the conditions in these two countries would be guilty of a number of gross errors. But try to put the question as a Marxist is bound to do: what is the specific peculiarity of the policy and tactics of the Russian Social-Democrats at the present time? We must preserve and strengthen the illegal Party—just as before the revolution. We must steadily prepare the masses for a new revolutionary crisis—as in the years 1897-1903. We must strengthen to the utmost the Party's ties with the masses, develop and utilise all kinds of workers' organisations for the furtherance of the socialist cause, as has always been the practice of all Social-Democratic parties. The specific peculiarity of the moment is, namely, that the old autocracy is making an attempt (an unsuccessful attempt) to solve new historic problems with the help of the Octobrist-Black-Hundred Duma. Hence, the specific tactical task of the Social-Democrats is to use this Duma for *their own* purposes, for spreading the ideas of revolution and socialism. The point is not that this specific task is particularly lofty, that it opens grand vistas, or that it equals or even approaches in importance the tasks which faced the proletariat in, say, the period of 1905-06. No. The point is that it is a special feature of the tactics of the present moment, marking its distinction from the period that is past or from that which is yet to come (for this coming period will *certainly* bring us specific tasks, more complex, more lofty, more interesting than that of utilising the Third Duma). We cannot be equal to the present situation, we cannot solve the whole assemblage of problems with which it confronts the Social-Democratic Party, unless we solve this specific problem of the moment, unless we convert the Black-Hundred-Octobrist Duma into an *instrument* for Social-Democratic propaganda.

The otzovist windbags, taking their cue from the Bolsheviks, talk, for instance, of taking account of the experience of the revolution. But they do not understand what they are talking about. They do not understand that taking account of the experience of the revolution *includes* defending the ideals and aims and methods of the revolution *from inside the Duma*. If we do not know how to *defend* these ideals, aims and methods from inside the Duma, through our working-class Party members who might enter and those who have already entered this Duma, it means that we are unable to make the *first* step towards politically taking account of the experience of the revolution (for what we are concerned with here is of course not a theoretical summing up of experience in books and researches). Our task is by no means ended by this first step. Incomparably more important than the first step will be the second and third steps, i.e., the conversion of the experience already gained by the masses into ideological stock-in-trade for new historic action. But if these otzovist windbags themselves speak of an "inter-revolutionary" period they should have understood (if they were able to think and reason things out in a Social-Democratic way) that "inter-revolutionary" signifies precisely that *elementary, preliminary tasks come on the order of the day.* "Inter-revolutionary" denotes as unsettled, indefinite situation when the old regime has become convinced that it is impossible to rule with the old instruments alone and *tries* to use a *new* instrument within the general framework of the old institutions. This is an internally contradictory, futile attempt, in which the autocracy is once more going towards inevitable failure, is once more leading us to a repetition of the glorious period and glorious battles of 1905. But it is going *not in the same way* as in 1897-1903, it is *leading* the people to revolution *not in the same way* as before 1905. It is this "not in the same way" that we must be able to understand; we must be able to modify our tactics, *supplementing* all the basic, general, primary and cardinal tasks of revolutionary Social-Democracy by one more task, not very ambitious, but a specific task of the present new period: the task of utilising the Black-Hundred Duma in a revolutionary Social-Democratic way.

Like any new task it seems more difficult than the others, because it requires of people not a simple repetition of slogans, learned by heart (beyond which Maximov and the otzovists are mentally bankrupt), but a certain amount of initiative, flexibility of mind, resourcefulness and independent work on a *novel* historical task. But in actual fact this task can appear particularly difficult only to people who are incapable of independent thought and independent effort: actually this task, like every specific task of a given moment, is easier than others because its solvability is determined entirely by the conditions of the given moment. In a period of "acute and increasing reaction" to solve the problem of organising "training schools and groups" in a

really serious way, i.e., one that really connects them with
the mass movement, that really subordinates them to it, is
quite impossible, for it is a task set stupidly by people who
have *copied* the formulation of it from a good pamphlet,
which was based on the conditions of a *different* period.
But to solve the problem of subordinating the speeches,
actions and policy of the Social-Democrats in the Third
Duma to the mass party and the interests of the masses *is
possible.* It is not easy, compared with the "easy" matter
of repeating things learned by heart, but it *can be done.*
However we exert all the forces of the Party now, we cannot solve the problem of a Social-Democratic (and not
anarchist) organisation of "training schools" at the present
"inter-revolutionary" moment, for the solution of this problem requires altogether different historical conditions. On
the contrary, by exerting all our forces we shall solve (and
we are already *beginning to solve*) the problem of utilising
the Third Duma in a revolutionary Social-Democratic way.
And we shall do so, O you otzovists and ultimatumists,
wronged by removal and the harshness of God, not in order
to put parliamentarism on some high pedestal, not to proclaim "parliamentarism at any price", but in order, *after*
the solution of the "inter-revolutionary" problem, corresponding to the present "inter-revolutionary" period, to
proceed to the solution of loftier revolutionary problems,
which will correspond to the higher, i.e., more revolutionary period of tomorrow.

III

These stupid outcries of Maximov and Co. about the Bolsheviks' standing for "parliamentarism at any price", sound
particularly queer in view of the actual history of otzovism.
What is queer is that the shout about exaggerated parliamentarism should come from the *very* people who have
developed and are developing a special trend *exclusively*
over the question of their attitude to parliamentarism! What
do you call yourselves, dear Maximov and Co.? You call
yourselves "otzovists", "ultimatumists", "boycottists". Maximov to this day is so proud of being a boycottist of the
Third Duma that he can't get over it, and his rare Party

utterances are invariably accompanied by the signature:
"Reporter on behalf of the boycottists at the July Conference of 1907".[158] One writer in olden times used to sign
himself: "Substantive state councillor and cavalier." Maximov
signs himself: "Reporter on behalf of the boycottists"—he,
too, is a cavalier, you see!

In the political situation of June 1907, when Maximov
advocated the boycott, the mistake was still quite a small
one. But when Maximov comes out in July 1909 with a
manifesto of sorts and persists in admiring his "boycottism"
in regard to the Third Duma, it is downright stupidity.
Boycottism, otzovism and ultimatumism—all these expressions in themselves imply the formation of a *trend* over the
question of the attitude to parliamentarism and *exclusively*
over this question. To make a separate stand on this question, to persist (two years after the Party has settled it in
principle!) in this separate stand, is a sign of unparalleled
narrow-mindedness. It is just those who behave in this
way, i.e., the "boycottists" (of 1909) and the otzovists
and the ultimatumists, who prove *thereby* that they
do not think like Social-Democrats, that they are putting parliamentarism on a special pedestal, that exactly
like the anarchists they make a *trend*, out of isolated formu-
las: boycott that Duma, recall your men from that Duma,
present an ultimatum to that group in the Duma. To act
like that is to be a caricature of a Bolshevik. Among Bolsheviks the trend is determined by their *common* attitude
to the Russian revolution and the Bolsheviks have emphatically declared a thousand times (as it were to forewarn
political infants) that to identify Bolshevism with boycottism
or *boyevism* is a stupid distortion and vulgarisation of the
views of revolutionary Social-Democracy. Our view that
Social-Democratic participation in the Third Duma is obligatory, for instance, follows *inevitably* from our attitude to
the present moment, to the attempts of the autocracy to
take a step forward along the path of creating a bourgeois
monarchy, to the significance of the Duma as an organisation of counter-revolutionary classes in a representative
institution on a national scale. Just as the anarchists display
an inverted parliamentary cretinism when they *separate* the
question of parliament from the whole question of bour-

geois society in general and try to create a trend from outcries against bourgeois parliamentarism (although criticism
of bourgeois parliamentarism is in principle on the same
level as criticism of the bourgeois press, bourgeois syndicalism and so forth), so our otzovists, ultimatumists and boycottists, in exactly the same way, display inverted Menshevism when they *form a separate* trend on the question of
the attitude to the Duma, on the question of methods of
combating deviations on the part of the Social-Democratic
group in the Duma (and not the deviations of bourgeois
literati, who come into the Social-Democratic movement
incidentally, and so on).

Supplement to *Proletary*   V. I. Lenin,
Nos. 47-48, September 11 (24),   *Collected Works*,
1909   Vol. 16, pp. 33-39

DIFFERENCES
IN THE EUROPEAN LABOUR MOVEMENT

I

The principal tactical differences in the present-day labour movement of Europe and America reduce themselves to a struggle against two big trends that are departing from Marxism, which has in fact become the dominant theory in this movement. These two trends are revisionism (opportunism, reformism) and anarchism (anarcho-syndicalism, anarcho-socialism). Both these departures from the Marxist theory and Marxist tactics that are dominant in the labour movement were to be observed in various forms and in various shades in all civilised countries during the more than half-century of history of the mass labour movement.

This fact alone shows that these departures cannot be attributed to accident, or to the mistakes of individuals or groups, or even to the influence of national characteristics and traditions, and so forth. There must be deep-rooted causes in the economic system and in the character of the development of all capitalist countries which constantly give rise to these departures. A small book, *The Tactical Differences in the Labour Movement* (*Die taktischen Differenzen in der Arbeiterbewegung*, Hamburg, Erdmann Dubber, 1909), published last year by a Dutch Marxist, Anton Pannekoek, represents an interesting attempt at a scientific investigation of these causes. In our exposition we shall acquaint the reader with Pannekoek's conclusions, which, it must be recognised, are quite correct.

One of the most profound causes that periodically give rise to differences over tactics is the very growth of the labour movement. If this movement is not measured by the criterion of some fantastic ideal, but is regarded as the practical movement of ordinary people, it will be clear that the enlistment of larger and larger numbers of new "recruits", the attraction of new sections of the working people must inevitably be accompanied by waverings in the sphere of theory and tactics, by repetitions of old mistakes, by a temporary reversion to antiquated views and antiquated methods, and so forth. The labour movement of every country periodically spends a varying amount of energy, attention and time on the "training" of recruits.

Furthermore, the rate at which capitalism develops varies in different countries and in different spheres of the national economy. Marxism is most easily, rapidly, completely and lastingly assimilated by the working class and its ideologists where large-scale industry is most developed. Economic relations which are backward, or which lag in their development, constantly lead to the appearance of supporters of the labour movement who assimilate only certain aspects of Marxism, only certain parts of the new world outlook, or individual slogans and demands, being unable to make a determined break with all the traditions of the bourgeois world outlook in general and the bourgeois-democratic world outlook in particular.

Again, a constant source of differences is the dialectical nature of social development, which proceeds in contradictions and through contradictions. Capitalism is progressive because it destroys the old methods of production and develops productive forces, yet at the same time, at a certain stage of development, it retards the growth of productive forces. It develops, organises, and disciplines the workers—and it crushes, oppresses, leads to degeneration, poverty, etc. Capitalism creates its own grave-digger, itself creates the elements of a new system, yet, at the same time, without a "leap" these individual elements change nothing in the general state of affairs and do not affect the rule of capital. It is Marxism, the theory of dialectical materialism, that is able to encompass these contradictions of living reality, of the living history of capitalism and the working-class movement. But, needless to say, the masses learn from life and not from books, and therefore certain individuals or groups constantly exaggerate, elevate to a one-sided theory, to a one-sided system of tactics, now one and now another feature of capitalist development, now one and now another "lesson" of this development.

Bourgeois ideologists, liberals and democrats, not understanding Marxism, and not understanding the modern labour movement, are constantly jumping from one futile extreme to another. At one time they explain the whole matter by asserting that evil-minded persons "incite" class against class—at another they console themselves with the idea that the workers' party is "a peaceful party of reform". Both anarcho-syndicalism and reformism must be regarded as a direct product of this bourgeois world outlook and its influence. They seize upon *one* aspect of the labour movement, elevate one-sidedness to a theory, and declare mutually exclusive those tendencies or features of this movement that are a specific peculiarity of a given period, of given conditions of working-class activity. But real life, real history, *includes* these different tendencies, just as life and development in nature include both slow evolution and rapid leaps, breaks in continuity.

The revisionists regard as phrase-mongering all arguments about "leaps" and about the working-class movement being antagonistic in principle to the whole of the old society. They regard reforms as a partial realisation of socialism. The anarcho-syndicalists reject "petty work", especially the utilisation of the parliamentary platform. In practice, the latter tactics amount to waiting for "great days" along with an inability to muster the forces which create great events. Both of them hinder the thing that is most important and most urgent, namely, to unite the workers in big, powerful and properly functioning organisations, capable of functioning well under *all* circumstances, permeated with the spirit of the class struggle, clearly realising their aims and trained in the true Marxist world outlook.

We shall here permit ourselves a slight digression and note in parenthesis, so as to avoid possible misunderstandings, that Pannekoek illustrates his analysis *exclusively* by examples taken from West-European history, especially the history of Germany and France, not referring to Russia *at all*. If at times it seems that he is alluding to Russia, it is only because the basic tendencies which give rise to definite departures from Marxist tactics are to be observed in our country too, despite the vast difference between Russia and the West in culture, everyday life, and historical and economic development.

Finally, an extremely important cause of differences among those taking part in the labour movement lies in changes in the tactics of the ruling classes in general and of the bourgeoisie in particular. If the tactics of the bourgeoisie were always uniform, or at least of the same kind, the working class would rapidly learn to reply to them by tactics just as uniform or of the same kind. But, as a matter of fact, in every country the bourgeoisie inevitably devises two systems of rule, two methods of fighting for its interests and of maintaining its domination, and these methods at times succeed each other and at times are interwoven in various combinations. The first of these is the method of force, the method which rejects all concessions to the labour movement, the method of supporting all the old and obsolete institutions, the method of irreconcilably rejecting reforms. Such is the nature of the conservative policy which in Western Europe is becoming less and less a policy of the landowning classes and more and more one of the varieties of bourgeois policy in general. The second is the method of "liberalism", of steps towards the development of political rights, towards reforms, concessions, and so forth.

The bourgeoisie passes from one method to the other not because of the malicious intent of individuals, and not accidentally, but owing to the fundamentally contradictory nature of its own position. Normal capitalist society cannot develop successfully without a firmly established representative system and without certain political rights for the population, which is bound to be distinguished by its relatively high "cultural" demands. These demands for a certain minimum of culture are created by the conditions of the capitalist mode of production itself, with its high technique, complexity, flexibility, mobility, rapid development of world competition, and so forth. In consequence, vacillations in the tactics of the bourgeoisie, transitions from the system of force to the system of apparent concessions have been characteristic of the history of all European countries during the last half-century, the various countries developing primarily the application of the one method or the other at definite periods. For instance, in the sixties and seventies of the nineteenth century Britain was the classical country of "liberal" bourgeois policy, Germany in the seventies and eighties adhered to the method of force, and so on.

When this method prevailed in Germany, a one-sided echo of this particular system of bourgeois government was the growth of anarcho-syndicalism, or anarchism, as it was then called, in the labour movement (the "Young"[159] at the beginning of the nineties, Johann Most at the beginning of the eighties). When in 1890 the change to "concessions" took place, this change, as is always the case, proved to be even more dangerous to the labour movement, and gave rise to an equally one-sided echo of bourgeois "reformism": opportunism in the labour movement. "The positive, real aim of the liberal policy of the bourgeoisie," Pannekoek says, "is to mislead the workers, to cause a split in their ranks, to convert their policy into an impotent adjunct of an impotent, always impotent and ephemeral, sham reformism."

Not infrequently, the bourgeoisie for a certain time achieves its object by a "liberal" policy, which, as Pannekoek justly remarks, is a "more crafty" policy. A part of the workers and a part of their representatives at times allow themselves to be deceived by seeming concessions. The revisionists declare that the doctrine of the class struggle is "antiquated", or begin to conduct a policy which is in fact a renunciation of the class struggle. The zigzags of bourgeois tactics intensify revisionism within the labour movement and not infrequently bring the differences within the labour movement to the point of an outright split.

All causes of the kind indicated give rise to differences over tactics within the labour movement and within the proletarian ranks. But there is not and cannot be a Chinese wall between the proletariat and the sections of the petty bourgeoisie in contact with it, including the peasantry. It is clear that the passing of certain individuals, groups and sections of the petty bourgeoisie into the ranks of the proletariat is bound, in its turn, to give rise to vacillations in the tactics of the latter.

The experience of the labour movement of various countries helps us to understand on the basis of concrete practical questions the nature of Marxist tactics; it helps the younger countries to distinguish more clearly the true class significance of departures from Marxism and to combat these departures more successfully.

Zvezda No. 1,
December 16, 1910
Signed *V. Ilyin*

V. I. Lenin,
Collected Works,
Vol. 16, pp. 347-52

From the Article AUGUST BEBEL

As soon as the German parliament was set up, Bebel was elected to it, although at the time he was still quite young—only twenty-seven years old. The fundamentals of parliamentary tactics for German (and international) Social-Democracy, tactics that never yield an inch to the enemy, never miss the slightest opportunity to achieve even small improvements for the workers and are at the same time implacable on questions of principle and always directed to the accomplishment of the final aim—the fundamentals of these tactics were elaborated by Bebel himself or under his direct leadership and with his participation.

Germany, united in the Bismarckian way, renovated in the Prussian, Junker way, responded to the successes of the workers' party with the Anti-Socialist Law. The legal conditions for the existence of the working-class party were destroyed and the party was outlawed. Difficult times were at hand. To persecution by the party's enemies was added an inner-party crisis—vacillation on the basic questions of tactics. At first the opportunists came to the fore; they allowed themselves to be frightened by the loss of the party's legality, and the mournful song they sang was that of rejecting full-blooded slogans and accusing themselves of having gone much too far, etc. Incidentally, one of the representatives of this opportunist trend, Höchberg, rendered financial aid to the party, which was still weak and could not immediately find its feet.

Marx and Engels launched a fierce attack from London against disgraceful opportunist shilly-shallying. Bebel showed himself to be a real party leader. He recognised the danger in good time, understood the correctness of the criticism by Marx and Engels and was able to direct the party on to the path of implacable struggle. The illegal newspaper *Der Sozialdemokrat* was established and was published first in Zurich and then in London; it was delivered weekly to Germany and had as many as 10,000 subscribers. Opportunist waverings were firmly stopped.

Another form of wavering was due to infatuation with Dühring at the end of the seventies of the last century. For a short time Bebel also shared that infatuation. Dühring's supporters, the most outstanding of whom was Most, toyed with "Leftism" and very soon slid into anarchism. Engels's sharp, annihilating criticism of Dühring's theories met with disapproval in many party circles and at one congress it was even proposed to close the columns of the central newspaper to that criticism.

All the viable socialist elements—headed, of course, by Bebel—soon realised that the "new" theories were rotten to the core and broke away from them and from all anarchist trends. Under the leadership of Bebel and Liebknecht the party learned to combine illegal and legal work. When the majority of the legally-existing Social-Democratic group in parliament adopted an opportunist position on the famous question of voting *for* the shipping subsidy, the illegal *Sozialdemokrat opposed* the group and, after a battle four weeks long, proved victorious.

The Anti-Socialist Law was defeated in 1890 after having been in operation for twelve years. A party crisis, very similar to that of the mid-seventies, again occurred. The opportunists under Vollmar, on the one hand, were prepared to take advantage of legality to reject full-blooded slogans and implacable tactics. The so-called "young ones", on the other hand, were toying with "Leftism", drifting towards anarchism. Considerable credit is due to Bebel and Liebknecht for offering the most resolute resistance to these waverings and making the party crisis a short-lived and not very serious one.

A period of rapid growth set in for the party, growth in

both breadth and depth, in the development of the trade union, co-operative, educational and other forms of organisation of the forces of the proletariat, as well as their political organisation. It is impossible to assess the gigantic practical work carried out in all these spheres by Bebel as a parliamentarian, agitator and organiser. It was by this work that Bebel earned his position as the undisputed and generally accepted leader of the party, the one who was closest to the working-class masses and most popular among them.

Severnaya Pravda No. 6   V. I. Lenin,
August 8, 1913,   *Collected Works,*
Signed: *U. I.*   Vol. 19, pp. 298-30

From HOW VERA ZASULICH DEMOLISHES
LIQUIDATIONISM [160]

V

"For the underground to be a useful force," writes Vera Zasulich in the conclusion to her excellent article, "the underground, even if it alone is called the party, must display an attitude towards the worker Social-Democrats, [i.e., towards the broad section in which Zasulich sees "all forces," and of which she declared: "we shall think of it and speak of it as the party"] similar to that of party officials to the party."

Think carefully over this statement, the gem of gems in an article so rich in gems. First Zasulich knows very well what is meant by a *party* in present-day Russia. But dozens of liquidator writers are continually assuring the public that they do not know it, with the result that disputes on the liquidation of the *Party* are so unbelievably confused by these gentry. Let readers who are interested in the fate of the working-class movement and oppose vulgar, commonplace liquidators turn to Vera Zasulich's article and gain from it the answer to the question that has been and is still being obscured—what is a party?

Secondly, examine Vera Zasulich's conclusion. The underground's attitude to the broad section should be that of party officials to the party, she tells us. May we ask what is the essence of the attitude of the officials of any association to that association? Obviously it is that the official does not carry out his own will (or that of a group or circle), but the will of the association.

How is the will of a broad section of several hundred thousands, or several million, to be determined? *It is abso-

lutely impossible to determine the will of a broad section that is not organised in an association—even a child would understand that. It is Vera Zasulich's misfortune, and that of the other liquidators, that they have taken a position on the inclined plane of organisational opportunism and are constantly sliding down into the swamp of the worst anarchism.

For anarchism is precisely what it is, in the fullest and most accurate meaning of the word, when Vera Zasulich declares that the liquidators *will think and speak* of the broad section as the party, and that the underground should display the attitude towards it that it would to a higher organisation, to a supreme arbiter on the question of "officials", etc., although she herself admits that the "broad section lacks only the opportunity of formally joining a party" and therefore "lacks· the opportunity of *forming a party*".

When an appeal is made to broad sections or to the masses *against* the organisation and at the same time the impossibility of organising those sections or masses *is admitted*, that is pure anarchism. The anarchists constitute one of the most harmful elements of the working-class movement because they are always shouting about the mass of the oppressed classes (or even about the oppressed masses in general), always ruining the good name of any socialist organisation but are themselves unable to create *any* other organisation as an alternative.

The Marxists have a fundamentally different view of the relation of the unorganised (and unorganisable for a lengthy period, sometimes decades) masses to the party, to organisation. It is to enable the mass of a *definite class* to learn to understand its own interests and its position, to learn to conduct its own policy, that there must be an organisation of the advanced elements of the class, immediately and at all costs, even though at first these elements constitute only a tiny fraction of the class. To do service to the masses and express *their* interests, having correctly conceived those interests, the advanced contingent, the organisation, must carry on all its activity among the masses, drawing from the masses all the best forces without any exception, at every step verifying carefully and objectively whether contact with the masses is being maintained and whether it is a live contact. In this way, and *only* in this way, does the advanced contingent train and enlighten the masses, expressing *their* interests, teaching them organisation and directing *all* the activities of the masses along the path of conscious class politics.

If the political activity of the masses as a whole, when directly or indirectly drawn into elections, or participating in them, should result in *all* the elected representatives of the workers being supporters of the underground and its political line, supporters of the Party, we have an objective fact *proving* the viability of our contact with the masses, proving the right of that organisation to be and to call itself the *sole* representative of the masses, and *sole* vehicle for the expression of the class interests of the masses. *Every* politically conscious worker, or rather, every group of workers, *was able* to participate in the elections and direct them one way or the other; and if the result is that the organisation that is ridiculed, cursed and treated with disdain by the liquidators has been *able to lead the masses*, that means that the attitude of our Party to the masses is correct in principle, it is the Marxist attitude.

The theory of the "*broad section* ... who lack *only* the opportunity of formally joining a party to found one" is an anarchist theory. The working class in Russia cannot consolidate and develop its movement if it does not struggle with the greatest determination against this theory, which corrupts the masses and destroys the very concept of organisation, the very principle of organisation.

The theory of the "broad section" *to replace* the party is an attempt to justify an extremely high-handed attitude towards and *mockery* of the mass working-class movement (furthermore, the mockers never fail to speak of the "masses" in their every phrase and to use "mass" freely as an adjective in all its cases). Everyone realises that the liquidators are using this theory to make it appear that *they*, their circle of intellectuals, represent and express the will of the "broad section". What, they would say, does the "narrow" party mean to us when we represent the "broad section"! What does an underground mean to us, an underground that carries with it a million workers to the polls, when we represent the broad section numbering, perhaps, millions and tens of millions!

The objective facts—the elections to the Fourth Duma, the appearance of workers' newspapers and the collections made on their behalf, the Metalworkers' Union in St. Petersburg, the shop assistants' congress[161]—serve to show clearly that the liquidators are a group of intellectuals that have fallen away from the working class. But the "theory of the broad section" enables the liquidators to get round all objective facts and fills their hearts with pride in their unacknowledged greatness . .

Prosveshcheniye No. 9,   V. I. Lenin,
September 1913,   *Collected Works*,
Signed: V. Ilyin   Vol. 19, pp. 407-410

From THE MANIFESTO OF THE C.C., R.S.D.L.P., "THE WAR AND RUSSIAN SOCIAL-DEMOCRACY"[162]

The opportunists have wrecked the decisions of the Stuttgart,[163] Copenhagen[164] and Basle[165] congresses, which made it binding on socialists of all countries to combat chauvinism in all and any conditions, made it binding on socialists to reply to any war begun by the bourgeoisie and governments, with intensified propaganda of civil war and social revolution. The collapse of the Second International is the collapse of opportunism, which developed from the features of a now bygone (and so-called "peaceful") period of history, and in recent years has come practically to dominate the International. The opportunists have long been preparing the ground for this collapse by denying the socialist revolution and substituting bourgeois reformism in its stead; by rejecting the class struggle with its inevitable conversion at certain moments into civil war, and by preaching class collaboration; by preaching bourgeois chauvinism under the guise of patriotism and the defence of the fatherland, and ignoring or rejecting the fundamental truth of socialism, long ago set forth in the *Communist Manifesto*, that the workingmen have no country;[166] by confining themselves, in the struggle against militarism, to a sentimental, philistine point of view, instead of recognising the need for a revolutionary war by the proletarians of all countries, against the bourgeoisie of all countries; by making a fetish of the necessary utilisation of bourgeois parliamentarianism and bourgeois legality, and forgetting that illegal forms of organisation and propaganda are imperative at times of crises. The natural "appendage" to opportunism—one that is just as bourgeois and hostile to the proletarian, i.e., the Marxist, point of view—namely, the anarcho-syndicalist trend, has been marked by a no less shamefully smug reiteration of the slogans of chauvinism, during the present crisis.

Written in September or
October 1914

V. I. Lenin,
Collected Works,
Vol. 21, pp. 31-32

Published in *Sotsial-Demokrat*
No. 33, November 1, 1914

From SOCIALISM AND WAR

Chapter I
THE PRINCIPLES OF SOCIALISM AND THE WAR OF 1914-1915

THE ATTITUDE OF SOCIALISTS TOWARDS WARS

Socialists have always condemned wars between nations as barbarous and brutal. Our attitude towards war, however, is fundamentally different from that of the bourgeois pacifists (supporters and advocates of peace) and of the anarchists. We differ from the former in that we understand the inevitable connection between wars and the class struggle within a country; we understand that wars cannot be abolished unless classes are abolished and socialism is created; we also differ in that we regard civil wars, i.e., wars waged by an oppressed class against the oppressor class, by slaves against slave-holders, by serfs against landowners, and by wage-workers against the bourgeoisie, as fully legitimate, progressive and necessary. We Marxists differ from both pacifists and anarchists in that we deem it necessary to study each war historically (from the standpoint of Marx's dialectical materialism) and separately. There have been in the past numerous wars which, despite all the horrors, atrocities, distress and suffering that inevitably accompany all wars, were progressive, i.e., benefited the development of mankind by helping to destroy most harmful and reactionary institutions (e.g., an autocracy or serfdom) and the most barbarous despotisms in Europe (the Turkish and the Russian).

Written in July-August 1915

Published in pamphlet form in
August 1915 by the *Sotsial-Demokrat*
Editorial Board in Geneva

V. I. Lenin,
Collected Works,
Vol. 21, p. 299

From THE TASKS OF THE OPPOSITION IN FRANCE
(LETTER TO COMRADE SAFAROV)

Anarchist phrase-mongering has always done a lot of harm in France. But now the anarchist-patriots, the anarchist-*chauvins*, like Kropotkin, Grave, Cornelissen and the other knights of *La Bataille Chauviniste*[167] will help to cure very many workers of anarchist phrase-mongering. Down with the socialist-patriots and socialist-*chauvins* and down also with anarchist-patriots and anarchist-*chauvins*! This call *will* be echoed in the hearts of the workers of France. Not anarchist phrase-mongering about revolution, but sustained, earnest, tenacious, persistent, systematic work of *everywhere* creating illegal organisations among the *workers*, of spreading *uncensored*, i.e., illegal, literature, of preparing the movement of the *masses* against their governments. This is what the working class of all countries needs!

It is not true to say that "the French are incapable" of carrying on illegal work regularly. It is *not* true! The French quickly learned to hide in the trenches; they will soon learn to do illegal work in the *new* conditions and systematically to build up a *revolutionary mass* movement.

Written on February 10, 1916

Published in French as a leaflet in Geneva in 1916

First published in Russian in *Proletarskaya Revolutsia* No. 4, 1924

V. I. Lenin,
Collected Works,
Vol. 22, p. 130

From a Review THE YOUTH INTERNATIONAL

2) On the question of the differences between socialists and anarchists in their attitude towards the state, Comrade Nota-Bene in his article (issue No. 6)[168] falls into a very serious error (as he also does on several other questions, for instance, our *reasons* for combating the "defence of the fatherland" slogan). The author wishes to present "a clear picture of the state in general" (together with that of the imperialist predatory state). He quotes several statements by Marx and Engels, and arrives at the following two conclusions, among others:

a) "... It is absolutely wrong to seek the difference between socialists and anarchists in the fact that the former are in favour of the state while the latter are against it. The real difference is that revolutionary Social-Democracy desires to organise social production on new lines, as centralised, i.e., technically the most progressive, method of production, whereas decentralised, anarchist production would mean retrogression to obsolete techniques, to the old form of enterprise." This is wrong. The author raises the question of the difference in the socialists' and anarchists' attitude *towards the state*. However, he answers *not* this question, but *another,* namely, the difference in their attitude towards the economic foundation of future society. That, of course, is an important and necessary question. But that is no reason to ignore the *main* point of difference between socialists and anarchists in their attitude towards

9*

the state. Socialists are in favour of utilising the present state and its institutions in the struggle for the emancipation of the working class, maintaining also that the state should be used for a specific form of transition from capitalism to socialism. This transitional form is the dictatorship of the proletariat, which is *also* a state.

The anarchists want to "abolish" the state, "blow it up" (*sprengen*) as Comrade Nota-Bene expresses it in one place, erroneously ascribing this view to the socialists. The socialists—unfortunately the author quotes Engels's relevant words rather incompletely—hold that the state will "wither away", will gradually "fall asleep" *after* the bourgeoisie has been expropriated.

Published in
Sbornik Sotsial-Demokrata
No. 2, December 1916
Signed: N. Lenin

V. I. Lenin,
Collected Works,
Vol. 23, pp. 165-166

From LETTERS FROM AFAR[169]

Third Letter
CONCERNING A PROLETARIAN MILITIA

It might be asked: What should be the function of the Soviets of Workers' Deputies? They "must be regarded as organs of insurrection, of revolutionary rule", we wrote in No. 47 of the Geneva *Sotsial-Demokrat*, of October 13, 1915.[170]

This theoretical proposition, deduced from the experience of the Commune of 1871 and of the Russian Revolution of 1905, must be explained and concretely developed on the basis of the practical experience of precisely the present stage of the present revolution in Russia.

We need revolutionary *government*, we need (for a certain transitional period) a *state*. This is what distinguishes us from the anarchists. The difference between the revolutionary Marxists and the anarchists is not only that the former stand for centralised, large-scale communist production, while the latter stand for disconnected small production. The difference between us precisely on the question of government, of the state, is that we are *for*, and the anarchists *against*, utilising revolutionary forms of the state in a revolutionary way for the struggle for socialism.

We need a state. But *not the kind* of state the bourgeoisie has created everywhere, from constitutional monarchies to the most democratic republics. And in this we differ from the opportunists and Kautskyites of the old, and decaying, socialist parties, who have distorted, or have forgotten, the lessons of the Paris Commune and the analysis of these lessons made by Marx and Engels.*

We need a state, but *not* the kind the bourgeoisie needs, with organs of government in the shape of a police force, an army and a bureaucracy (officialdom) separate from and opposed to the people. All bourgeois revolutions merely perfected *this* state machine, merely transferred *it* from the hands of one party to those of another.

The proletariat, on the other hand, if it wants to uphold the gains of the present revolution and proceed further, to win peace, bread and freedom must "*smash*", to use Marx's expression, this "ready-made" state machine and substitute a new one for it by *merging* the police force, the army and the bureaucracy with *the entire armed people*. Following the path indicated by the experience of the Paris Commune of 1871 and the Russian Revolution of 1905, the proletariat must organise and arm *all* the poor, exploited sections of the population in order that they *themselves* should take the organs of state power directly into their own hands, in order that *they themselves should constitute* these organs of state power.

And the workers of Russia have already *taken* this path in the first stage of the first revolution, in February-March 1917. The whole task now is clearly to understand what this new path is, to proceed along it further, boldly, firmly and perseveringly.

Written on March 11 (24)   V. I. Lenin,
1917   *Collected Works*,
                                             Vol. 23, pp. 324-326
First published in the magazine
The Communist International
Nos. 3-4, 1924

---

* In one of my next letters, or in a special article, I will deal in detail with this analysis, given in particular in Marx's *The Civil War in France*, in Engels's preface to the third edition of that work, in the letters: Marx's of April 12, 1871, and Engels's of March 18-28, 1875, and also with the utter distortion of Marxism by Kautsky in his controversy with Pannekoek in 1912 on the question of the so-called "destruction of the state".**

** See pp. 270-85 of this volume.—*Ed.*

From LETTERS ON TACTICS

First Letter
ASSESSMENT OF THE PRESENT SITUATION

... But are we not in danger of falling into subjectivism, of wanting to arrive at the socialist revolution by "skipping" the bourgeois-democratic revolution—which is not yet completed and has not yet exhausted the peasant movement?

I might be incurring this danger if I said: "No Tsar, but a *workers'* government."[171] But I did *not* say that, I said something else. I said that there *can be no* government (barring a bourgeois government) in Russia *other than* that of the Soviets of Workers', Agricultural Labourers', Soldiers', and Peasants' Deputies. I said that power in Russia now can pass from Guchkov and Lvov *only* to these Soviets. And in these Soviets, as it happens, it is the peasants, the soldiers, i.e., petty bourgeoisie, who preponderate, to use a scientific, Marxist term, a class characterisation, and not a common, man-in-the-street, professional characterisation.

In my theses, I absolutely ensured myself against skipping over the peasant movement, which has not outlived itself, or the petty-bourgeois movement in general, against any *playing* at "seizure of power" by a workers' government, against any kind of Blanquist adventurism; for I pointedly referred to the experience of the Paris Commune. And this experience, as we know, and as Marx proved at length in 1871 and Engels in 1891,[172] absolutely excludes Blanquism, absolutely ensures the direct, immediate and unquestionable rule of the *majority* and the activity of the masses only to the extent that the majority itself acts *consciously*.

In the theses, I very definitely reduced the question to one of a *struggle for influence within* the Soviets of

Workers', Agricultural Labourers', Peasants', and Soldiers' Deputies. To leave no shadow of doubt on this score, I *twice* emphasised in the theses the need for patient and persistent "explanatory" work "adapted to the *practical* needs of the *masses*".

Ignorant persons or renegades from Marxism, like Mr. Plekhanov, may shout about anarchism, Blanquism, and so forth. But those who want to think and learn cannot fail to understand that Blanquism means the seizure of power by a minority, whereas the Soviets are *admittedly* the direct and immediate organisation of the *majority* of the people. Work confined to a struggle for influence *within* these Soviets cannot, simply *cannot*, stray into the swamp of Blanquism. Nor can it stray into the swamp of anarchism, for anarchism denies *the need for a state and state power* in the period of *transition* from the rule of the bourgeoisie to the rule of the proletariat, whereas I, with a precision that precludes any possibility of misinterpretation, *advocate* the need for a state in this period, although, in accordance with Marx and the lessons of the Paris Commune, I advocate not the usual parliamentary bourgeois state, but a state *without* a standing army, *without* a police opposed to the people, *without* an officialdom placed above the people.

When Mr. Plekhanov, in his newspaper *Yedinstvo*, shouts with all his might that this is anarchism, he is merely giving further proof of his break with Marxism.

Challenged by me in *Pravda* (No. 26) to tell us what Marx and Engels taught on the subject in 1871, 1872 and 1875,[173] Mr. Plekhanov can only preserve silence on the question at issue and shout out abuse after the manner of the enraged bourgeoisie.

Mr. Plekhanov, the ex-Marxist, has *absolutely* failed to understand the Marxist doctrine of the state. Incidentally, the germs of this lack of understanding are also to be found in his German pamphlet on anarchism.[174]

Written between
April 8 and 13
(21 and 26), 1917

Published in Petrograd
by Priboi Publishers
in April 1917

V. I. Lenin,
Collected Works,
Vol. 24, pp. 48-50

From THE TASKS OF THE PROLETARIAT IN OUR REVOLUTION

(DRAFT PLATFORM FOR THE PROLETARIAN PARTY)

WHAT SHOULD BE THE NAME OF OUR PARTY— ONE THAT WILL BE CORRECT SCIENTIFICALLY AND HELP TO CLARIFY THE MIND OF THE PROLETARIAT POLITICALLY?

19. I now come to the final point, the name of our Party. We must call ourselves the *Communist Party*—just as Marx and Engels called themselves.

We must repeat that we are Marxists and that we take as our basis the *Communist Manifesto,* which has been distorted and betrayed by the Social-Democrats on two main points: (1) the working men have no country: "defence of the fatherland" in an imperialist war is a betrayal of socialism; and (2) the Marxist doctrine of the state has been distorted by the Second International.

The name "Social-Democracy" is *scientifically* incorrect as Marx frequently pointed out, in particular, in the *Critique of the Gotha Programme* in 1875, and as Engels reaffirmed in a more popular form in 1894.[175] From capitalism mankind can pass directly only to socialism, i.e., to the social ownership of the means of production and the distribution of products according to the amount of work performed by each individual. Our Party looks farther ahead: socialism must inevitably evolve gradually into communism, upon the banner of which is inscribed the motto, "From each according to his ability, to each according to his needs".

That is my first argument.

Here is the second: the second part of the name of our Party (Social-*Democrats*) is also scientifically incorrect. Democracy is a form of *state*, whereas we Marxists are opposed to *every kind* of state.

The leaders of the Second International (1889-1914), Plekhanov, Kautsky and their like, have vulgarised and distorted Marxism.

Marxism differs from anarchism in that it recognises *the need for a state* for the purpose of the transition to socialism; but (and here is where we differ from Kautsky and Co.) *not a state of the type* of the usual parliamentary bourgeois-democratic republic, but a state like the Paris Commune of 1871 and the Soviets of Workers' Deputies of 1905 and 1917.

My third argument: *living reality*, the revolution, has *already actually* established in our country, albeit in a weak and embryonic form, precisely this new type of "state", which is not a state in the proper sense of the word.

This is *already* a matter of the practical action of the people, and not merely a theory of the leaders.

The state in the proper sense of the term is domination over the people by contingents of armed men divorced from the people.

Our *emergent*, new state is also a state, for we too need contingents of armed men, we too need the *strictest* order, and must *ruthlessly* crush by force all attempts at either a tsarist or a Guchkov-bourgeois counter-revolution.

But our *emergent* new state is *no longer* a state in the proper sense of the term, for in some parts of Russia these contingents of armed men are *the masses themselves*, the entire people, and not certain privileged persons placed over the people, and divorced from the people, and for all practical purposes undisplaceable.

We must look forward, and not backward to the usual bourgeois type of democracy, which consolidated the rule of the bourgeoisie with the aid of the old, *monarchist* organs of administration, the police, the army and the bureaucracy.

We must look forward to the emergent new democracy. which is already ceasing to be a democracy, for democracy means the domination of the people, and the armed people cannot dominate themselves.

The term democracy is not only scientifically incorrect when applied to a Communist Party; it has now, since March 1917, simply become *blinkers* put on the eyes of the revolutionary people and *preventing* them from boldly and freely, on their own initiative, building up the new: the Soviets of Workers', Peasants', and all other Deputies, as *the sole power* in the "state" and as the harbinger of the "withering away" of the state *in every form*.

My fourth argument: we must reckon with the actual situation in which socialism finds itself internationally.

It is not what it was during the years 1871 to 1914, when Marx and Engels knowingly put up with the inaccurate, opportunist term "Social-Democracy". For *in those days*, after the defeat of the Paris Commune, history made slow organisational and educational work the task of the day. Nothing else was possible. The anarchists were then (as they are now) fundamentally wrong not only theoretically, but also economically and politically. The anarchists misjudged the character of the times, for they failed to understand the world situation: the worker of Britain corrupted by imperialist profits, the Commune defeated in Paris, the recent (1871) triumph of the bourgeois national movement in Germany, the age-long sleep of semi-feudal Russia.

Marx and Engels gauged the times accurately; they understood the international situation; they understood that the approach to the beginning of the social revolution must be *slow*.

We, in our turn, must also understand the specific features and tasks of the new era. Let us not imitate those sorry Marxists of whom Marx said: "I have sown dragon's teeth and harvested fleas."[176]

The objective inevitability of capitalism which grew into imperialism brought about the imperialist war. The war has brought mankind to the *brink of a precipice*, to the brink of the destruction of civilisation, of the brutalisation and destruction of more millions, countless millions, of human beings.

The *only* way out is through a proletarian revolution.

At the very moment when such a revolution is beginning, when it is taking its first hesitant, groping steps, steps betraying too great a confidence in the bourgeoisie, at such a moment the majority (that is the truth, that is a fact) of the "Social-Democratic" leaders, of the "Social-Democratic" parliamentarians, of the "Social-Democratic" newspapers— and these are precisely the *organs* that influence the people—

have *deserted* socialism, have *betrayed* socialism and have gone over to the side of "their own" national bourgeoisie.

The people have been confused, led astray and deceived by *these* leaders.

And we shall aid and abet that deception if we retain the old and out-of-date Party name, which is as decayed as the Second International!

Granted that "many" workers *understand* Social-Democracy in an honest way; but it is time to learn how to distinguish the subjective from the objective.

Subjectively, such Social-Democratic workers are most loyal leaders of the proletarians.

Objectively, however, the world situation is such that the old name of our Party *makes it easier* to fool the people and *impedes* the onward march; for at every step, in every paper, in every parliamentary group, the masses see *leaders*, i.e., people whose voices carry farthest and whose actions are most conspicuous; yet they are all "would-be Social-Democrats", they are all "for unity" with the betrayers of socialism, with the social-chauvinists; and they are all presenting for payment the old bills issued by "Social-Democracy"....

And what are the arguments against?... We'll be confused with the Anarchist-Communists, they say....

Why are we not afraid of being confused with the Social-Nationalists, the Social-Liberals, or the Radical-Socialists, the foremost bourgeois party in the French Republic and the most adroit in the bourgeois deception of the people?... We are told: The people are used to it, the workers have come to "love" *their* Social-Democratic Party.

That is the only argument. But it is an argument that dismisses the science of Marxism, the tasks of the morrow in the revolution, the objective position of world socialism, the shameful collapse of the Second International, and the harm done to the practical cause by the packs of "would-be Social-Democrats" who surround the proletarians.

It is an argument of routinism, an argument of inertia, an argument of stagnation.

But we are out to rebuild the world. We are out to put an end to the imperialist world war into which hundreds of millions of people have been drawn and in which the interests of billions and billions of capital are involved, a war which cannot end in a truly democratic peace without the greatest proletarian revolution in the history of mankind.

Yet we are afraid of our own selves. We are loth to cast off the "dear old" soiled shirt. . . .

But it is time to cast off the soiled shirt and to put on clean linen.

Petrograd, April 10, 1917

Published in Petrograd
as a pamphlet by
Priboi Publishers
in September 1917

V. I. Lenin,
Collected Works,
Vol. 24, pp. 84-88

From THE STATE AND REVOLUTION

THE MARXIST THEORY OF THE STATE AND THE TASKS OF THE PROLETARIAT IN THE REVOLUTION

Chapter III

THE STATE AND REVOLUTION EXPERIENCE OF THE PARIS COMMUNE OF 1871. MARX'S ANALYSIS

3. ABOLITION OF PARLIAMENTARISM

"The Commune," Marx wrote, "was to be a working, not a parliamentary, body, executive and legislative at the same time. . . .

"Instead of deciding once in three or six years which member of the ruling class was to represent and repress [ver- und zertreten] the people in parliament, universal suffrage was to serve the people constituted in communes, as individual suffrage serves every other employer in the search for workers, foremen and accountants for his business."[177]

Owing to the prevalence of social-chauvinism and opportunism, this remarkable criticism of parliamentarism, made in 1871, also belongs now to the "forgotten words" of Marxism. The professional Cabinet Ministers and parliamentarians, the traitors to the proletariat and the "practical" socialists of our day, have left all criticism of parliamentarism to the anarchists, and, on this wonderfully reasonable ground, they denounce *all* criticism of parliamentarism as "anarchism"!! It is not surprising that the proletariat of the "advanced" parliamentary countries, disgusted with such "socialists" as the Scheidemanns, Davids, Legiens, Sembats, Renaudels, Hendersons, Vanderveldes, Staunings, Brantings, Bissolatis and Co., has been with increasing frequency giving its sympathies to anarcho-syndicalism, in spite of the fact that the latter is merely the twin brother of opportunism.

For Marx, however, revolutionary dialectics was never the empty fashionable phrase, the toy rattle, which Plekhanov, Kautsky and others have made of it. Marx knew how to break with anarchism ruthlessly for its inability to make use even of the "pigsty" of bourgeois parliamentarism, especially when the situation was obviously not revolutionary; but at the same time he knew how to subject parliamentarism to genuinely revolutionary proletarian criticism.

To decide once every few years which member of the ruling class is to repress and crush the people through parliament—this is the real essence of bourgeois parliamentarism, not only in parliamentary-constitutional monarchies, but also in the most democratic republics. . . .

4. ORGANISATION OF NATIONAL UNITY

"In a brief sketch of national organisation which the Commune had no time to develop, it states explicitly that the Commune was to be the political form of even the smallest village. . . ." The communes were to elect the "National Delegation" in Paris.

". . . The few but important functions which would still remain for a central government were not to be suppressed, as has been deliberately mis-stated, but were to be transferred to communal, i.e., strictly responsible, officials.

". . . National unity was not to be broken, but, on the contrary, organised by the communal constitution; it was to become a reality by the destruction of state power which posed as the embodiment of that unity yet wanted to be independent of, and superior to, the nation, on whose body it was but a parasitic excrescence. While the merely repressive organs of the old governmental power were to be amputated, its legitimate functions were to be wrested from an authority claiming the right to stand above society, and restored to the responsible servants of society."[178]

The extent to which the opportunists of present-day Social-Democracy have failed—perhaps it would be more true to say, have refused—to understand these observations of Marx is best shown by that book of Herostratean fame of the renegade Bernstein, *The Premises of Socialism and the Tasks*

of the Social-Democrats. It is in connection with the above
passage from Marx that Bernstein wrote that "as far as its
political content is concerned", this programme "displays,
in all its essential features, the greatest similarity to the
federalism of Proudhon.... In spite of all the other points
of difference between Marx and the 'petty-bourgeois' Proudhon [Bernstein places the word "petty-bourgeois" in inverted
commas to make it sound ironical] on these points, their
lines of reasoning run as close as could be". Of course, Bernstein continues, the importance of the municipalities is growing, but "it seems doubtful to me whether the first job of
democracy would be such a dissolution [Auflösung] of the
modern states and such a complete transformation
[Umwandlung] of their organisation as is visualised by Marx
and Proudhon (the formation of a National Assembly from
delegates of the provincial or district assemblies, which, in
their turn, would consist of delegates from the communes),
so that consequently the previous mode of national representation would disappear". (Bernstein, *Premises*, German
edition, 1899, pp. 134 and 136.)

To confuse Marx's views on the "destruction of state power,
a parasitic excrescence", with Proudhon's federalism is
positively monstrous! But it is no accident, for it never occurs
to the opportunist that Marx does not speak here at all about
federalism as opposed to centralism, but about smashing the
old, bourgeois state machine which exists in all bourgeois
countries.

The only thing that does occur to the opportunist is what
he sees around him, in an environment of petty-bourgeois
philistinism and "reformist" stagnation, namely, only
"municipalities"! The opportunist has even grown out of the
habit of thinking about proletarian revolution.

It is ridiculous. But the remarkable thing is that nobody
argued with Bernstein on this point. Bernstein has been
refuted by many, especially by Plekhanov in Russian literature and by Kautsky in European literature, but neither of
them has said *anything* about *this* distortion of Marx by
Bernstein.

The opportunist has so much forgotten how to think in a
revolutionary way and to dwell on revolution that he attributes "federalism" to Marx, whom he confuses with the

founder of anarchism, Proudhon. As for Kautsky and Plekhanov, who claim to be orthodox Marxists and defenders of
the theory of revolutionary Marxism, they are silent on this
point! Here is one of the roots of the extreme vulgarisation
of the views on the difference between Marxism and anarchism, which is characteristic of both the Kautskyites and the
opportunists, and which we shall discuss again later.

There is not a trace of federalism in Marx's above-quoted
observations on the experience of the Commune. Marx agreed
with Proudhon on the very point that the opportunist Bernstein did not see. Marx disagreed with Proudhon on the very
point on which Bernstein found a similarity between them.

Marx agreed with Proudhon in that they both stood for
the "smashing" of the modern state machine. Neither the
opportunists nor the Kautskyites wish to see the similarity
of views on this point between Marxism and anarchism (both
Proudhon and Bakunin) because this is where they have
departed from Marxism.

Marx disagreed both with Proudhon and Bakunin precisely
on the question of federalism (not to mention the dictatorship of the proletariat). Federalism as a principle follows
logically from the petty-bourgeois views of anarchism. Marx
was a centralist. There is no departure whatever from
centralism in his observations just quoted. Only those who
are imbued with the philistine "superstitious belief" in the
state can mistake the destruction of the bourgeois state
machine for the destruction of centralism!

Now if the proletariat and the poor peasants take state
power into their own hands, organise themselves quite freely
in communes, and *unite* the action of all the communes in
striking at capital, in crushing the resistance of the capitalists, and in transferring the privately-owned railways,
factories, land and so on to the *entire* nation, to the whole
of society, won't that be centralism? Won't that be the most
consistent democratic centralism and, moreover, proletarian
centralism?

Bernstein simply cannot conceive of the possibility of
voluntary centralism, of the voluntary amalgamation of the
communes into a nation, of the voluntary fusion of the
proletarian communes, for the purpose of destroying bourgeois rule and the bourgeois state machine. Like all philis-

tines, Bernstein pictures centralism as something which can
be imposed and maintained solely from above, and solely by
the bureaucracy and the military clique.

As though foreseeing that his views might be distorted,
Marx expressly emphasised that the charge that the Commune had wanted to destroy national unity, to abolish the
central authority, was a deliberate fraud. Marx purposely
used the words: "National unity was ... to be organised",
so as to oppose conscious, democratic, proletarian centralism
to bourgeois, military, bureaucratic centralism. ...

Chapter IV
CONTINUATION.
SUPPLEMENTARY EXPLANATIONS OF ENGELS

1. THE HOUSING QUESTION

... Speaking of the Blanquists' adoption of the fundamental position of Marxism after the Commune and under
the influence of its experience, Engels, in passing, formulates
this position as follows:

"... Necessity of political action by the proletariat and
of its dictatorship as the transition to the abolition of
classes and, with them, of the state...." (P. 55.)*

Addicts to hair-splitting criticism, or bourgeois "extermi-
nators of Marxism", will perhaps see a contradiction between
this *recognition* of the "abolition of the state" and repudiation of this formula as an anarchist one in the above passage
from *Anti-Dühring*. It would not be surprising if the opportunists classed Engels, too, as an "anarchist", for it is becoming increasingly common with the social-chauvinists to accuse
the internationalists of anarchism.

Marxism has always taught that with the abolition of classes
the state will also be abolished. The well-known passage
on the "withering away of the state" in *Anti-Dühring*
accuses the anarchists not simply of favouring the abolition
of the state, but of preaching that the state can be abolished
"overnight".

---

* See p. 90 of this volume.—*Ed.*

As the now prevailing "Social-Democratic" doctrine completely distorts the relation of Marxism to anarchism on the question of the abolition of the state, it will be particularly useful to recall a certain controversy in which Marx and Engels came out against the anarchists.

2. CONTROVERSY WITH THE ANARCHISTS

This controversy took place in 1873. Marx and Engels contributed articles against the Proudhonists, "autonomists" or "anti-authoritarians", to an Italian socialist annual, and it was not until 1913 that these articles appeared in German in *Neue Zeit*.[179]

"If the political struggle of the working class assumes revolutionary forms," wrote Marx, ridiculing the anarchists for their repudiation of politics, "and if the workers set up their revolutionary dictatorship in place of the dictatorship of the bourgeoisie, they commit the terrible crime of violating principles, for in order to satisfy their wretched, vulgar everyday needs and to crush the resistance of the bourgeoisie, they give the state a revolutionary and transient form, instead of laying down their arms and abolishing the state...." (*Neue Zeit*, Vol. XXXII, 1, 1913-14, p. 40.)*

It was solely against this kind of "abolition" of the state that Marx fought in refuting the anarchists! He did not at all oppose the view that the state would disappear when classes disappeared, or that it would be abolished when classes were abolished. What he did oppose was the proposition that the workers should renounce the use of arms, organised violence, *that is, the state,* which is to serve to "crush the resistance of the bourgeoisie".

To prevent the true meaning of his struggle against anarchism from being distorted, Marx expressly emphasised the "revolutionary and *transient* form" of the state which the proletariat needs. The proletariat needs the state only temporarily. We do not at all differ with the anarchists on

_____

* See p. 95 of this volume.—*Ed.*

the question of the abolition of the state as the *aim*. We maintain that, to achieve this aim, we must temporarily make use of the instruments, resources and methods of state power *against* the exploiters, just as the temporary dictatorship of the oppressed class is necessary for the abolition of classes. Marx chooses the sharpest and clearest way of stating his case against the anarchists: After overthrowing the yoke of the capitalists, should the workers "lay down their arms", or use them against the capitalists in order to crush their resistance? But what is the systematic use of arms by one class against another if not a "transient form" of state?

Let every Social-Democrat ask himself: Is *that* how he has been posing the question of the state in controversy with the anarchists? Is *that* how it has been posed by the vast majority of the official socialist parties of the Second International?

Engels expounds the same ideas in much greater detail and still more popularly. First of all he ridicules the muddled ideas of the Proudhonists, who called themselves "anti-authoritarians", i.e., repudiated all authority, all subordination, all power. Take a factory, a railway, a ship on the high seas, said Engels: is it not clear that not one of these complex technical establishments, based on the use of machinery and the systematic co-operation of many people, could function without a certain amount of subordination and, consequently, without a certain amount of authority or power?

"... When I counter the most rabid anti-authoritarians with these arguments, the only answer they can give me is the following: Oh, that's true, except that here it is not a question of authority with which we vest our delegates, *but of a commission!* These people imagine they can change a thing by changing its name. ..."*

Having thus shown that authority and autonomy are relative terms, that the sphere of their application varies with the various phases of social development, that it is absurd to take them as absolutes, and adding that the sphere of application of machinery and large-scale production is steadily expanding, Engels passes from the general discussion of authority to the question of the state.

---

* See p. 102 of this volume.—*Ed.*

"Had the autonomists," he wrote, "contented themselves with saying that the social organisation of the future would allow authority only within the bounds which the conditions of production make inevitable, one could have come to terms with them. But they are blind to all facts that make authority necessary and they passionately fight the word.

"Why do the anti-authoritarians not confine themselves to crying out against political authority, the state? All Socialists are agreed that the state, and with it political authority, will disappear as a result of the coming social revolution, that is, that public functions will lose their political character and become mere administrative functions of watching over social interests. But the anti-authoritarians demand that the political state be abolished at one stroke, even before the social relations that gave birth to it have been destroyed. They demand that the first act of the social revolution shall be the abolition of authority.

"Have these gentlemen ever seen a revolution? A revolution is certainly the most authoritarian thing there is; it is an act whereby one part of the population imposes its will upon the other part by means of rifles, bayonets and cannon, all of which are highly authoritarian means. And the victorious party must maintain its rule by means of the terror which its arms inspire in the reactionaries. Would the Paris Commune have lasted more than a day if it had not used the authority of the armed people against the bourgeoisie? Cannot we, on the contrary, blame it for having made too little use of that authority? Therefore, one of two things: either the anti-authoritarians don't know what they are talking about, in which case they are creating nothing but confusion. Or they do know, and in that case they are betraying the cause of the proletariat. In either case they serve only reaction." (p. 39.)*

This argument touches upon questions which should be examined in connection with the relationship between politics and economics during the withering away of the state (the next chapter is devoted to this). These questions are: the transformation of public functions from political into simple

---

* See p. 103 of this volume.—*Ed.*

functions of administration, and the "political state". This last term, one particularly liable to cause misunderstanding, indicates the process of the withering away of the state: at a certain stage of this process, the state which is withering away may be called a non-political state.

Again, the most remarkable thing in this argument of Engels is the way he states his case against the anarchists. Social-Democrats, claiming to be disciples of Engels, have argued on this subject against the anarchists millions of times since 1873, but they have *not* argued as Marxists could and should. The anarchist idea of the abolition of the state is muddled and *non-revolutionary*—that is how Engels put it. It is precisely the revolution in its rise and development, with its specific tasks in relation to violence, authority, power, the state, that the anarchists refuse to see.

The usual criticism of anarchism by present-day Social-Democrats has boiled down to the purest philistine banality: "We recognise the state, whereas the anarchists do not!" Naturally, such banality cannot but repel workers who are at all capable of thinking and revolutionary-minded. What Engels says is different. He stresses that all socialists recognise that the state will disappear as a result of the socialist revolution. He then deals specifically with the question of the revolution—the very question which, as a rule, the Social-Democrats evade out of opportunism, leaving it, so to speak, exclusively for the anarchists "to work out". And when dealing with this question, Engels takes the bull by the horns; he asks: should not the Commune have made *more* use of the *revolutionary* power of the *state*, that is, of the proletariat armed and organised as the ruling class?

Prevailing official Social-Democracy usually dismissed the question of the concrete tasks of the proletariat in the revolution either with a philistine sneer, or, at best, with the sophistic evasion: "The future will show". And the anarchists were justified in saying about such Social-Democrats that they were failing in their task of giving the workers a revolutionary education. Engels draws upon the experience of the last proletarian revolution precisely for the purpose of making a most concrete study of what should be done by the proletariat, and in what manner, in relation to both the banks and the state.

3. LETTER TO BEBEL

One of the most, if not *the* most, remarkable observation on the state in the works of Marx and Engels is contained in the following passage in Engels's letter to Bebel dated March 18-28, 1875. This letter, we may observe in parenthesis, was, as far as we know, first published by Bebel in the second volume of his memoirs (*Aus meinem Leben*), which appeared in 1911, i.e., thirty-six years after the letter had been written and sent.

Engels wrote to Bebel criticising that same draft of the Gotha Programme which Marx criticised in his famous letter to Bracke. Referring specially to the question of the state, Engels said:

"The free people's state has been transformed into the free state. Taken in its grammatical sense, a free state is one where the state is free in relation to its citizens, hence a state with a despotic government. The whole talk about the state should be dropped, especially since the Commune, which was no longer a state in the proper sense of the word. The 'people's state' has been thrown in our faces by the anarchists to the point of disgust, although already Marx's book against Proudhon[180] and later the *Communist Manifesto* say plainly that with the introduction of the socialist order of society the state dissolves of itself [sich auflöst] and disappears. As the state is only a transitional institution which is used in the struggle, in the revolution, to hold down one's adversaries by force, it is sheer nonsense to talk of a 'free people's state'; so long as the proletariat still *needs* the state, it does not need it in the interests of freedom but in order to hold down its adversaries, and as soon as it becomes possible to speak of freedom the state as such ceases to exist. We would therefore propose replacing *state* everywhere by *Gemeinwesen*, a good old German word which can very well take the place of the French word *commune*." (Pp. 321-22 of the German original.)*

---

* See p. 153 of this volume.—*Ed.*

It should be borne in mind that this letter refers to the party programme which Marx criticised in a letter dated only a few weeks later than the above (Marx's letter is dated May 5, 1875),[181] and that at the time Engels was living with Marx in London. Consequently, when he says "we" in the last sentence, Engels undoubtedly, in his own as well as in Marx's name, suggests to the leader of the German workers' party that the word "state" *be struck out of the programme* and replaced by the word "*community*".

What a howl about "anarchism" would be raised by the leading lights of present-day "Marxism", which has been falsified for the convenience of the opportunists, if such an amendment of the programme were suggested to them!

Let them howl. This will earn them the praises of the bourgeoisie.

And we shall go on with our work. In revising the programme of our Party, we must by all means take the advice of Engels and Marx into consideration in order to come nearer the truth, to restore Marxism by ridding it of distortions, to guide the struggle of the working class for its emancipation more correctly. Certainly no one opposed to the advice of Engels and Marx will be found among the Bolsheviks. The only difficulty that may perhaps arise will be in regard to the term. In German there are two words meaning "community", of which Engels used the one which does *not* denote a single community, but their totality, a system of communities. In Russian there is no such word, and we may have to choose the French word "commune", although this also has its drawbacks.

"The Commune was no longer a state in the proper sense of the word"—this is the most theoretically important statement Engels makes. After what has been said above, this statement is perfectly clear. The Commune *was ceasing* to be a state since it had to suppress, not the majority of the population, but a minority (the exploiters). It had smashed the bourgeois state machine. In place of a *special* coercive force the population itself came on the scene. All this was a departure from the state in the proper sense of the word. And had the Commune become firmly established, all traces of the state in it would have "withered away" of themselves; it would not have had to "abolish" the institutions of the

THE STATE AND REVOLUTION

state—they would have ceased to function as they ceased to have anything to do.

"The 'people's state' has been thrown in our faces by the anarchists." In saying this, Engels above all has in mind Bakunin and his attacks on the German Social-Democrats. Engels admits that these attacks were justified *insofar* as the "people's state" was as much an absurdity and as much a departure from socialism as the "free people's state". Engels tried to put the struggle of the German Social-Democrats against the anarchists on the right lines, to make this struggle correct in principle, to rid it of opportunist prejudices concerning the "state". Unfortunately, Engels's letter was pigeon-holed for thirty-six years. We shall see farther on that, even after this letter was published, Kautsky persisted in virtually the same mistakes against which Engels had warned.

Bebel replied to Engels in a letter dated September 21, 1875, in which he wrote, among other things, that he "fully agreed" with Engels's opinion of the draft programme, and that he had reproached Liebknecht with readiness to make concessions (p. 334 of the German edition of Bebel's memoirs, Vol. II). But if we take Bebel's pamphlet, *Our Aims*, we find there views on the state that are absolutely wrong.

"The state must ... be transformed from one based on *class rule* into a *people's state*." (*Unsere Ziele*, German edition, 1886, p. 14.)

This was printed in the *ninth* (the ninth!) edition of Bebel's pamphlet! It is not surprising that opportunist views on the state, so persistently repeated, were absorbed by the German Social-Democrats, especially as Engels's revolutionary interpretations had been safely pigeon-holed, and all the conditions of life were such as to "wean" them from revolution for a long time.

Chapter VI
THE VULGARISATION
OF MARXISM BY THE OPPORTUNISTS

The question of the relation of the state to the social revolution, and of the social revolution to the state, like the question of revolution generally, was given very little attention by the leading theoreticians and publicists of the

Second International (1889-1914). But the most characteristic thing about the process of the gradual growth of opportunism that led to the collapse of the Second International
in 1914 is the fact that even when these people were
squarely faced with this question they *tried to evade* it or
ignored it.

In general, it may be said that *evasiveness* over the question of the relation of the proletarian revolution to the state—
an evasiveness which benefited and fostered opportunism—
resulted in the *distortion* of Marxism and in its complete
vulgarisation.

To characterise this lamentable process, if only briefly,
we shall take the most prominent theoreticians of Marxism:
Plekhanov and Kautsky.

1. PLEKHANOV'S CONTROVERSY WITH THE ANARCHISTS

Plekhanov wrote a special pamphlet on the relation of
anarchism to socialism, entitled *Anarchism and Socialism*,
which was published in German in 1894.

In treating this subject, Plekhanov contrived completely
to evade the most urgent, burning, and most politically
essential issue in the struggle against anarchism, namely, the
relation of the revolution to the state, and the question of
the state in general! His pamphlet falls into two distinct
parts: one of them is historical and literary, and contains
valuable material on the history of the ideas of Stirner,
Proudhon and others; the other is philistine, and contains
a clumsy dissertation on the theme that an anarchist cannot
be distinguished from a bandit.

It is a most amusing combination of subjects and most
characteristic of Plekhanov's whole activity on the eve of the
revolution and during the revolutionary period in Russia.
In fact, in the years 1905 to 1917, Plekhanov revealed himself as a semi-doctrinaire and semi-philistine who, in politics,
trailed in the wake of the bourgeoisie.

We have seen how, in their controversy with the anarchists, Marx and Engels with the utmost thoroughness
explained their views on the relation of revolution to the
state. In 1891, in his foreword to Marx's *Critique of the
Gotha Programme*, Engels wrote that "we"—that is, Engels

and Marx—"were at that time, hardly two years after The
Hague Congress of the [First] International, engaged in the
most violent struggle against Bakunin and his anarchists".

The anarchists had tried to claim the Paris Commune as
their "own", so to say, as a corroboration of their doctrine;
and they completely misunderstood its lessons and Marx's
analysis of these lessons. Anarchism has given nothing even
approximating true answers to the concrete political questions: Must the old state machine be *smashed*? And *what*
should be put in its place?

But to speak of "anarchism and socialism" while completely evading the question of the state, and *disregarding*
the whole development of Marxism before and after the
Commune, meant inevitably slipping into opportunism. For
what opportunism needs most of all is that the two questions
just mentioned should *not* be raised at all. That *in itself* is
a victory for opportunism.

3. KAUTSKY'S CONTROVERSY WITH PANNEKOEK

In opposing Kautsky, Pannekoek came out as one of the
representatives of the "Left radical" trend which included
Rosa Luxemburg, Karl Radek and others. Advocating revolutionary tactics, they were united in the conviction that
Kautsky was going over to the "Centre", which wavered in
an unprincipled manner between Marxism and opportunism.
This view was proved perfectly correct by the war, when
this "Centrist" (wrongly called Marxist) trend, or Kautsky-
ism, revealed itself in all its repulsive wretchedness.

In an article touching on the question of the state, entitled
"Mass Action and Revolution" (*Neue Zeit*, 1912, Vol. XXX,
2), Pannekoek described Kautsky's attitude as one of "passive
radicalism", as "a theory of inactive expectancy". "Kautsky
refuses to see the process of revolution," wrote Pannekoek
(p. 616). In presenting the matter in this way, Pannekoek
approached the subject which interests us, namely, the tasks
of the proletarian revolution in relation to the state.

"The struggle of the proletariat," he wrote, "is not merely a struggle
against the bourgeoisie *for* state power, but a struggle *against* state
power.... The content of this [the proletarian] revolution is the destruction and dissolution [Auflösung] of the instruments of power of the state

with the aid of the instruments of power of the proletariat (p. 544). The struggle will cease only when, as the result of it, the state organisation is completely destroyed. The organisation of the majority will then have demonstrated its superiority by destroying the organisation of the ruling minority." (p. 548).

The formulation in which Pannekoek presented his ideas suffers from serious defects. But its meaning is clear nonetheless, and it is interesting to note *how* Kautsky combated it.

"Up to now," he wrote, "the antithesis between the Social-Democrats and the anarchists has been that the former wished to win state power while the latter wished to destroy it. Pannekoek wants to do both." (p. 724.)

Although Pannekoek's exposition lacks precision and concreteness—not to speak of other shortcomings of his article which have no bearing on the present subject—Kautsky seized precisely on the point of *principle* raised by Pannekoek; and *on this fundamental* point of *principle* Kautsky completely abandoned the Marxist position and went over wholly to opportunism. His definition of the distinction between the Social-Democrats and the anarchists is absolutely wrong; he completely vulgarises and distorts Marxism.

The distinction between the Marxists and the anarchists is this: (1) The former, while aiming at the complete abolition of the state, recognise that this aim can only be achieved after classes have been abolished by the socialist revolution, as the result of the establishment of socialism, which leads to the withering away of the state. The latter want to abolish the state completely overnight, not understanding the conditions under which the state can be abolished. (2) The former recognise that after the proletariat has won political power it must completely destroy the old state machinery and replace it by a new one consisting of an organisation of the armed workers, after the type of the Commune. The latter, while insisting on the destruction of the state machine, have a very vague idea of *what* the proletariat will put in its place and *how* it will use its revolutionary power. The anarchists even deny that the revolutionary proletariat should use the state power, they reject its revolutionary dictatorship. (3) The former demand that the proletariat be trained for revolution by utilising the present state. The anarchists reject this.

In this controversy, it is not Kautsky but Pannekoek who represents Marxism, for it was Marx who taught that the proletariat cannot simply win state power in the sense that the old state apparatus passes into new hands, but must smash this apparatus, must break it and replace it by a new one.

Kautsky abandons Marxism for the opportunist camp, for this destruction of the state machine, which is utterly unacceptable to the opportunists, completely disappears from his argument, and he leaves a loophole for them in that "conquest" may be interpreted as the simple acquisition of a majority....

Marx's critico-analytical genius saw in the practical measures of the Commune the *turning-point* which the opportunists fear and do not want to recognise because of their cowardice, because they do not want to break irrevocably with the bourgeoisie, and which the anarchists do not want to see, either because they are in a hurry or because they do not understand at all the conditions of great social changes. "We must not even think of destroying the old state machine; how can we do without ministries and officials?" argues the opportunist, who is completely saturated with philistinism and who, at bottom, not only does not believe in revolution, in the creative power of revolution, but lives in mortal dread of it (like our Mensheviks and Socialist-Revolutionaries).

"We must think *only* of destroying the old state machine; it is no use probing into the *concrete* lessons of earlier proletarian revolutions and analysing *what* to put in the place of what has been destroyed, and *how*," argues the anarchist (the best of the anarchists, of course, and not those who, following the Kropotkins and Co., trail behind the bourgeoisie). Consequently, the tactics of the anarchist become the tactics of *despair* instead of a ruthlessly bold revolutionary effort to solve concrete problems while taking into account the practical conditions of the mass movement.

Marx teaches us to avoid both errors; he teaches us to act with supreme boldness in destroying the entire old state machine, and at the same time he teaches us to put the question concretely: the Commune was able in the space of a few weeks to *start* building a *new*, proletarian state machine by introducing such-and-such measures to provide wider democracy and to uproot bureaucracy. Let us learn revolutionary boldness from the Communards; let us see in their practical measures the *outline* of really urgent and immediately possible measures, and then, *following this road*, we shall achieve the complete destruction of bureaucracy.

Written in August-September, 1917; Section 3 of Chapter II earlier than December 1918

Published as a book in Petrograd by Zhizn i Znaniye Publishers

V. I. Lenin, *Collected Works*, Vol. 25, pp. 422-488 passim

From THE IMMEDIATE TASKS
OF THE SOVIET GOVERNMENT

THE SIGNIFICANCE OF THE STRUGGLE
FOR COUNTRY-WIDE ACCOUNTING AND CONTROL

The state, which for centuries has been an organ for oppression and robbery of the people, has left us a legacy of the people's supreme hatred and suspicion of everything that is connected with the state. It is very difficult to overcome this, and only a Soviet government can do it. Even a Soviet government, however, will require plenty of time and enormous perseverance to accomplish it. This "legacy" is especially apparent in the problem of accounting and control —the fundamental problem facing the socialist revolution on the morrow of the overthrow of the bourgeoisie. A certain amount of time will inevitably pass before the people, who feel free for the first time now that the landowners and the bourgeoisie have been overthrown, will understand—not from books, but from their own, *Soviet* experience—will understand and *feel* that without comprehensive state accounting and control of the production and distribution of goods, the power of the working people, the freedom of the working people, *cannot* be maintained, and that a return to the yoke of capitalism is *inevitable*.

All the habits and traditions of the bourgeoisie, and of the petty bourgeoisie in particular, also oppose *state* control, and uphold the inviolability of "sacred private property", of "sacred" private enterprise. It is now particularly clear to us how correct is the Marxist thesis that anarchism and anarcho-syndicalism are *bourgeois* trends, how irreconcilably opposed they are to socialism, proletarian dictatorship and communism. The fight to instil into the people's minds the idea of *Soviet* state control and accounting, and to carry out this idea in practice; the fight to break with the rotten past, which taught the people to regard the procurement of bread and clothes as a "private" affair, and buying and selling as a transaction "which concerns only myself"—is a great fight of world-historic significance, a fight between socialist consciousness and bourgeois-anarchist spontaneity.

We have introduced workers' control as a law, but this law is only just beginning to operate and is only just beginning to penetrate the minds of broad sections of the proletariat. In our agitation we do not sufficiently explain that lack of accounting and control in the production and distribution of goods means the death of the rudiments of socialism, means the embezzlement of state funds (for all property belongs to the state and the state is the Soviet state in which power belongs to the majority of the working people). We do not sufficiently explain that carelessness in accounting and control is downright aiding and abetting the German and the Russian Kornilovs, who can overthrow the power of the working people *only* if we fail to cope with the task of accounting and control, and who, with the aid of the whole of the rural bourgeoisie, with the aid of the Constitutional-Democrats, the Mensheviks and the Right Socialist-Revolutionaries, are "watching" us and waiting for an opportune moment to attack us. And the advanced workers and peasants do not think and speak about this sufficiently. Until workers' control has become a fact, until the advanced workers have organised and carried out a victorious and ruthless crusade against the violators of this control, or against those who are careless in matters of control, it will be impossible to pass from the first step (from workers' control) to the second step towards socialism, i.e., to pass on to workers' regulation of production. . . .

"HARMONIOUS ORGANISATION" AND DICTATORSHIP

The resolution adopted by the recent Moscow Congress of Soviets advanced as the primary task of the moment the establishment of a "harmonious organisation", and the tightening of discipline.[182] Everyone now readily "votes for" and "subscribes to" resolutions of this kind; but usually people do not think over the fact that the application of such resolutions calls for coercion—coercion precisely in the form of dictatorship. And yet it would be extremely stupid and absurdly utopian to assume that the transition from capitalism to socialism is possible without coercion and without dictatorship. Marx's theory very definitely opposed this petty-bourgeois-democratic and anarchist absurdity long ago. And Russia of 1917-18 confirms the correctness of Marx's theory in this respect so strikingly, palpably and imposingly that only those who are hopelessly dull or who have obstinately decided to turn their backs on the truth can be under any misapprehension concerning this. Either the dictatorship of Kornilov (if we take him as the Russian type of bourgeois Cavaignac), or the dictatorship of the proletariat—any other choice is *out of the question* for a country which is developing at an extremely rapid rate with extremely sharp turns and amidst desperate ruin created by one of the most horrible wars in history. Every solution that offers a middle path is either a deception of the people by the bourgeoisie—for the bourgeoisie dare not tell the truth, dare not say that they need Kornilov—or an expression of the dull-wittedness of the petty-bourgeois democrats, of the Chernovs, Tseretelis and Martovs, who chatter about the unity of democracy, the dictatorship of democracy, the general democratic front, and similar nonsense. Those whom even the progress of the Russian Revolution of 1917-18 has not taught that a middle course is impossible, must be given up for lost.

On the other hand, it is not difficult to see that during every transition from capitalism to socialism, dictatorship is necessary for two main reasons, or along two main channels. Firstly, capitalism cannot be defeated and eradicated without the ruthless suppression of the resistance of the exploiters, who cannot at once be deprived of their wealth, of their advantages of organisation and knowledge, and consequently for a fairly long period will inevitably try to overthrow the hated rule of the poor; secondly, every great revolution, and a socialist revolution in particular, even if there is no external war, is inconceivable without internal war, i.e., civil war, which is even more devastating than

10—1130

external war, and involves thousands and millions of cases of wavering and desertion from one side to another, implies a state of extreme indefiniteness, lack of equilibrium and chaos. And of course, all the elements of disintegration of the old society, which are inevitably very numerous and connected mainly with the petty bourgeoisie (because it is the petty bourgeoisie that every war and every crisis ruins and destroys first), are bound to "reveal themselves" during such a profound revolution. And these elements of disintegration *cannot* "reveal themselves" otherwise than in an increase of crime, hooliganism, corruption, profiteering and outrages of every kind. To put these down requires time and *requires an iron hand*.

There has not been a single great revolution in history in which the people did not instinctively realise this and did not show salutary firmness by shooting thieves on the spot. The misfortune of previous revolutions was that the revolutionary enthusiasm of the people, which sustained them in their state of tension and gave them the strength to suppress ruthlessly the elements of disintegration, did not last long. The social, i.e., the class, reason for this instability of the revolutionary enthusiasm of the people was the weakness of the proletariat, which *alone* is able (if it is sufficiently numerous, class-conscious and disciplined) to win over to its side *the majority* of the working and exploited people (the majority of the poor, to speak more simply and popularly) and retain power sufficiently long to suppress completely all the exploiters as well as all the elements of disintegration.

It was this historical experience of all revolutions, it was this world-historic—economic and political—lesson that Marx summed up when he gave his short, sharp, concise and expressive formula: dictatorship of the proletariat. And the fact that the Russian revolution has been correct in its approach to this world-historic task *has been proved* by the victorious progress of the Soviet form of organisation among all the peoples and tongues of Russia. For Soviet power is nothing but an organisational form of the dictatorship of the proletariat, the dictatorship of the advanced class, which raises to a new democracy and to independent participation in the administration of the state tens upon tens of millions of working and exploited people, who by their own experience learn to regard the disciplined and class-conscious vanguard of the proletariat as their most reliable leader.

Dictatorship, however, is a big word, and big words should not be thrown about carelessly. Dictatorship is iron rule, government that is revolutionarily bold, swift and ruthless in suppressing both exploiters and hooligans. But our government is excessively mild, very often it resembles jelly more than iron. We must not forget for a moment that the bourgeois and petty-bourgeois element is fighting against the Soviet system in two ways; on the one hand, it is operating from without, by the methods of the Savinkovs, Gotzes, Gegechkoris and Kornilovs, by conspiracies and rebellions, and by their filthy "ideological" reflection, the flood of lies and slander in the Constitutional-Democratic, Right Socialist-Revolutionary and Menshevik press; on the other hand, this element operates from within and takes advantage of every manifestation of disintegration, of every weakness, in order to bribe, to increase indiscipline, laxity and chaos. The nearer we approach the complete military suppression of the bourgeoisie, the more dangerous does the element of petty-bourgeois anarchy become. And the fight against this element cannot be waged solely with the aid of propaganda and agitation, solely by organising competition and by selecting organisers. The struggle must also be waged by means of coercion.

Written between
April 13 and 26, 1918

Published on April 28, 1918
in *Pravda* No. 83 and in
Supplement to *Izvestia UTSiK* No. 85
Signed: N. Lenin

V. I. Lenin,
Collected Works,
Vol. 27, pp. 263-66

REMARKS ON THE DRAFT "PROPOSITIONS CONCERNING THE MANAGEMENT OF NATIONALISED ENTERPRISES"

Communism demands and presupposes maximum centralisation of large-scale industry throughout the country. The all-Russia centre must unconditionally, therefore, be given the right to place all enterprises of a given branch under its direct control. The regional centres will determine their functions depending on local, everyday and other conditions in accordance with the instructions and decisions of the centre.

To deprive the all-Russia centre of the right of immediate control over all enterprises of a given branch in all parts of the country, as is implied in the commission's draft proposals, would be regional anarcho-syndicalism, and not communism.

Written June 2, 1918

First published in 1959
in *Lenin Miscellany* XXXVI

V. I. Lenin,
Collected Works,
Fifth Russ. ed.,
Vol. 36, p. 392

ON REVIVING RAIL TRANSPORT
Draft Decree of the C.P.C.

After an exchange of opinions on the question of reviving rail transport the Council of People's Commissars decrees: Comrade Nevsky is instructed, in consultation with colleagues strictly adhering to a Soviet, genuinely socialist and not syndicalist, policy, to place before the Council of People's Commissars at an early date practical proposals on the struggle against syndicalism and slackness, on measures for exposing and penalising those who violate Soviet policy, on measures to establish the precise responsibility of each person in a position of authority for performing his duties to practical effect, and on measures to draw comrades capable of management into the conduct of such work.

The appointment of a Collegium in the Commissariat for Railways is to be postponed in view of the failure to publish the decree.

Written June 14, 1918

First published in 1933,
in *Lenin Miscellany XXI*

V. I. Lenin,
Collected Works,
Fifth Russ. ed.,
Vol. 36, p. 423

To Comrade Sylvia Pankhurst, London

August 28, 1919

Dear Comrade,

I received your letter of July 16, 1919, only yesterday. I am extremely grateful to you for the information about Britain and will try to fulfil your request, i.e., reply to your question.

I have no doubt at all that many workers who are among the best, most honest and sincerely revolutionary members of the proletariat are enemies of parliamentarism and of any participation in Parliament. The older capitalist culture and bourgeois democracy in any country, the more understandable this is, since the bourgeoisie in old parliamentary countries has excellently mastered the art of hypocrisy and of fooling the people in a thousand ways, passing off bourgeois parliamentarism as "democracy in general" or as "pure democracy" and so on, cunningly concealing the million threads which bind Parliament to the stock exchange and the capitalists, utilising a venal mercenary press and exercising the power of money, the power of capital in every way.

There is no doubt that the Communist International and the Communist Parties of the various countries would be making an irreparable mistake if they repulsed those workers who stand for Soviet power, but who are against participation in the parliamentary struggle. If we take the problem in its general form, theoretically, then it is this very programme, i.e., the struggle for Soviet power, for the

Soviet republic, which is able to unite, and today must certainly unite, all sincere, honest revolutionaries from among the workers. Very many anarchist workers are now becoming sincere supporters of Soviet power, and that being so, it proves them to be our best comrades and friends, the best of revolutionaries, who have been enemies of Marxism only through misunderstanding, or, more correctly, not through misunderstanding but because the official socialism prevailing in the epoch of the Second International (1889-1914) betrayed Marxism, lapsed into opportunism, perverted Marx's revolutionary teachings in general and his teachings on the lessons of the Paris Commune of 1871 in particular. I have written in detail about this in my book *The State and Revolution*[184] and will therefore not dwell further on the problem.

What if in a certain country those who are Communists by their convictions and their readiness to carry on revolutionary work, sincere partisans of Soviet power (the "Soviet system", as non-Russians sometimes call it), cannot unite owing to disagreement over participation in Parliament?

I should consider such disagreement immaterial at present, since the struggle for Soviet power is the political struggle of the proletariat in its highest, most class-conscious, most revolutionary form. It is better to be with the revolutionary workers when they are mistaken over some partial or secondary question than with the "official" socialists or Social-Democrats, if the latter are not sincere, firm revolutionaries, and are unwilling or unable to conduct revolutionary work among the working masses, but pursue correct tactics in regard to that partial question. And the question of parliamentarism is now a partial, secondary question. Rosa Luxemburg and Karl Liebknecht were, in my opinion, correct when they defended participation in the elections to the German bourgeois parliament, to the constituent National Assembly, at the January 1919 Conference of the Spartacists in Berlin, *against* the majority at the Conference.[185] But, of course, they were still more correct when they preferred remaining with the Communist Party, which was making a partial mistake, to siding with the direct traitors to socialism, like Scheidemann and his party, or with those servile souls, doctrinaires, cowards, spineless accomplices of the bourgeoisie, and reformists in practice, such as Kautsky, Haase, Däuming and all this "party" of German "Independents".[186]

I am personally convinced that to renounce participation in the parliamentary elections is a mistake on the part of the revolutionary workers of Britain, but better to make that mistake than to delay the formation of a big workers' Communist Party in Britain out of all the trends and elements, listed by you, which sympathise with Bolshevism and sincerely support the Soviet Republic. If, for example, among the B.S.P.[187] there were sincere Bolsheviks who refused, because of differences over participation in Parliament, to merge at once in a Communist Party with trends 4, 6 and 7, then these Bolsheviks, in my opinion, would be making a mistake a thousand times greater than the mistaken refusal to participate in elections to the British bourgeois parliament. In saying this I naturally assume that trends 4, 6 and 7, taken together, are really connected with the *mass* of the workers, and are not *merely* small intellectual groups, as is often the case in Britain. In this respect particular importance probably attaches to the Workers Committees and Shop Stewards, which, one should imagine, are closely connected with the *masses*.

Unbreakable ties with the mass of the workers, the ability to agitate unceasingly among them, to participate in every strike, to respond to every demand of the masses—this is the chief thing for a Communist Party, especially in such a country as Britain, where until now (as incidentally is the case in all imperialist countries) participation in the socialist movement, and the labour movement generally, has been confined chiefly to a thin top crust of workers, the labour aristocracy, most of whom are thoroughly and hopelessly spoiled by reformism and are held back by bourgeois and imperialist prejudices. Without a struggle against this stratum, without the destruction of every trace of its prestige among the workers, without convincing the masses of the utter bourgeois corruption of this stratum, there can be no question of a serious communist workers' movement. This applies to Britain, France, America and Germany.

Those working-class revolutionaries who make parliamentarism the centre of their attacks are quite right inasmuch as these attacks serve to express their denial in principle of bourgeois parliamentarism and bourgeois democracy. Soviet power, the Soviet republic—this is what the workers' revolution has put in place of bourgeois democracy, this is the form of transition from capitalism to socialism, the form of the dictatorship of the proletariat. And criticism of parliamentarism is not only legitimate and necessary, as giving the case for the transition to Soviet power, but is quite correct, as being the recognition of the historically conditional and limited character of parliamentarism, its connection with capitalism and capitalism alone, of its progressive character as compared with the Middle Ages, and of *its reactionary character as compared with Soviet power*.

But the critics of parliamentarism in Europe and America, when they are anarchists or anarcho-syndicalists, are very often wrong insofar as they reject *all participation* in elections and parliamentary activity. Here they simply show their lack of revolutionary experience. We Russians, who have lived through two great revolutions in the twentieth century, are well aware what importance parliamentarism can have, and actually does have during a revolutionary period in general and *in the very midst of a revolution* in particular. Bourgeois parliaments must be abolished and replaced by Soviet bodies. There is no doubt about that. There is no doubt now, after the experience of Russia, Hungary, Germany and other countries, that this *absolutely must take place* during a proletarian revolution. Therefore, systematically to prepare the working masses for this, to explain to them in advance the importance of Soviet power, to conduct propaganda and agitation for it—all this is the *absolute* duty of the worker who wants to be a revolutionary in deeds. But we Russians fulfilled *that* task, operating in the parliamentary arena, *too*. In the tsarist, fake, landowners' Duma our representatives knew how to carry on revolutionary and republican propaganda. In just the same way *Soviet propaganda* can and must *be carried on* in and from within bourgeois parliaments.

Perhaps that will not be easy to achieve at once in this or that parliamentary country. But that is another question. Steps must be taken to ensure that these correct tactics are mastered by the revolutionary workers in all countries. And if the workers' party is really *revolutionary*, if it is really a *workers'* party (that is, connected with the masses, with the majority of the working people, with the *rank and file* of the proletariat and not merely with its top crust), if it is really a *party*, i.e., a firmly, effectively knit *organisation of the revolutionary vanguard*, which knows how to carry on revolutionary work among the masses by all possible means, then such a party will surely be able to keep *its own* parliamentarians in hand, to make of them real revolutionary propagandists, such as Karl Liebknecht was, and not opportunists, not those who corrupt the proletariat with bourgeois methods, bourgeois customs, bourgeois ideas or bourgeois poverty of ideas.

If that failed to be achieved in Britain at once, if, in addition, no union of the supporters of Soviet power proved possible in Britain because of a difference over parliamentarism and only because of that, then I should consider a good step forward to complete unity the immediate formation of *two* Communist Parties, i.e., two parties which stand for the transition from bourgeois parliamentarism to Soviet power. Let one of these parties recognise participation in the bourgeois parliament, and the other reject it; this disagreement is now so immaterial that the most reasonable thing would be not to split over it. But even the joint existence of two such parties would be immense progress as compared with the present situation, would most likely be a transition to complete unity and the speedy victory of communism.

Soviet power in Russia has not only shown by the experience of almost two years that the dictatorship of the proletariat is possible *even* in a peasant country and is capable, by creating a strong army (the best proof that organisation and order prevail), of holding out in unbelievably, exceptionally difficult conditions.

Soviet power has done more: it has already achieved a moral victory *throughout* the world, for the working masses everywhere, although they get only tiny fragments of the truth about Soviet power, although they hear thousands and millions of false reports about Soviet power, *are already in favour of Soviet power*. It is already understood by the proletariat of the whole world that this power is the power of the working people, that it alone is salvation from capitalism, from the yoke of capital, from wars between the imperialists, that it leads to lasting peace.

That is why defeats of individual Soviet republics by the imperialists are possible, but it is impossible to conquer the world Soviet movement of the proletariat.

With communist greetings,

N. Lenin

P.S.—The following cutting from the Russian press will give you an example of our information about Britain:

"London, 25, 8 (via Beloostrov). The London correspondent of the Copenhagen paper *Berlinske Tidende* wires on August 3rd concerning the Bolshevik movement in Britain: 'The strikes which have occurred in the last few days and the recent revelations have shaken the confidence of the British in the immunity of their country to Bolshevism. At present the press is vigorously discussing this question, and the government is making every effort to establish that a "conspiracy" has existed for quite a long time and has had for its aim neither more nor less than the overthrow of the existing system. The British police have arrested a revolutionary bureau which, according to the press, had both money and arms at its disposal. *The Times* publishes the contents of certain documents found on the arrested men. They contain a complete revolutionary programme, according to which the entire bourgeoisie are to be disarmed; arms and ammunition are to be obtained for Soviets of Workers' and Red Army Deputies and a Red Army formed; all government posts are to be filled by workers. Furthermore, it was planned to set up a revolutionary tribunal for political criminals and persons guilty of cruelly treating prisoners. All foodstuffs were to be confiscated. Parliament and other organs of public government were to be dissolved and revolutionary Soviets created in their place. The working day was to be lowered to six hours and the minimum weekly wage raised to £7. All state and other debts were to be annulled. All banks, industrial and commercial enterprises and means of transport were to be declared nationalised.'"

If this is true, then I must offer the British imperialists and capitalists, in the shape of their organ, the richest newspaper in the world, *The Times*, my respectful gratitude and thanks for their excellent propaganda in behalf of Bolshevism. Carry on in the same spirit, gentlemen of *The Times*, you are splendidly leading Britain to the victory of Bolshevism!

Published in September 1919 in the magazine *The Communist International*

V. I. Lenin, *Collected Works*, Vol. 29, pp. 561-66

Comrades, before the war it seemed that the main division in the working-class movement was the division into socialists and anarchists. Not only did it seem so; it was so. In the protracted period that preceded the imperialist war and the revolution, no objective revolutionary situation existed in the overwhelming majority of European countries. What had to be done at that time was to use this slow process for revolutionary preparation. The socialists began it, but the anarchists did not see the need for it. The war created a revolutionary situation, and the old division proved to be outdated. On the one hand, the top leaders of anarchism and socialism became chauvinists; they showed what it meant to defend their own bourgeois robbers against other bourgeois robbers, both of whom were responsible for the loss of millions of lives in the war. On the other hand, new trends arose among the rank and file of the old parties—against the war, against imperialism and for social revolution. A most profound crisis thus developed owing to the war; both the anarchists and the socialists split, because the parliamentary leaders of the socialists were in the chauvinist wing while an ever-growing minority of the rank and file left them and began to take the side of the revolution.

Thus the working-class movement in all countries followed a new line, not the line of the anarchists and the socialists, but one that could lead to the dictatorship of the proletariat.

This split had become apparent throughout the world and had started before the Third International was founded.

If our Party has been successful it is because it came into being when the situation was revolutionary and when the labour movement was already in existence in all countries; and we therefore see now that a split has taken place in socialism and anarchism. All over the world, this is leading to communist workers participating in the formation of new organisations and to their uniting in the Third International. That is the most correct attitude.

Disagreements are again arising, for example, over the question of using parliaments, but since the experience of the Russian revolution and the Civil War, since the figure of Liebknecht and his role and importance among parliamentarians, have become known to the world, it is absurd to reject the revolutionary use of parliaments. It has become clear to people of the old way of thinking that the question of the state cannot be presented in the old way, that the old, bookish approach to this question has been succeeded by a new one based on practice and born of the revolutionary movement.

A united and centralised force of the proletariat must be counterposed to the united and centralised force of the bourgeoisie. The question of the state has thus now been shifted to a new plane, and the old disagreement has begun to lose its meaning. The old division of the working-class movement has yielded to new ones, the attitude towards Soviet government and to the dictatorship of the proletariat having assumed prime importance.

The Soviet Constitution is clear evidence of what the Russian revolution has produced. Our experience and the study of it have shown that all the groups of the old issues are now reduced to one: for or against Soviet rule, either for bourgeois rule, for democracy (for those forms of democracy which promise equality between the well-fed and the hungry, equality between the capitalist and the worker at the ballot-box, between the exploiters and the exploited, and serve to camouflage capitalist slavery), or for proletarian rule, for the ruthless suppression of the exploiters, for the Soviet state.

Only supporters of capitalist slavery can favour bourgeois

democracy. We can see that in the whiteguard literature of Kolchak and Denikin. Many Russian cities have been cleared of this filth, and the literature collected and sent to Moscow. When you scan the writings of Russian intellectuals like Chirikov, or of bourgeois thinkers like Y. Trubetskoi, it is interesting to see that they help Denikin and at the same time argue about the Constituent Assembly, equality, etc. These arguments about the Constituent Assembly are of service to us; when they conducted this propaganda among the whiteguard rank and file they helped us in the same way as the entire course of the Civil War, all the events, helped us. By their own arguments they proved that Soviet rule is backed by sincere revolutionaries who sympathise with the struggle against the capitalists. That has been made perfectly clear during the Civil War.

After the experience gained, after what has happened in Russia, Finland and Hungary, after a year's experience in the democratic republics, in Germany, one cannot object to, and write disquisitions about, the need for a central authority, for dictatorship and a united will to ensure that the vanguard of the proletariat shall close its ranks, develop the state and place it upon a new footing, while firmly holding the reins of power. Democracy has completely exposed itself; that is why signs of the strengthening of the communist movement for Soviet rule, for the dictatorship of the proletariat, have increased tremendously in all countries and have taken on the most diverse forms.

This has reached a point where such parties as the German Independents and the French Socialist Party, which are dominated by leaders of the old type who failed to understand either the new propaganda or the new conditions, and have not in the least changed their parliamentary activity, but are turning it into a means of dodging important issues and engaging the workers' attention with parliamentary debates—even these leaders have to recognise the dictatorship of the proletariat and Soviet power. This is because the masses of the workers are making themselves felt and forcing them to recognise it.

You know from the speeches of other comrades that the breakaway of the German Party of Independents, the recognition of the dictatorship of the proletariat and of Soviet government was the last decisive blow dealt to the Second International. Taking the existing state of affairs into consideration, it may be said that the Second International has been killed, and that the proletarian masses in Germany, Britain and France are taking the side of the Communists. In Britain there is also a party of Independents which persists in adhering to legality and in condemning the violence of the Bolsheviks. A discussion forum was recently opened in their newspaper. Well, the question of Soviets is being discussed 'here, and next to an article printed in British working-class newspapers we see an article by an Englishman who refuses to reckon with the theory of socialism and persists in his stupid contempt for theory, but who, taking the conditions of life in Britain into consideration, reaches a definite conclusion and says that they cannot condemn the Soviets, but should support them.

This shows that things have begun to change even among the backward sections of the workers in countries like Britain, and it may be said that the old forms of socialism have been killed for ever.

Europe is not moving towards revolution the way we did, although essentially Europe is going through the same experience. In its own way, every country must go through, and has begun to go through, an internal struggle against its own Mensheviks and against its own opportunists and Socialist-Revolutionaries, which exist under different names to a greater or lesser degree in all countries.

A brief newspaper report
was published on March 7, 1920
in *Pravda* No. 52 and *Izvestia UTSiK*
No. 52

V. I. Lenin,
Collected Works,
Vol. 30, pp. 320-23

Published in full
in the magazine
The Communist International
No. 10, June 14, 1920
Signed: N. Lenin

From "LEFT-WING" COMMUNISM—
AN INFANTILE DISORDER[18]

IV

THE STRUGGLE AGAINST WHICH ENEMIES WITHIN THE WORKING-CLASS MOVEMENT HELPED BOLSHEVISM DEVELOP, GAIN STRENGTH, AND BECOME STEELED

First and foremost, the struggle against opportunism, which in 1914 definitely developed into social-chauvinism and definitely sided with the bourgeoisie, against the proletariat. Naturally, this was Bolshevism's principal enemy within the working-class movement. It still remains the principal enemy on an international scale. The Bolsheviks have been devoting the greatest attention to this enemy. This aspect of Bolshevik activities is now fairly well known abroad too.

It was, however, different with Bolshevism's other enemy within the working-class movement. Little is known in other countries of the fact that Bolshevism took shape, developed and became steeled in the long years of struggle against *petty-bourgeois revolutionism,* which smacks of anarchism, or borrows something from the latter and, in all essential matters, does not measure up to the conditions and requirements of a consistently proletarian class struggle. Marxist theory has established—and the experience of all European revolutions and revolutionary movements has fully confirmed —that the petty proprietor, the small master (a social type existing on a very extensive and even mass scale in many European countries), who, under capitalism, always suffers oppression and very frequently a most acute and rapid deterioration in his conditions of life, and even ruin, easily goes to revolutionary extremes, but is incapable of perseverance, organisation, discipline and steadfastness. A petty bourgeois driven to frenzy by the horrors of capitalism is a social phenomenon which, like anarchism, is characteristic of all capitalist countries. The instability of such revolutionism, its barrenness, and its tendency to turn rapidly into submission, apathy, phantasms, and even a frenzied infatuation with one bourgeois fad or another—all this is common knowledge. However, a theoretical or abstract recognition of these truths does not at all rid revolutionary parties of old errors, which always crop up at unexpected occasions, in somewhat new forms, in a hitherto unfamiliar garb or surroundings, in an unusual—a more or less unusual—situation.

Anarchism was not infrequently a kind of penalty for the opportunist sins of the working-class movement. The two monstrosities complemented each other. And if in Russia—despite the more petty-bourgeois composition of her population as compared with the other European countries—anarchism's influence was negligible during the two revolutions (of 1905 and 1917) and the preparations for them, this should no doubt stand partly to the credit of Bolshevism, which has always waged a most ruthless and uncompromising struggle against opportunism. I say "partly", since of still greater importance in weakening anarchism's influence in Russia was the circumstance that in the past (the seventies of the nineteenth century) it was able to develop inordinately and to reveal its absolute erroneousness, its unfitness to serve the revolutionary class as a guiding theory.

When it came into being in 1903, Bolshevism took over the tradition of a ruthless struggle against petty-bourgeois, semi-anarchist (or dilettante-anarchist) revolutionism, a tradition which had always existed in revolutionary Social-Democracy and had become particularly strong in our country during the years 1900-03, when the foundations for a mass party of the revolutionary proletariat were being laid in Russia. Bolshevism took over and carried on the struggle against a party which, more than any other, expressed the tendencies of petty-bourgeois revolutionism, namely, the "Socialist-Revolutionary" Party, and waged that struggle on three main issues. First, that party, which rejected Marxism, stubbornly refused (or, it might be more correct to say: was unable) to understand the need for a strictly objective

appraisal of the class forces and their alignment, before
taking any political action. Second, this party considered
itself particularly "revolutionary", or "Left", because of its
recognition of individual terrorism, assassination—something
that we Marxists emphatically rejected. It was, of course,
only on grounds of expediency that we rejected individual
terrorism, whereas people who were capable of condemning
"on principle" the terror of the Great French Revolution, or,
in general, the terror employed by a victorious revolutionary party which is besieged by the bourgeoisie of the whole
world, were ridiculed and laughed to scorn by Plekhanov in
1900-03, when he was a Marxist and a revolutionary. Third,
the "Socialist-Revolutionaries" thought it very "Left" to
sneer at the comparatively insignificant opportunist sins of
the German Social-Democratic Party, while they themselves
imitated the extreme opportunists of that party, for example,
on the agrarian question, or on the question of the dictatorship of the proletariat.

History, incidentally, has now confirmed on a vast and
world-wide scale the opinion we have always advocated,
namely, that German *revolutionary* Social-Democracy (note
that as far back as 1900-03 Plekhanov demanded Bernstein's
expulsion from the Party, and in 1913 the Bolsheviks, always
continuing this tradition, exposed Legien's[189] baseness, vileness and treachery) *came closest* to being the party the revolutionary proletariat needs in order to achieve victory. Today,
in 1920, after all the ignominious failures and crises of the
war period and the early post-war years, it can be plainly
seen that, of all the Western parties, the German revolutionary Social-Democrats produced the finest leaders, and recovered and gained new strength more rapidly than the
others did. This may be seen in the instances both of the
Spartacists and the Left, proletarian wing of the Independent Social-Democratic Party of Germany, which is waging
an incessant struggle against the opportunism and spinelessness of the Kautskys, Hilferdings, Ledebours and Cris-
piens. If we now cast a glance to take in a complete historical period, namely, from the Paris Commune to the First
Socialist Soviet Republic, we shall find that Marxism's attitude to anarchism in general stands out most definitely and
unmistakably. In the final analysis, Marxism proved to be

correct, and although the anarchists rightly pointed to the opportunist views on the state prevalent among most of the socialist parties, it must be said, first, that this opportunism was connected with the distortion, and even deliberate suppression, of Marx's views on the state (in my book, *The State and Revolution*, I pointed out that for thirty-six years, from 1875 to 1911, Bebel withheld a letter by Engels, which very clearly, vividly, bluntly and definitively exposed the opportunism of the current Social-Democratic views on the state); second, that the rectification of these opportunist views, and the recognition of Soviet power and its superiority to bourgeois parliamentary democracy proceeded most rapidly and extensively among those trends in the socialist parties of Europe and America that were most Marxist.

The struggle that Bolshevism waged against "Left" deviations within its own Party assumed particularly large proportions on two occasions: in 1908, on the question of whether or not to participate in a most reactionary "parliament" and in the legal workers' societies, which were being restricted by most reactionary laws; and again in 1918 (the Treaty of Brest-Litovsk),[190] on the question of whether one "compromise" or another was permissible.

In 1908 the "Left" Bolsheviks were expelled from our Party for stubbornly refusing to understand the necessity of participating in a most reactionary "parliament". The "Lefts"—among whom there were many splendid revolutionaries who subsequently were (and still are) commendable members of the Communist Party—based themselves particularly on the successful experience of the 1905 boycott. When, in August 1905, the tsar proclaimed the convocation of a consultative "parliament",[191] the Bolsheviks called for its boycott, in the teeth of all the opposition parties and the Mensheviks, and the "parliament" was in fact swept away by the revolution of October 1905. The boycott proved correct at the time, not because non-participation in reactionary parliaments is correct in general, but because we accurately appraised the objective situation, which was leading to the rapid development of the mass strikes first into a political strike, then into a revolutionary strike, and finally into an uprising. Moreover, the struggle centred at that time on the question of whether the convocation of the first representative assembly should be left to the tsar, or an attempt should be made to wrest its convocation from the old regime. When there was not, and could not be, any certainty that the objective situation was of a similar kind, and when there was no certainty of a similar trend and the same rate of development, the boycott was no longer correct.

The Bolsheviks' boycott of "parliament" in 1905 enriched the revolutionary proletariat with highly valuable political experience and showed that, when legal and illegal, parliamentary and non-parliamentary forms of struggle are combined, it is sometimes useful and even essential to reject parliamentary forms. It would, however, be highly erroneous to apply this experience blindly, imitatively and uncritically to *other* conditions and *other* situations. The Bolsheviks' boycott of the Duma in 1906 was a mistake, although a minor and easily remediable one.* The boycott of the Duma in 1907, 1908 and subsequent years was a most serious error and difficult to remedy, because, on the one hand, a very rapid rise of the revolutionary tide and its conversion into an uprising was not to be expected, and, on the other hand, the entire historical situation attendant upon the renovation of the bourgeois monarchy called for legal and illegal activities being combined. Today, when we look back at this fully completed historical period, whose connection with subsequent periods has now become quite clear, it becomes most obvious that in 1908-14 the Bolsheviks *could not have* preserved (let alone strengthened and developed) the core of the revolutionary party of the proletariat, had they not upheld, in a most strenuous struggle, the viewpoint that it was *obligatory* to combine legal and illegal forms of struggle, and that it was *obligatory* to participate even in a most reactionary parliament and in a number of other institutions hemmed in by reactionary laws (sick benefit societies, etc.).

In 1918 things did not reach a split. At that time the "Left" Communists formed only a separate group or "fac-

---

* What applies to individuals also applies—with necessary modifications—to politics and parties. It is not he who makes no mistakes that is intelligent. There are no such men, nor can there be. It is he whose errors are not very grave and who is able to rectify them easily and quickly that is intelligent.

tion" within our Party, and that not for long. In the same year, 1918, the most prominent representatives of "Left Communism"[192], for example, Comrades Radek and Bukharin, openly acknowledged their error. It had seemed to them that the Treaty of Brest-Litovsk was a compromise with the imperialists, which was inexcusable on principle and harmful to the party of the revolutionary proletariat. It was indeed a compromise with the imperialists, but it was a compromise which, under the circumstances, *had to be made*.

Today, when I hear our tactics in signing the Brest-Litovsk Treaty being attacked by the Socialist-Revolutionaries, for instance, or when I hear Comrade Lansbury say, in a conversation with me, "Our British trade union leaders say that if it was permissible for the Bolsheviks to compromise, it is permissible for them to compromise too", I usually reply by first of all giving a simple and "popular" example:

Imagine that your car is held up by armed bandits. You hand them over your money, passport, revolver and car. In return you are rid of the pleasant company of the bandits. That is unquestionably a compromise. "*Do ut des*" (I "give" you money, fire-arms and a car "so that you give" me the opportunity to get away from you with a whole skin). It would, however, be difficult to find a sane man who would declare such a compromise to be "inadmissible on principle", or who would call the compromiser an accomplice of the bandits (even though the bandits might use the car and the fire-arms for further robberies). Our compromise with the bandits of German imperialism was just that kind of compromise.

But when, in 1914-18 and then in 1918-20, the Mensheviks and Socialist-Revolutionaries in Russia, the Scheidemannites (and to a large extent the Kautskyites) in Germany, Otto Bauer and Friedrich Adler (to say nothing of the Renners and Co.) in Austria, the Renaudels and Longuets and Co. in France, the Fabians,[193] the Independents and the Labourites in Britain entered into *compromises* with the bandits of their own bourgeoisie, and sometimes of the "Allied" bourgeoisie, and *against* the revolutionary proletariat of their own countries, all these gentlemen were actually acting as *accomplices in banditry*.

The conclusion is clear: to reject compromises "on principle", to reject the permissibility of compromises in general, no matter of what kind, is childishness, which it is difficult even to consider seriously. A political leader who desires to be useful to the revolutionary proletariat must be able to distinguish *concrete* cases of compromises that are inexcusable and are an expression of opportunism and *treachery*; he must direct all the force of criticism, the full intensity of merciless exposure and relentless war, against *these concrete* compromises, and not allow the past masters of "practical" socialism and the parliamentary Jesuits to dodge and wriggle out of responsibility by means of disquisitions on "compromises in general". It is in this way that the "leaders" of the British trade unions, as well as of the Fabian society and the "Independent" Labour Party, dodge responsibility *for the treachery they have perpetrated*, for having made a *compromise* that is really tantamount to the worst kind of opportunism, treachery and betrayal.

There are different kinds of compromises. One must be able to analyse the situation and the concrete conditions of each compromise, or of each variety of compromise. One must learn to distinguish between a man who has given up his money and fire-arms to bandits so as to lessen the evil they can do and to facilitate their capture and execution, and a man who gives his money and fire-arms to bandits so as to share in the loot. In politics this is by no means always as elementary as it is in this childishly simple example. However, anyone who is out to think up for the workers some kind of recipe that will provide them with cut-and-dried solutions for all contingencies, or promises that the policy of the revolutionary proletariat will never come up against difficult or complex situations, is simply a charlatan.

To leave no room for misinterpretation, I shall attempt to outline, if only very briefly, several fundamental rules for the analysis of concrete compromises.

The party which entered into a compromise with the German imperialists by signing the Treaty of Brest-Litovsk had been evolving its internationalism in practice ever since the end of 1914. It was not afraid to call for the defeat of the tsarist monarchy and to condemn "defence of country" in a war between two imperialist robbers. The parliamentary representatives of this party preferred exile in Siberia to taking a road leading to ministerial portfolios in a bourgeois government.[194] The revolution that overthrew tsarism and established a democratic republic put this party to a new and tremendous test—it did not enter into any agreements with its "own" imperialists, but prepared and brought about their overthrow. When it had assumed political power, this party did not leave a vestige of either landed or capitalist ownership. After making public and repudiating the imperialists' secret treaties, this party proposed peace to *all* nations, and yielded to the violence of the Brest-Litovsk robbers only after the Anglo-French imperialists had torpedoed the conclusion of a peace, and after the Bolsheviks had done everything humanly possible to hasten the revolution in Germany and other countries. The absolute correctness of this compromise, entered into by such a party in such a situation, is becoming ever clearer and more obvious with every day.

The Mensheviks and the Socialist-Revolutionaries in Russia (like all the leaders of the Second International throughout the world, in 1914-20) began with treachery—by directly or indirectly justifying "defence of country", i.e., the defence of *their own* predatory bourgeoisie. They continued their treachery by entering into a coalition with the bourgeoisie of *their own* country, and fighting, together with *their own* bourgeoisie, against the revolutionary proletariat of their own country. Their bloc, first with Kerensky and the Cadets, and then with Kolchak and Denikin in Russia—like the bloc of their *confrères* abroad with the bourgeoisie of *their* respective countries—was in fact desertion to the side of the bourgeoisie, against the proletariat. From beginning to end, *their* compromise with the bandits of imperialism meant their becoming *accomplices* in imperialist banditry.

X
SEVERAL CONCLUSIONS

... The history of the working-class movement now shows that, in all countries, it is about to go through (and is already going through) a struggle waged by communism—

emergent, gaining strength and advancing towards victory—
against, primarily, Menshevism, i.e., opportunism and social-
chauvinism (the home brand in each particular country),
and then as a complement, so to say, Left-wing communism.
The former struggle has developed in all countries, apparently without any exception, as a duel between the Second
International (already virtually dead) and the Third International. The latter struggle is to be seen in Germany, Great
Britain, Italy, America (at any rate, a certain *section* of the
Industrial Workers of the World[195] and of the anarcho-
syndicalist trends uphold the errors of Left-wing communism
alongside of an almost universal and almost unreserved
acceptance of the Soviet system), and in France (the attitude
of a section of the former syndicalists towards the political
party and parliamentarianism, also alongside of the acceptance of the Soviet system); in other words, the struggle is
undoubtedly being waged, not only on an international, but
even on a world-wide scale.

But while the working-class movement is everywhere going
through what is actually the same kind of preparatory school
for victory over the bourgeoisie, it is achieving that development in its *own way* in each country. The big and advanced
capitalist countries are travelling this road *far more rapidly*
than did Bolshevism, to which history granted fifteen years
to prepare itself for victory, as an organised political trend.
In the brief space of a year, the Third International has
already scored a decisive victory; it has defeated the yellow,
social-chauvinist Second International, which only a few
months ago was incomparably stronger than the Third International, seemed stable and powerful, and enjoyed every
possible support—direct and indirect, material (Cabinet
posts, passports, the press) and ideological—from the world
bourgeoisie.

It is now essential that Communists of every country
should quite consciously take into account both the fundamental objectives of the struggle against opportunism and
"Left" doctrinairism, and the *concrete features* which this
struggle assumes and must inevitably assume in each country,
in conformity with the specific character of its economics,
politics, culture, and national composition (Ireland, etc.),
its colonies, religious divisions, and so on and so forth. Dis-

satisfaction with the Second International is felt everywhere and is spreading and growing, both because of its opportunism and because of its inability or incapacity to create a really centralised and really leading centre capable of directing the international tactics of the revolutionary proletariat in its struggle for a world Soviet republic. It should be clearly realised that such a leading centre can never be built up on stereotyped, mechanically equated, and identical tactical rules of struggle. As long as national and state distinctions exist among peoples and countries—and these will continue to exist for a very long time to come, even after the dictatorship of the proletariat has been established on a world-wide scale—the unity of the international tactics of the communist working-class movement in all countries demands, not the elimination of variety or the suppression of national distinctions (which is a pipe dream at present), but an application of the *fundamental* principles of communism (Soviet power and the dictatorship of the proletariat), which will *correctly modify* these principles in certain *particulars*, correctly adapt and apply them to national and national-state distinctions. To seek out, investigate, predict, and grasp that which is nationally specific and nationally distinctive, in the *concrete manner* in which each country should tackle a *single* international task: victory over opportunism and Left doctrinairism within the working-class movement; the overthrow of the bourgeoisie; the establishment of a Soviet republic and a proletarian dictatorship—such is the basic task in the historical period that all the advanced countries (and not they alone) are going through. The chief thing—though, of course, far from everything—the chief thing has already been achieved: the vanguard of the working class has been won over, has ranged itself on the side of Soviet government and against parliamentarism, on the side of the dictatorship of the proletariat and against bourgeois democracy. All efforts and all attention should now be concentrated on the *next* step, which may seem—and from a certain viewpoint actually is—less fundamental, but, on the other hand, is actually closer to a practical accomplishment of the task. That step is: the search after forms of the *transition* or the *approach* to the proletarian revolution.

The proletarian vanguard has been won over ideologically. That is the main thing. Without this, not even the first step towards victory can be made. But that is still quite a long way from victory. Victory cannot be won with a vanguard alone. To throw only the vanguard into the decisive battle, before the entire class, the broad masses have taken up a position either of direct support for the vanguard, or at least of sympathetic neutrality towards it and of precluded support for the enemy, would be, not merely foolish but criminal. Propaganda and agitation alone are not enough for an entire class, the broad masses of the working people, those oppressed by capital, to take up such a stand. For that, the masses must have their own political experience. Such is the fundamental law of all great revolutions, which has been confirmed with compelling force and vividness, not only in Russia but in Germany as well. To turn resolutely towards communism, it was necessary, not only for the ignorant and often illiterate masses of Russia, but also for the literate and well-educated masses of Germany, to realise from their own bitter experience the absolute impotence and spinelessness, the absolute helplessness and servility to the bourgeoisie, and the utter vileness of the government of the paladins of the Second International; they had to realise that a dictatorship of the extreme reactionaries (Kornilov in Russia; Kapp and Co. in Germany) is inevitably the only alternative to a dictatorship of the proletariat.

The immediate objective of the class-conscious vanguard of the international working-class movement, i.e., the Communist parties, groups and trends, is to be able to *lead* the broad masses (who are still, for the most part, apathetic, inert, dormant and convention-ridden) to their new position, or, rather, to be able to lead, *not only* their own party but also these masses in their advance and transition to the new position. While the first historical objective (that of winning over the class-conscious vanguard of the proletariat to the side of Soviet power and the dictatorship of the working class) could not have been reached without a complete ideological and political victory over opportunism and social-chauvinism, the second and immediate objective, which consists in being able to lead the *masses* to a new position ensuring the victory of the vanguard in the revolution, cannot be reached without the liquidation of Left doctrinairism, and without a full elimination of its errors. . . .

Written in April-May 1920

Published as a pamphlet
by Petrograd State Publishers
in June 1920

V. I. Lenin,
Collected Works,
Vol. 31, pp. 31-39, 90-93

From THESES ON THE FUNDAMENTAL TASKS
OF THE SECOND CONGRESS
OF THE COMMUNIST INTERNATIONAL[196]

18. The Second Congress of the Third International considers erroneous the views on the Party's relation to the class and to the masses, and the view that it is not obligatory for Communist parties to participate in bourgeois parliaments and in reactionary trade unions. These views have been refuted in detail in special decisions of the present Congress, and advocated most fully by the Communist Workers' Party of Germany,[197] and partly by the Communist Party of Switzerland, by *Kommunismus*, organ of the East-European Secretariat of the Communist International in Vienna, by the now dissolved secretariat in Amsterdam,[198] by several Dutch comrades, by several Communist organisations in Great Britain, as, for example, the Workers' Socialist Federation,[199] etc., and also by the Industrial Workers of the World in the USA and the Shop Stewards' Committees in Great Britain, etc.

Nevertheless, the Second Congress of the Third International considers it possible and desirable that those of the above-mentioned organisations which have not yet officially affiliated to the Communist International should do so immediately; for in the present instance, particularly as regards the Industrial Workers of the World in the USA and Australia, as well as the Shop Stewards' Committees in Great Britain, we are dealing with a profoundly proletarian and mass movement, which in all essentials actually stands by the basic principles of the Communist International. The erroneous views held by these organisations regarding participation in bourgeois parliaments can be explained, not so much by the influence of elements coming from the bourgeoisie, who bring their essentially petty-bourgeois views into the movement—views such as anarchists often hold—as by the political inexperience of proletarians who are quite revolutionary and connected with the masses.

For this reason, the Second Congress of the Third International requests all Communist organisations and groups in the Anglo-Saxon countries, even if the Industrial Workers of the World and the Shop Stewards' Committees do not immediately affiliate to the Third International, to pursue a very friendly policy towards these organisations, to establish closer contacts with them and the masses that sympathise with them, and to explain to them in a friendly spirit—on the basis of the experience of all revolutions, and particularly of the three Russian revolutions of the twentieth century—the erroneousness of their views as set forth above, and not to desist from further efforts to amalgamate with these organisations to form a single Communist party.

19. In this connection, the Congress draws the attention of all comrades, particularly in the Latin and Anglo-Saxon countries, to the fact that, since the war, a profound ideological division has been taking place among anarchists all over the world regarding the attitude to be adopted towards the dictatorship of the proletariat and Soviet government. Moreover, a proper understanding of these principles is particularly to be seen among proletarian elements that have often been impelled towards anarchism by a perfectly legitimate hatred of the opportunism and reformism of the parties of the Second International. That understanding is growing the more widespread among them, the more familiar they become with the experience of Russia, Finland, Hungary, Latvia, Poland and Germany.

The Congress therefore considers it the duty of all Communists to do everything to help all proletarian mass elements to abandon anarchism and come over to the side of the Third International. The Congress points out that the measure in which genuinely Communist parties succeed in winning mass proletarian elements rather than intellectual, and petty-bourgeois elements away from anarchism, is a criterion of the success of those Parties.

July 4, 1920

Written July 4, 1920

Published in the journal
The Communist International
No. 2

V. I. Lenin,
Collected Works,
Vol. 31, pp. 199-201

From the Article THE PARTY CRISIS[200]

Bukharin and Co.'s theses [are] an all-time low in *ideological* disintegration. We have here one of those "turns" which in the old days Marxists used to call "not so much historical as hysterical". Thesis 17 says: "At the present time, these nominations must be made *mandatory*" (that is, the trade unions' nominations to the respective "chief administrations and central boards").

This is a clean break with communism and a transition to syndicalism. It is, in essence, a repetition of Shlyapnikov's "unionise the state" slogan, and means transferring the Supreme Economic Council apparatus piecemeal to the respective trade unions. To say, "I propose *mandatory* nominations", is exactly the same as saying, "I appoint".

Communism says: The Communist Party, the vanguard of the proletariat, leads the non-Party workers' masses, educating, preparing, teaching and training the masses ("school" of communism)—first the workers and then the peasants—to enable them eventually to concentrate in their hands the administration of the whole national economy.

Syndicalism hands over to the mass of non-Party workers, who are compartmentalised in the industries, the management of their industries ("the chief administrations and central boards"), thereby making the Party superfluous, and failing to carry on a sustained campaign either in training the masses or in *actually* concentrating in *their* hands the management *of the whole national economy*.

The Programme of the R.C.P. says: "The trade unions *should eventually arrive*" (which means that they are not yet there or even on the way) "at a *de facto* concentration in their hands" (in *their*, that is, the hands of the trade unions, that is, the hands of the fully organised *masses*; anyone will see how far we have still to go even to the very first approaches to this *de facto* concentration) ... concentration of what? "of the whole administration of the whole national economy, as a single economic entity" (hence, not branches of industry, or even industry as a whole, but industry *plus* agriculture, etc. Are we anywhere near to actually concentrating the management of agriculture in the hands of the trade unions?). The R.C.P. Programme then speaks of the "ties" between the "central state administration" and the "broad masses of toilers", and of the "*participation* of the trade unions in running the economy".

Why have a Party, if industrial management is to be appointed ("mandatory nomination") by the trade unions nine-tenths of whose members are non-Party workers? Bukharin has talked himself into a logical, theoretical and practical implication of a split in the Party, or, rather, a breakaway of the syndicalists from the Party.

Trotsky, who had been "chief" in the struggle, has now been "outstripped" and entirely "eclipsed" by Bukharin, who has thrown the struggle into an altogether new balance by talking himself into a mistake that is much more serious than all of Trotsky's put together.

Written January 19, 1921
Pravda No. 13,
January 21, 1921
Signed: *N. Lenin*

V. I. Lenin,
Collected Works,
Vol. 32, pp. 49-51

At the Eighth Congress of Soviets, I said that we ought to have less politics. When I said that I thought we would have no more political mistakes, but here we are, three years after the Soviet revolution, talking about syndicalism. This is a shame. If I had been told six months ago that I would be writing about syndicalism, I would have said that I preferred to write about the Donbas. Now we are being distracted, and the Party is being dragged back. A small mistake is growing into a big one. That is where Comrade Shlyapnikov comes in. Point 16 of Comrade Trotsky's theses gives a correct definition of Shlyapnikov's mistake.

In an effort to act the buffer, Bukharin clutched at Shlyapnikov, but it would have been better for him to clutch at a straw. He promises the unions mandatory nominations, which means they are to have the final say in appointments. But that is exactly what Shlyapnikov is saying. Marxists have been combating syndicalism all over the world. We have been fighting in the Party for over twenty years, and we have given the workers visual proof that the Party is a special kind of thing which needs forward-looking men prepared for sacrifice; that it does make mistakes, but corrects them; that it guides and selects men who know the way and the obstacles before us. It does not deceive the workers. It never makes promises that cannot be kept. And if you skip the trade unions you will make a hash of everything we have achieved over the past three years. Comrade Bukharin, with whom I discussed this mistake, said: "Comrade Lenin, you are picking on us."

I take mandatory nominations to mean that they will be made under the direction of the Party's Central Committee. But in that case, what are the rights we are giving them? There will then be no chance of having a bloc. The workers and the peasants are two distinct classes. Let us talk about vesting the rights in the trade unions when electricity has spread over the whole country—if we manage to achieve this in twenty years it will be incredibly quick work, for it cannot be done quickly. To talk about it before then will be deceiving the workers. The dictatorship of the proletariat is the most stable thing in the world because it has won confidence by its deeds, and because the Party took great care to prevent diffusion.

What does that mean?

Does every worker know how to run the state? People working in the practical sphere know that this is not true, that millions of our organised workers are going through what we always said the trade unions were, namely, a school of communism and administration. When they have attended this school for a number of years they will have learned to administer, but the going is slow. We have not even abolished illiteracy. We know that workers in touch with peasants are liable to fall for non-proletarian slogans. How many of the workers have been engaged in government? A few thousand throughout Russia and no more. If we say that it is not the Party but the trade unions that put up the candidates and administrate, it may sound very democratic and might help us to catch a few votes, but not for long. It will be fatal for the dictatorship of the proletariat.

Read the decision of the Second Congress of the Comintern. Its resolutions and decisions have gone round the world. The recent Socialist Congress in France revealed that we have won a majority in a country where chauvinism is most virulent; we have split the Party and ejected the corrupt leaders, and we did this in opposition to the syndicalists.* And all the best workers and leaders there have adopted our

---

* See pp. 326-29 of this volume.—*Ed.*

theory. Even syndicalists—revolutionary syndicalists—are siding with us all over the world. I myself have met American syndicalists who, after a visit to this country, say: "Indeed, you cannot lead the proletariat without a Party." You all know that this is a fact. And it is quite improper for the proletariat to rush into the arms of syndicalism and talk about mandatory nominations to "all-Russia producers' congresses". This is dangerous and jeopardises the Party's guiding role. Only a very small percentage of the workers in the country are now organised. The majority of the peasants will follow the Party because its policy is correct, and because, during the Brest peace ordeal, it was capable of making temporary sacrifices and retreats, which was the right thing to do. Are we to throw all this away? Was it all a windfall? No, it was all won by the Party in decades of hard work. Everybody believes the word of the Bolsheviks, who have had twenty years of Party training.

To govern you need an army of steeled revolutionary Communists. We have it, and it is called the Party. All this syndicalist nonsense about mandatory nominations of producers must go into the wastepaper basket. To proceed on those lines would mean thrusting the Party aside and making the dictatorship of the proletariat in Russia impossible. This is the view I believe it to be my Party duty to put to you. It is, in my opinion, enunciated in the form of practical propositions in the platform called *Draft Decision of the Tenth Congress of the R.C.P.* . . . .

Published in the *Bulletin Utorogo vserossiiskogo syezda gornorabochikh (Bulletin of the Second All-Russia Congress of Miners)* No. 1, January 25, 1921

V. I. Lenin,
Collected Works,
Vol. 32, pp. 60-62

From ONCE AGAIN ON THE TRADE UNIONS, THE CURRENT SITUATION AND THE MISTAKES OF TROTSKY AND BUKHARIN

During the discussion it was Comrade Shlyapnikov and his group, the so-called Workers' Opposition,[201] who showed the most pronounced syndicalist trend. This being an obvious deviation from communism and the Party, we shall have to reckon with it, talk it over, and make a special propaganda effort to explain the error of these views and the danger of making such mistakes. Comrade Bukharin, who actually coined the syndicalist phrase "mandatory nominations" (by trade unions to management bodies), tries to vindicate himself in today's issue of *Pravda*, but I'm afraid his line of defence is highly ineffective and quite wrong. He wants us to know, you see, that he deals with the role of the Party in his other points. I should think so! If it were otherwise it would have been more than just a *mistake*, requiring correction and allowing some slight rectification: it would have been withdrawal from the Party. When you say "mandatory nominations" but neglect to add, there and then, that they are *not* mandatory for the Party, you have a syndicalist deviation, and that is *in*compatible with communism and the Party Programme. If you add: "mandatory but *not* for the Party" you are giving the non-Party workers a false sense of having some increase in their rights, whereas in fact there will be no change at all. The longer Comrade Bukharin persists in his deviation from communism—a deviation that is wrong theoretically and deceptive politically—the more deplorable will be the fruits of his obstinacy. You cannot maintain an untenable proposition. The Party does not object to the extension of the rights of the non-Party workers in general, but a little reflection will show what can and what cannot be done in this respect.

In the discussion by the Communist group of the Second All-Russia Miners' Congress, Shlyapnikov's platform was defeated despite the backing it got from Comrade Kiselyov, who commands special prestige in that union: our platform won 137 votes, Shlyapnikov's, 62, and Trotsky's, 8. The syndicalist malaise must and will be cured.

Written January 25, 1921

Published as a pamphlet
on January 25, 26, 1921 by the Press
Department of the Moscow Soviet
of Workers', Peasants' and
Red Army Deputies
Signed: *N. Lenin*

V. I. Lenin,
Collected Works,
Vol. 32, pp. 106-07

PRELIMINARY DRAFT RESOLUTION OF THE TENTH CONGRESS OF THE R.C.P. ON THE SYNDICALIST AND ANARCHIST DEVIATION IN OUR PARTY

1. A syndicalist and anarchist deviation has been definitely revealed in our Party in the past few months. It calls for the most resolute measures of ideological struggle and also for purging the Party and restoring its health.

2. The said deviation is due partly to the influx into the Party of former Mensheviks, and also of workers and peasants who have not yet fully assimilated the communist world outlook. Mainly, however, this deviation is due to the influence exercised upon the proletariat and on the Russian Communist Party by the petty-bourgeois element, which is exceptionally strong in our country, and which inevitably engenders vacillation towards anarchism, particularly at a time when the condition of the masses has greatly deteriorated as a consequence of the crop failure and the devastating effects of war, and when the demobilisation of the army numbering millions sets loose hundreds and hundreds of thousands of peasants and workers unable immediately to find regular means of livelihood.

3. The most theoretically complete and clearly defined expression of this deviation (*or*: one of the most complete, etc., expressions of this deviation) is the theses and other literary productions of the so-called Workers' Opposition group. Sufficiently illustrative of this is, for example, the following thesis propounded by this group: "The organisation of the management of the national economy is the function

of an All-Russia Congress of Producers organised in industrial unions which shall elect a central body to run the whole of the national economy of the Republic."

The ideas at the bottom of this and numerous similar statements are radically wrong in theory, and represent a complete break with Marxism and communism, with the practical experience of all semi-proletarian revolutions and of the present proletarian revolution.

First, the concept "producer" combines proletarians with semi-proletarians and small commodity producers, thus radically departing from the fundamental concept of the class struggle and from the fundamental demand that a precise distinction be drawn between classes.

Secondly, the bidding for or flirtation with the non-Party masses, which is expressed in the above-quoted thesis, is an equally radical departure from Marxism.

Marxism teaches—and this tenet has not only been formally endorsed by the whole of the Communist International in the decisions of the Second (1920) Congress of the Comintern on the role of the political party of the proletariat, but has also been confirmed in practice by our revolution—that only the political party of the working class, i.e., the Communist Party, is capable of uniting, training and organising a vanguard of the proletariat and of the whole mass of the working people that alone will be capable of withstanding the inevitable petty-bourgeois vacillations of this mass and the inevitable traditions and relapses of narrow craft unionism or craft prejudices among the proletariat, and of guiding all the united activities of the whole of the proletariat, i.e., of leading it politically, and through it, the whole mass of the working people. Without this the dictatorship of the proletariat is impossible.

The wrong understanding of the role of the Communist Party in its relation to the non-Party proletariat, and in the relation of the first and second factors to the whole mass of working people, is a radical theoretical departure from communism and a deviation towards syndicalism and anarchism, and this deviation permeates all the views of the Workers' Opposition group.

4. The Tenth Congress of the Russian Communist Party declares that it also regards as radically wrong all attempts

on the part of the said group and of other persons to defend
their fallacious views by referring to Paragraph 5 of the
economic section of the Programme of the Russian Communist Party, which deals with the role of the trade unions. This
paragraph says that "the trade unions should eventually
arrive at a *de facto* concentration in their hands of the whole
administration of the whole national economy, as a single
economic entity" and that they will "ensure in this way
indissoluble ties between the central state administration, the
national economy and the broad masses of working people",
"drawing" these masses "into direct economic management".

This paragraph in the Programme of the Russian Communist Party also says that a prerequisite for the state at
which the trade unions "should eventually arrive" is the
process whereby they increasingly "divest themselves of the
narrow craft-union spirit" and embrace the majority "and
eventually all" of the working people.

Lastly, this paragraph in the Programme of the Russian
Communist Party emphasises that "on the strength of the
laws of the R.S.F.S.R., and established practice, the trade
unions participate in all the local and central organs of
industrial management".

Instead of studying the practical experience of participation in administration, and instead of developing this
experience further, strictly in conformity with successes
achieved and mistakes rectified, the syndicalists and
anarchists advance as an immediate slogan "congresses or a
congress of producers" "to elect" the organs of economic
management. Thus, the leading, educational and organising
role of the Party in relation to the trade unions of the proletariat, and of the latter to the semi-petty-bourgeois and
even wholly petty-bourgeois masses of working people, is
completely evaded and eliminated, and instead of continuing and correcting the practical work of building new forms
of economy already begun by the Soviet state, we get petty-
bourgeois-anarchist disruption of this work, which can only
lead to the triumph of the bourgeois counterrevolution.

5. In addition to the theoretical fallacies and a radically
wrong attitude towards the practical experience of economic
organisation already begun by the Soviet government, the
Congress of the Russian Communist Party discerns in the

views of this and similar groups and persons a gross political mistake and a direct political danger to the very existence of the dictatorship of the proletariat.

In a country like Russia, the overwhelming preponderance of the petty-bourgeois element and the devastation, impoverishment, epidemics, crop failures, extreme want and hardship inevitably resulting from the war, engender particularly sharp vacillations in the temper of the petty-bourgeois and semi-proletarian masses. First they incline towards a strengthening of the alliance between these masses and the proletariat, and then towards bourgeois restoration. The experience of all revolutions in the eighteenth, nineteenth, and twentieth centuries shows most clearly and convincingly that the only possible result of these vacillations—if the unity, strength and influence of the revolutionary vanguard of the proletariat is weakened in the slightest degree—will be the restoration of the power and property of the capitalists and landowners.

Hence, the views of the Workers' Opposition and of like-minded elements are not only wrong in theory, but are an expression of petty-bourgeois and anarchist wavering in practice, and actually weaken the consistency of the leading line of the Communist Party and help the class enemies of the proletarian revolution.

6. In view of all this, the Congress of the R.C.P., emphatically rejecting the said ideas, as being expressive of a syndicalist and anarchist deviation, deems it necessary:

First, to wage an unswerving and systematic struggle against these ideas;

Secondly, to recognise the propaganda of these ideas as being incompatible with membership of the R.C.P.

Instructing the C.C. of the Party strictly to enforce these decisions, the Congress at the same time points out that special publications, symposiums, etc., can and should provide space for a most comprehensive exchange of opinion between Party members on all the questions herein indicated.

First published in 1923
in N. Lenin (V. Ulyanov),
Works, Vol. XVIII, Part I

V. I. Lenin,
Collected Works,
Vol. 32, pp. 245-48

REPORT ON PARTY UNITY
AND THE ANARCHO-SYNDICALIST DEVIATION
TO THE TENTH CONGRESS OF THE R.C.P.(B.)
March 16, 1921

Comrades, I do not think there is any need to say a great deal on this question because the subjects on which an official pronouncement must now be made on behalf of the Party Congress, that is, on behalf of the whole Party, were touched upon in all the questions discussed at the Congress. The resolution "On Unity"[202] largely contains a characterisation of the political situation. You must have all read the printed text of this resolution that has been distributed. Point 7, which introduces an exceptional measure, namely, the right to expel a member from the Central Committee by a two-thirds majority of a general meeting of members of the C.C., alternate members and members of the Central Control Commission, is not for publication. This measure was repeatedly discussed at private conferences at which representatives of all shades expressed their opinions. Let us hope, comrades, that it will not be necessary to apply this point: but it is necessary to have it, in view of the new situation, when we are on the eve of a new and fairly sharp turn, and want to abolish all traces of separatism.

Let me now deal with the resolution on syndicalist and anarchist deviations. It is the question touched upon in point 4 of the Congress agenda. The definition of our attitude to certain trends, or deviations in thinking, is the pivot of the whole resolution. By saying "deviations", we emphasise that we do not as yet regard them as something that has crystallised and is absolutely and fully defined, but merely as the beginning of a political trend of which the Party must give its appraisal. Point 3 of the resolution on the syndicalist and anarchist deviation, copies of which you all probably have, evidently contains a misprint (judging by the remarks, it has been noticed). It should read: "illustrative of this is, for example, the following thesis of the Workers' Opposition: 'The organisation of the management of the national economy is the function of an All-Russia Congress of Producers organised in industrial unions which shall elect a central body to run the whole of the national economy of the Republic.' " We have repeatedly discussed this point during the Congress, at restricted conferences as well as the open general sessions of the Congress. I think we have already made it clear that it is quite impossible to defend this point on the plea that Engels had spoken of an association of producers, because it is quite obvious, and an exact quotation of the appropriate passage will prove, that Engels was referring to a classless communist society. That is something we all take for granted. Once society is rid of classes, only the producers remain, without any division into workers and peasants. And we know perfectly well from all the works of Marx and Engels that they drew a very clear distinction between the period in which classes still exist and that in which they no longer do. Marx and Engels used to ridicule the idea that classes could disappear before communism, and said that communism alone meant their abolition.

The position is that we are the first to raise the question of abolishing classes in the practical plane, and that two main classes remain in this peasant country—the working class and the peasantry. Alongside of them, however, are whole groups left over from capitalism.

Our Programme definitely says that we are taking the first steps and shall have a number of transitional stages. But in the practical work of Soviet administration and in the whole history of the revolution we have constantly had graphic illustrations of the fact that it is wrong to give theoretical definitions of the kind the opposition has given in this case. We know perfectly well that classes have remained in our country and will remain for a long time to come; and that

in a country with a predominantly peasant population they
are bound to remain for many, many years. It will take us
at least ten years to organise large-scale industry to produce
a reserve and secure control of agriculture. This is the
shortest period even if the technical conditions are exceptionally favourable. But we know that our conditions are
terribly unfavourable. We have a plan for building up Russia on the basis of modern large-scale industry: it is the
electrification plan drawn up by our scientists. The shortest
period provided for in that plan is ten years, and this is
based on the assumption that conditions will be something
like normal. But we know perfectly well that we do not
have such conditions and it goes without saying that ten
years is an extremely short period for us. We have reached
the very core of the question: the situation is such that classes
hostile to the proletariat will remain, so that in practice
we cannot now create that which Engels spoke about. There
will be a dictatorship of the proletariat. Then will come the
classless society.

Marx and Engels sharply challenged those who tended to
forget class distinctions and spoke about producers, the
people, or working people in general. Anyone who has read
Marx and Engels will recall that in all their works they
ridicule those who talk about producers, the people, working
people in general. There are no working people or workers
in general; there are either small proprietors who own the
means of production, and whose mentality and habits are
capitalistic—and they cannot be anything else—or wage-
workers with an altogether different cast of mind, wage-
workers in large-scale industry, who stand in antagonistic
contradiction to the capitalists and are ranged in struggle
against them.

We have approached this question after three years of
struggle, with experience in the exercise of the political
power of the proletariat, and knowledge of the enormous
difficulties existing in the relationships between classes,
which are still there, and with remnants of the bourgeoisie
filling the cracks and crevices of our social fabric, and holding office in Soviet institutions. In the circumstances the
appearance of a platform containing the theses I have read
to you is a clear and obvious syndicalist-anarchist deviation.

That is no exaggeration: I have carefully weighed my words.
A deviation is not yet a full-blown trend. A deviation is
something that can be rectified. People have somewhat
strayed or are beginning to stray from the path, but can still
be put right. That, in my opinion, is what the Russian word
uklon means. It emphasises that there is nothing final in it
as yet, and that the matter can be easily rectified; it shows
a desire to sound a warning and to raise the question on
principle in all its scope. If anyone has a better word to
express this idea, let us have it, by all means. I hope we shall
not start arguing over words. We are essentially examining
this thesis as the main one, so as not to go chasing after a
mass of similar ideas, of which the Workers' Opposition group
has a great many. We will leave our writers, and the leaders
of this trend to go into the matter, for at the end of the
resolution we make a point of saying that special publications
and symposiums can and should give space to a more
comprehensive exchange of opinion between Party members
on all the questions indicated. We cannot now afford to put
off the question. We are a party fighting in acute difficulties.
We must say to ourselves: if our unity is to be more solid,
we must condemn a definite deviation. Since it has come to
light, it should be brought out and discussed. If a comprehensive discussion is necessary, let us have it, by all means;
we have the men to give chapter and verse on every point,
and if we find it relevant and necessary, we shall raise this
question internationally as well, for you all know and have
just heard the delegate of the Communist International say
in his report that there is a certain Leftist deviation in the
ranks of the international revolutionary working-class movement. The deviation we are discussing is identical with the
anarchist deviation of the German Communist Workers'
Party, the fight against which was clearly revealed at the
last Congress of the Communist International.[203] Some of the
terms used there to qualify it were stronger than "deviation".
You know that this is an international question. That is why
it would be wrong to have done with it by saying, "Let's
have no more discussions. Full stop." But a theoretical discussion is one thing, and the Party's political line—a political
struggle—is another. We are not a debating society. Of
course, we are able to publish symposiums and special publi-

cations and will continue to do so but our first duty is to
carry on the fight against great odds, and that needs unity.
If we are to have proposals, like organising an "All-Russia
Congress of Producers", introduced into the political discussion and struggle, we shall be unable to march forward
united and in step. That is not the policy we have projected
over the next few years. It is a policy that would disrupt
the Party's team-work, for it is wrong not only in theory,
but also in its incorrect definition of the relations between
classes—the crucial element which was specified in the resolution of the Second Congress of the Communist International,[204] and without which there is no Marxism. The situation today is such that the non-Party element is yielding to
the petty-bourgeois vacillations which are inevitable in Russia's present economic condition. We must remember that
in some respects the internal situation presents a greater
danger than Denikin and Yudenich; and our unity must not
be formal but must go deep down below the surface. If we
are to create this unity, a resolution like the one proposed is
indispensable.

The next very important thing in my opinion is Point 4
of this resolution, which gives an interpretation of our
Programme. It is an authentic interpretation, that is, the
author's interpretation. Its author is the Congress, and that
is why it must give its interpretation in order to put a stop
to all this wavering, and to the tricks that are sometimes
being played with our Programme, as if what it says about
the trade unions is what some people would like it to say.
You have heard Comrade Ryazanov's criticism of the Programme—let us thank the critic for his theoretical researches.
You have heard Comrade Shlyapnikov's criticism. That is
something we must not ignore. I think that here, in this
resolution, we have exactly what we need just now. We
must say on behalf of the Congress, which endorses the Programme and which is the Party's supreme organ: here is what
we understand the Programme to mean. This, I repeat, does
not cut short theoretical discussion. Proposals to amend the
Programme may be made; no one has suggested that this
should be prohibited. We do not think that our Programme
is so perfect as not to require any modification whatever; but
just now we have no formal proposals, nor have we allocated

any time for the examination of this question. If we read the Programme carefully we shall find the following: "The trade unions ... should eventually arrive at a *de facto* concentration", etc. The words "should eventually arrive at a *de facto* concentration", should be underlined. And a few lines above that we read: "On the strength of the laws ... the trade unions participate in all the local and central organs of industrial management." We know that it took decades to build up capitalist industry, with the assistance of all the advanced countries of the world. Are we so childish as to think that we can complete this process so quickly at this time of dire distress and impoverishment, in a country with a mass of peasants, with workers in a minority, and a proletarian vanguard bleeding and in a state of prostration? We have not even laid the main foundation, we have only begun to give an experimental definition of industrial management with the participation of the trade unions. We know that want is the principal obstacle. It is not true to say that we are not enlisting the masses; on the contrary, we give sincere support to anyone among the mass of workers with the least sign of talent, or ability. All we need is for the conditions to ease off ever so little. We need a year or two, at least, of relief from famine. This is an insignificant period of time in terms of history but in our conditions it is a long one. A year or two of relief from famine, with regular supplies of fuel to keep the factories running, and we shall receive a hundred times more assistance from the working class, and far more talent will arise from its ranks than we now have. No one has or can have any doubts about this. The assistance is not forthcoming at present, but not because we do not want it. In fact, we are doing all we can to get it. No one can say that the government, the trade unions, or the Party's Central Committee have missed a single opportunity to do so. But we know that the want in the country is desperate, that there is hunger and poverty everywhere, and that this very often leads to passivity. Let us not be afraid to call a spade a spade: it is these calamities and evils that are hindering the rise of mass energy. In such a situation, when the statistics tell us that 60 per cent of the members of management boards are workers, it is quite impossible to try to interpret the words in the Programme—"The trade unions ... should eventually arrive at a *de facto* concentration", etc.—*à la* Shlyapnikov.

An authentic interpretation of the Programme will enable us to combine the necessary tactical solidarity and unity with the necessary freedom of discussion, and this is emphasised at the end of the resolution. What does it say in essence? Point 6 reads:

"In view of all this, the Congress of the R.C.P., emphatically rejecting the said ideas, as being expressive of a syndicalist and anarchist deviation, deems it necessary, first, to wage an unswerving and systematic struggle against these ideas; secondly, to recognise the propaganda of these ideas as being incompatible with membership of the R.C.P.

"Instructing the C.C. of the Party strictly to enforce these decisions, the Congress at the same time points out that special publications, symposiums, etc., can and should provide space for a most comprehensive exchange of opinion between Party members on all the questions herein indicated."

Do you not see—you all who are agitators and propagandists in one way or another—the difference between the propaganda of ideas within political parties engaged in struggle, and the exchange of opinion in special publications and symposiums? I am sure that everyone who takes the trouble to understand this resolution will see the difference. And we hope that the representatives of this deviation whom we are taking into the Central Committee will treat the decisions of the Party Congress as every class-conscious disciplined Party member does. We hope that with their assistance we, in the Central Committee, shall look into this matter, without creating a special situation. We shall investigate and decide what it is that is going on in the Party—whether it is the propaganda of ideas within a political party engaged in struggle, or the exchange of opinion in special publications and symposiums. There is the opportunity for anyone interested in a meticulous study of quotations from Engels. We have theoreticians who can always give the Party useful advice. That is necessary. We shall publish two or three big collections—that is useful and absolutely necessary. But is this anything like the propaganda of ideas, or a conflict of platforms? How can these two things be confused? They will not be confused by anyone who desires to understand our political situation.

Do not hinder our political work, especially in a difficult situation, but go on with your scientific research. We shall be very happy to see Comrade Shlyapnikov supplement his recent book on his experiences in the underground revolutionary struggle with a second volume written in his spare time over the next few months and analysing the concept of "producer". But the present resolution will serve as our landmark. We opened the widest and freest discussion. The platform of the Workers' Opposition was published in the central organ of the Party in 250,000 copies. We have weighed it up from all sides, we have elected delegates on its basis, and finally we have convened this Congress, which, summing up the political discussion, says: "The deviation has come to light, we shall not play hide-and-seek, but shall say openly: a deviation is a deviation and must be straightened out. We shall straighten it out, and the discussion will be a theoretical one."

That is why I renew and support the proposal that we adopt both these resolutions, consolidate the unity of the Party, and give a correct definition to what should be dealt with by Party meetings, and what individuals—Marxists, Communists who want to help the Party by looking into theoretical questions—are free to study in their spare time.

Pravda No. 68,
March 30, 1921

V. I. Lenin,
Collected Works,
Vol. 32, pp. 249-56

From A LETTER TO THE GERMAN COMMUNISTS

... The difficult position of the Communist Party of Germany is aggravated at the present moment by the breakaway of the not very good Communists on the left (the Communist Workers' Party of Germany, K.A P.D.) and on the right (Paul Levi and his little magazine *Unser Weg* or *Sowjet*).

Beginning with the Second Congress of the Communist International, the "Leftists" or "K.A.P.-ists" have received sufficient warning from us in the international arena. Until sufficiently strong, experienced and influential Communist Parties have been built, at least in the principal countries, the participation of semi-anarchist elements in our international congresses has to be tolerated, and is to some extent even useful. It is useful insofar as these elements serve as a clear "warning" to inexperienced Communists, and also insofar as they themselves are still capable of learning. All over the world, anarchism has been splitting up—not since yesterday, but since the beginning of the imperialist war of 1914-18—into two trends: one pro-Soviet, and the other anti-Soviet; one in favour of the dictatorship of the proletariat, and the other against it. We must allow this process of disintegration among the anarchists to go on and come to a head. Hardly anyone in Western Europe has experienced anything like a big revolution. There, the experience of great revolutions has been almost entirely forgotten, and the

transition from the desire to be revolutionary and from talk
(and resolutions) about revolution to real revolutionary work
is very difficult, painful and slow.

It goes without saying, however, that the semi-anarchist
elements can and should be tolerated only within certain
limits. In Germany, we tolerated them for quite a long time.
The Third Congress of the Communist International[205]
faced them with an ultimatum and fixed a definite time limit.
If they have now voluntarily resigned from the Communist
International, all the better. Firstly, they have saved us the
trouble of expelling them. Secondly, it has now been demonstrated most conclusively and most graphically, and proved
with precise facts to all vacillating workers, and all those
who have been inclined towards anarchism because of their
hatred for the opportunism of the old Social-Democrats, that
the Communist International has been patient, that it has
not expelled anarchists immediately and unconditionally,
and that it has given them an attentive hearing and helped
them to learn.

We must now pay less attention to the K.A.P.-ists. By
polemising with them we merely give them publicity. They
are too unintelligent; it is wrong to take them seriously; and
it is not worth being angry with them. They have no influence among the masses, and will acquire none, unless we
make mistakes. Let us leave this tiny trend to die a natural
death; the workers themselves will realise that it is worth-
less. Let us propagate and implement, with greater effect,
the organisational and tactical decisions of the Third
Congress of the Communist International, instead of giving
the K.A.P.-ists publicity by arguing with them. The infantile disorder of "Leftism" is passing and will pass away as
the movement grows.

Written August 14, 1921

Published in German in
the newspaper *Die Rote Fahne*
No. 384, August 22, 1921

Published in Russian in
*The Bulletin of the Executive
Committee of the Communist
International* No. 3

V. I. Lenin,
Collected Works,
Vol. 32, pp. 514-15

NOTES

[1] The essay, which Engels left unfinished, was intended for the fifth issue of the *Neue Rheinische Zeitung. Politisch-ökonomische Revue.* It was prompted by individualistic and anarchistic articles written by Eduard Meyen, Julius Faucher, Ludwig Buhl and Max Stirner. These Young Hegelians were since 1842 members of the group "The Free" in Berlin, and since the early fifties they centred around the newspaper *Abend-Post.* Rejection of universal suffrage and parliamentary representation together with extreme individualism and the glorification of anarchy as the embodiment of a "superior democracy" and "free association of men" were characteristic features of their political views. The *Abend-Post* systematically attacked "the law-abiding people within the ranks of democracy" as well as socialism, communism and the "terror of the revolution". These anarchistic and semi-anarchistic ideas became fairly widespread among a section of the petty-bourgeois German emigrants.   p. 27

[2] This passage is taken from the review by Marx and Engels of *Le socialisme et l'impôt.* Par Emile de Girardin, Paris 1850 (See Marx/Engels, *Werke*, Band 7, Berlin 1960, pp. 288/289).   p. 27

[3] Engels presumably alludes to Karl Grün and Arnold Ruge, who translated some of Proudhon's works into German and publicised them in the press.   p. 28

[4] In 1850 Ludwig Simon and Karl Vogt (both were members of the Stuttgart Parliament, and Vogt was also one of the five Imperial Regents) published articles in the *Deutsche Monatsschrift* (Stuttgart), in which they extolled anarchy and advocated the abolition of all state institutions.   p. 28

[5] The French revolution of February 1848.   p. 28

[6] A reference to the uprisings of March 1848, which took place in many German states and initiated the German revolution of 1848 and 1849.   p. 28

[7] In the review of Girardin's book mentioned in Note 2.   p. 29

[8] From Wieland's poem *Oberon*.   p. 29

[9] Published in Paris in 1851.   p. 32

[10] The Mountain (*La Montagne*), a name given to a group of revolutionary democrats during the French Revolution who were linked with
the Jacobin club and sat on the highest benches in the National
Convention.   p. 32

[11] Pierre Joseph Proudhon, *Idée générale de la révolution au XIXe
siècle*, Paris 1851.   p. 39

[12] *Neue Preussische Zeitung* (also known as *Kreuz-Zeitung*)—German
daily published in Berlin from June 1848; organ of the reactionary
court camarilla and the Prussian landed aristocracy.   p. 40

[13] *Manifesto of the Communist Party* by Karl Marx and Frederick
Engels.   p. 40

[14] *Die Klassenkämpfe in Frankreich 1848 bis 1850*, published in the *Neue
Rheinische Zeitung. Politisch-ökonomische Revue* in 1850.   p. 40

[15] *Misère de la philosophie. Réponse à la philosophie de la misère de
M. Proudhon*. Par Karl Marx, Paris 1847.   p. 40

[16] The General Council of the International discussed the Austro-
Prussian War of 1866 at its meetings on June 19 and 26 and on
July 17, 1866. Finally the following amended resolution was passed
unanimously:
      "That the Central Council of the International Working Men's
Association consider the present conflict on the Continent to be one
between Governments and advise working men to be neutral, and
to associate themselves with a view to acquire strength by unity and
to use the strength so acquired in working out their social and political emancipation." (See *The General Council of the First International 1864-1866, The London Conference, 1865, Minutes*, Moscow,
p. 213.)   p. 41

[17] *Model phalanstery* (Phalanstère modèle)—name given to the utopian
socialist communities described by Fourier.   p. 41

[18] *Congress at Geneva*—the first Congress of the International Working
Men's Association, which met from September 3 to 8, 1866. The 60
delegates present represented the General Council and various sections
of the International and workers' associations in Britain, France,
Germany and Switzerland. The "Instructions for the Delegates of the
Provisional General Council", which was regarded as the official
report of the Council, was written by Marx. The Proudhonists, who
comprised nearly a third of the delegates, opposed their own
programme to the Council's official report. Nevertheless six of the
nine points listed by Marx in the "Instructions" were incorporated
in the resolutions passed by the Congress, i.e., on international co-
ordination of efforts, limitation of the working day, juvenile and
children's labour (both sexes), co-operative labour, trade unions and
standing armies. A compromise resolution on the Polish question

moved by Johann Philipp Becker was adopted. The Congress also
endorsed the "Rules and Administrative Regulations of the International Working Men's Association".   p. 43

[19] "The abolition of the right of inheritance" was demanded by various
followers of Saint-Simon. This demand was clearly formulated by
Saint Amand Bazard in his book *Doctrine de Saint-Simon. Première
année. Exposition. 1829.* Paris 1830, pp. 143-169.   p. 45

[20] The police seized this letter of Engels when Cafiero was arrested in
August 1871. The letter, which was written in English, was translated
into Italian by the police and filed with other documents relating
to the Neapolitan Section of the International. The following note
was found on the Italian version: "Letter written by Engels, seized
from Mr. Carlo Cafiero. Translation from the English. Copy."
  The copy was found in 1946 by the Italian historian Aldo Romano
among documents of the prefecture in the government archives at
Naples. Engels's original letter has not been traced.   p. 47

[21] Following the report about the defeat of the French army at Sedan,
a revolt broke out in Lyons on September 4, 1870. Bakunin, who
arrived in the city on September 15, attempted to seize the leadership
of the uprising and to put his anarchistic programme into practice,
but failed because he had no connections with the proletariat and
lacked a definite plan of action.   p. 47

[22] *The International Alliance of Socialist Democracy* (L'Alliance
internationale de la démocratie socialiste) was founded by Bakunin
in Geneva in October 1868. A detailed account of the activities of
this organisation is given in the pamphlet *L'Alliance de la démocratie
socialiste et l'Association internationale des travailleurs* written by
Marx and Engels and published in 1873.   p. 48

[23] The Franco-Prussian war and afterwards the persecutions of members
of the International made it impossible to hold the annual Congress
of the International; a Conference was therefore organised in London
from September 17 to 23, 1871, to deal with urgent matters.   p. 51

[24] On September 20, 1871, at the sixth meeting of the London Conference
Vaillant tabled a motion which stressed that political and social
problems were closely linked and that it was necessary to unite the
forces of the workers on a political basis. Marx and Engels (see
pp. 51-52 of this volume) who spoke during the discussion supported
this motion. The Conference instructed the General Council to draw
up the final version of the resolution, and on October 7, 1871, a
special committee was set up for this purpose of which Engels was
a member.
  The main part of the resolution was later incorporated (as Article
7a) in the General Rules of the International Working Men's Association by decision of the Hague Congress of 1872. (See p. 83 of
this volume.)   p. 53

[25] See "General Rules and Administrative Regulations of the International Working Men's Association". In: *The General Council of the
First International 1870-1871, Minutes,* Moscow, p. 451.   p. 53

[26] See "Inaugural Address of the Working Men's International Association". In: *The General Council of the First International 1864-1866, Minutes,* Moscow, p. 286.   p. 53

[27] See *Procès-verbaux du congrès de l'Association Internationale des Travailleurs réuni à Lausanne du 2 au 8 septembre 1867,* Chaux-de-Fonds 1867, p. 19.   p. 53

[28] This refers to the plebiscite held on May 8, 1870, by Napoleon III in an effort to strengthen his shaky position. The demagogical manoeuvre of the government was exposed in a manifesto issued on April 24, 1870, by the Paris Federation of the International which called upon the workers to refrain from voting.

The members of the Paris Federation were arrested on the eve of the plebiscite and accused of plotting to assassinate Napoleon III. The trial, which took place from June 22 to July 5, 1870, showed that the accusation was completely unfounded.

See *The General Council of the First International 1868-1870, Minutes,* pp. 231-232.   p. 53

[29] Marx refers to the following resolutions passed by the London Conference of the International in September 1871: "Political Action of the Working Class" (IX) (see pp. 53-54 of this volume), "Alliance de la démocratie socialiste" (The Alliance of Socialist Democracy) (XVI), "Split in the French-Speaking Part of Switzerland" (XVII) and presumably to points 1, 2 and 3 of Resolution II, "Designations of National Councils, etc.".   p. 56

[30] Following the news of the defeat of the French army at Sedan, mass demonstrations took place in Paris on September 4, 1870, leading to the downfall of the Second Empire and the proclamation of a republic. The newly formed government, however, contained monarchists as well as moderate republicans. The policy of this government, which was headed by Trochu, the Military Governor of Paris, and strongly influenced by Thiers, reflected the defeatist sentiments current among the French bourgeois and landowning strata and their fear of the masses and led to national betrayal and to a deal with a hostile foreign power.   p. 57

[31] The Basle Congress of the International Working Men's Association was held from September 6 to 11, 1869. Among other things, the Congress voted a number of decisions designed to strengthen the organisation of the International and to extend the powers of the General Council.   p. 58

[32] This article is a reply to the "Circulaire à toutes les fédérations de l'Association Internationale des Travailleurs" (Circular to All Federations of the International Working Men's Association) which was adopted by the Sonvillier Congress (in November 1871) of the Bakuninist Swiss Jura Federation. Among the numerous organisations of the International who rejected the Sonvillier circular were the German, British, Dutch and United States sections and also that of Milan. A number of Spanish sections which were influenced by Bakunin were not prepared to agree openly with the circular.   p. 60

[33] The revolutionary actions of 1870 and 1871.   p. 60

[34] The London Conference of the I.W.A. which was held from September
17 to 23, 1871. (See also Note 23.)   p. 61

[35] Versailles was the seat of the Thiers Government which fought and
defeated the Paris Commune and subsequently killed many thousands
of Communards.   p. 62

[36] *Brunswick criminal court*—five members of the Brunswick Committee
of the Social-Democratic Workers' Party, i.e., Bracke, Bonhorst, Spier,
Kühn and Gralle, as well as the printer Sievers, were tried at the
Brunswick district court in October 1871.
    They were arrested on September 9, 1870, for issuing a manifesto
addressed to the German working class in which they called upon
it to prevent the annexation of Alsace and Lorraine and to bring
about an honourable peace with the French Republic. They were
sentenced to various terms of imprisonment.   p. 63

[37] *Black cabinet* (Cabinet noir)—a secret office set up by Louis XIV in
France to enable the authorities to inspect the correspondence of
the citizens. Similar institutions existed in Prussia, Austria and
other European states.   p. 63

[38] The Sonvillier Circular.   p. 67

[39] The London Conference of the I.W.A. held in September 1871. p. 67

[40] This refers to the Congress held by the bourgeois pacifist League for
Peace and Freedom in Berne in September 1868, which Bakunin
tried to persuade to accept his muddled socialist programme aimed
at the "social and economic equalisation of classes", the abolition of
the State and of the right of inheritance, etc. When the majority
rejected his plan he quitted the League and set up the International
Alliance of Socialist Democracy.   p. 69

[41] This refers to the resolutions adopted at the Fourth Congress of the
I.W.A. which was held in Basle in September 1869.   p. 70

[42] The circular gives a detailed account of the disruptive activities of
the International Alliance of Socialist Democracy. This organisation,
which was headed by Bakunin, intensified its efforts to bring about
a split in the International especially after the London Conference
of the I.W.A. held in September 1871.
    The circular was printed in French and sent to all sections of the
International.   p. 72

[43] The name is derived from Icarie, a utopian country described by
Etienne Cabet in his book *Voyage en Icarie*.   p. 72

[44] Jules Favre's circular of May 26, 1871, instructed the diplomatic
representatives of France abroad to request European governments
to treat Communards who had emigrated as ordinary criminals and
have them arrested and extradited.
    Dufaure moved a Bill drafted by an *ad hoc* committee of the
French National Assembly making membership of the International

punishable by imprisonment. The Bill was passed by the Assembly
on March 14, 1872. p. 73

[45] Engels refers to the Congress of the Bakuninist Swiss Jura Federation
held in Sonvillier on November 12, 1871. p. 75

[46] See Karl Marx, "Inaugural Address of the Working Men's International Association". In: *The General Council of the First International
1864-1866, Minutes*, Moscow, pp. 277-287. p. 75

[47] François Sacase's report was made on February 5, 1872. p. 77

[48] Letters to Cafiero written by Engels in the autumn of 1871 were
indeed handed over by Cafiero to James Guillaume, the editor of
the *Bulletin de la Fédération jurassienne.* p. 78

[49] In connection with the preparations for the Hague Congress it became
especially important to expose the disruptive activities of the Alliance
of Socialist Democracy.
At the meeting of the Sub-Committee of the General Council
on July 5, 1872, at which documents relating to the clandestine
activity of the Alliance were discussed, it was decided that the
General Council should be asked to propose to the next congress
the expulsion of Bakunin and the other members of the Alliance.
Marx and Engels were requested to edit the observations made during the discussion and submit them to the General Council. On
August 6, 1872, at the General Council meeting, Engels read the
report of the Sub-Committee on the Alliance. A spirited discussion
ensued, during which several Council members objected to its
publication before the case of the Alliance had been examined.
According to the Minutes: "the Chairman proposed that the report
of the Sub-Committee as read by Citizen Engels be accepted, which
was declared to be carried by twelve votes for and eight votes
against."
There exists a French and English version of the Draft Address
in Engels's handwriting. p. 80

[50] *The Hague Congress of the International Working Men's Association*
met from September 2 to 7, 1872. It was attended by 65 delegates
from 15 national organisations.
The official text of the resolutions was drawn up by Marx and
Engels, who were members of the committee set up to prepare the
resolutions for publication.
Engels's manuscript containing the final text of all resolutions in
French has been preserved. p. 83

[51] After the Hague Congress of the I.W.A. Marx and other delegates
went to Amsterdam to meet the local section of the International. At
a meeting held on September 8, 1872, Marx delivered a speech in
German and French. Dutch, Belgian, French and German newspapers
published reports of this speech which they had received from their
correspondents. The speech was most fully reported in the Belgian
and French newspapers, and the texts were identical. p. 84

[52] This refers to the mandates given to the delegates representing the Jura Federation at the Hague Congress of the I.W.A. in 1872. p. 86

[53] *La Federación*—a Spanish weekly, organ of the Barcelona Federation of the International, published from 1869 to 1873; it was strongly influenced by the Bakuninists. p. 86

[54] Engels's work *The Housing Question* consists of a series of articles, which were first published in the Social-Democratic paper *Der Volksstaat* and then reissued in pamphlet form in 1873. A second revised edition was published in Switzerland in 1887. p. 88

[55] *Blanquists*—followers of a trend in the French socialist movement headed by Louis Auguste Blanqui (1805-1881), outstanding revolutionary and spokesman of utopian communism.
   Lenin wrote that the Blanquists expected "that mankind will be emancipated from wage slavery, not by the proletarian class struggle, but through a conspiracy hatched by a small minority of intellectuals" (see V. I. Lenin, *Collected Works*, Vol. 10, p. 392). They abandoned action by a revolutionary party in favour of activities by a handful of conspirators, failed to take into account the concrete situation for a successful uprising and neglected to establish links with the masses. p. 90

[56] G. Hegel, *Wissenschaft der Logik*, Th. 1, Abt. 2. In: *Werke*. Vollst. Ausg. durch einen Verein von Freunden des Verewigten. Bd. 4-5. Berlin 1834, S. 15, 75, 145. p. 90

[57] Mülberger's articles, published in the beginning of 1872 in the *Volksstaat*, were later reissued as a booklet under the title: A. Mülberger, *Die Wohnungsfrage. Eine soziale Skizze*, Leipzig 1872. p. 93

[58] Engels paraphrases a line from Dante's *Divina commedia* (see Dante, *The Divine Comedy*, Hell, Song III, Verse 3). p. 102

[59] This report was written in French by Marx and Engels in collaboration with Lafargue between April and July 1873. It was first published as a booklet under the title *L'Alliance de la démocratie socialiste et l'Association internationale des travailleurs*, Londres, Hambourg 1873. p. 105

[60] Among the documents relating to the activities of the secret Alliance which Marx and Engels submitted to the Hague Congress of the I.W.A. was a letter by Nechayev written in February 1870. The letter, which was addressed to Lyubavin, was written on Bakunin's instructions and in the name of a non-existent Russian revolutionary organisation. It threatened Lyubavin, who was making arrangements for the publication of the first volume of Marx's *Capital* in Russia, with retaliatory measures, if he did not release Bakunin from his obligations with regard to the Russian translation of Volume One of *Capital*. In August 1872 the letter was sent by Lyubavin via Danielson to Marx. p. 105

[61] An allusion to the Congress of the League for Peace and Freedom. p. 106

[62] This is a quotation from the anonymous article "Noch einiges über Bakunin", which was published in *Tagwacht* No. 40, October 5, 1872.

p. 107

[63] The Programme was published in Section XI of this work. p. 107

[64] There were three grades of membership in the Alliance: I. International Brothers; II. National Brothers; III. The partly secret, partly public organisation of the International Alliance of Socialist Democracy.

The International Brothers comprised a relatively small number of "initiates", to whom members of the other two grades were subordinated. p. 108

[65] See note 21. p. 108

[66] Large student demonstrations took place in many universities, especially in Petersburg and Moscow, against new university regulations issued by the government in 1861. The student movement, which reached unprecedented dimensions, was suppressed, many students were arrested and either put into prison or banished to Siberia.

p. 112

[67] *Ignorantines*—a name given to members of a religious order founded in Rheims in 1680. It was the duty of its members to teach the children of the poor, but the children received mainly religious instruction and had an extremely meagre knowledge of any other subject. p. 113

[68] This and the following quotations are from Bakunin's leaflets "Postanovka revolutsionnogo voprosa" (Statement of the Revolutionary Issue) and "Nachala revolutsii" (Revolutionary Principles), both published in 1869. p. 113

[69] *Izdaniya obshchestva "Narodnoi raspravy"* No. 2 (Issue No. 2, published by Narodnaya Rasprava), St. Petersburg, 1870, p. 9. Issue No. 2, like that of No. 1, was printed in Geneva. p. 116

[70] The article was written by Nechayev and published in *Izdaniya obshchestva "Narodnoi raspravy"* No. 2. p. 118

[71] A reference to the theocratic state set up by the Jesuits in South America in the sixteenth and seventeenth centuries; it was mainly situated in what is now Paraguay. p. 120

[72] Two of the dates in the Prefatory Note are incorrect, i.e., the republic was proclaimed on February 11, not February 12, 1873, and the elections to the Constituent Assembly took place on May 10, not April 10, 1873. p. 126

[73] *The New Madrid Federation* was founded on July 8, 1872, by the editors of the weekly *La Emancipación* who had been expelled from the Madrid Federation by the anarchist majority on account of articles published in *La Emancipación* which exposed the activities of the Bakuninist Alliance in Spain. p. 128

[74] The Congress of the I.W.A. held in Geneva from September 8 to 13, 1873.   p. 128

[75] Engels refers to the Alliance of Socialist Democracy. For details about this organisation see *The Alliance of Socialist Democracy and the International Working Men's Association* (see pp. 105-122 of this volume and Note 22).   p. 128

[76] A reference to the constitutional monarchists who supported King Amadeo, a protégé of the great European powers.   p. 130

[77] *Alfonsists*—a group connected with the reactionary strata of big landowners, the clergy and the big bourgeoisie. It supported the Bourbon pretender to the Spanish throne, who under the name of Alfonso XII became king in 1874.   p. 130

[78] *Carlists*—a clerical absolutist group, partisans of Don Carlos (1788-1855) who claimed the Spanish throne on the death of his brother Ferdinand VII. Backed by the military and the Catholic clergy and supported by the backward peasants in some parts of the country, the Carlists started a civil war, which lasted from 1833 to 1840, and virtually became a fight between feudal Catholic elements and bourgeois liberals. After the death of Don Carlos the Carlists supported the claims of his descendants. In 1872 during the political crisis and the intensification of the class struggle, the Carlists again became more active and a new civil war broke out, which ended only in 1876.   p. 130

[79] See Frederick Engels, *The Condition of the Working-Class in England.* In: Karl Marx and Frederick Engels, *On Britain*, Moscow 1962.   p. 132

[80] The Congress of the anarchists held in Geneva from September 1 to 6, 1873.   p. 132

[81] *Solidarité révolutionnaire*—an anarchist weekly published in French in Barcelona from June to September 1873. It was the organ of the Revolutionary Socialist Propaganda Committee for Southern France, which was set up by Alerini and Brousse, to advocate anarchist ideas in France and among the Communard emigrants.   p. 134

[82] *General Association of German Workers*—the first national organisation of German workers, founded at the Congress of Workers' Organisations held in Leipzig in 1863. The Association was from the outset strongly influenced by Lassalle, who was its first Chairman. Its principal aims were struggle for universal suffrage and peaceful parliamentary activities.   p. 134

[83] After the Cordoba Congress of 1872 the anarchist organisations in Spain were headed by the Federal Commission, whose report was published in *L'Internationale* of August 24, 1873.   p. 134

[84] Shakespeare, *King Henry IV*, Part I, Act V, Scene 4.   p. 135

[85] A reference to the peasant war in Germany (1524 to 1525).   p. 140

[86] See Frederick Engels, *Der deutsche Bauernkrieg* (*The Peasant War in Germany*) and *Die deutsche Reichsverfassungskampagne.*   p. 140

[87] *Lettres à un français sur la crise actuelle.* Neuchâtel 1870. The pamphlet was published anonymously by Bakunin.   p. 140

[88] Marx began precising Bakunin's *Gosudarstvennost i anarkhiya* (Geneva 1873) soon after the publication of the book. The conspectus is part of a large notebook called by Marx "Russica II, 1875", containing synopses of various works of Russian writers.   p. 147

[89] The Free People's State was a slogan of the German Social-Democrats in the seventies. For a Marxist criticism of this slogan see Engels's letter to Bebel of March 18-28, 1875 (p. 153 of this volume), also Marx, *Critique of the Gotha Programme* (Section IV) and Lenin, *The State and Revolution,* Chapter I, Section 4, and Chapter IV, Section 3 (pp. 270-285 of this volume).   p. 152

[90] Karl Marx, *Misère de la philosophie. Réponse à la philosophie de la misère de M. Proudhon.* Paris 1847. See Karl Marx, *The Poverty of Philosophy. Answer to the "Philosophy of Poverty" by M. Proudhon,* Moscow 1962.   p. 153

[91] *Manifest der Kommunistischen Partei.* London 1848. See Karl Marx and Frederick Engels, *Manifesto of the Communist Party,* Moscow 1969.   p. 153

[92] This is a reference to the German translation of *L'Alliance de la démocratie socialiste et l'Association internationale des travailleurs* by Marx and Engels; see this volume, pp. 105-122.   p. 154

[93] This and the quotations following it are from Bakunin's letter to Francisco Mora, the Spanish socialist, written on April 5, 1872. It was published together with other documents in Section XI of *L'Alliance de la démocratie socialiste et l'Association internationale des travailleurs* by Marx and Engels.   p. 154

[94] Heinrich Heine, "Junge Leiden", a poem published in *Buch der Lieder.*   p. 155

[95] *La Plebe*—Italian paper, which was edited by Enrico Bignami and published in Lodi from 1868 to 1875 and in Milan from 1875 to 1883. Engels contributed to its columns from 1871 to 1873 and from 1877 to 1879 and corresponded regularly with Bignami.   p. 156

[96] *Bulletin de la Fédération jurassienne de l'Association internationale des travailleurs*—organ of the Swiss anarchists, published in French in Sonvillier from 1872 to 1878; its editor was Guillaume.   p. 157

[97] The 12 candidates of the Socialist Workers' Party elected to the German Reichstag on January 10, 1877, received nearly 500,000 votes.   p. 159

[98] It was prepared by the Italian Committee of Social Revolution, a Bakuninist organisation. A few days before the date fixed for the rising its chief organiser A. Kosta was arrested. This forced the conspirators headed by Bakunin to speed up their preparations.

On August 7, 1874, leaflets of the Committee were distributed in Bologna calling upon the people to take up arms and overthrow the existing social order. The insurrection was to have taken place that night, but only a small armed force rose in Bologna and several other Italian towns. These were quickly disarmed by the government troops, and Bakunin himself fled the country.   p. 160

[99] In 1877 the anarchists seized Letino, a small town, but the rising was quickly put down by the police.   p. 160

[100] The socialist Congress held at Ghent from September 9 to 16, 1877, was an attempt to unite the various socialist movements throughout the world.   p. 161

[101] This refers to the New Madrid Federation. See Note 73.   p. 162

[102] *O Protesto*—a Portuguese socialist weekly founded in Lisbon in 1875.   p. 163

[103] The reference is to the *Narodna Volya* which was published in Smederevo (Serbia) from October 1875 to June 1876.   p. 166

[104] The miners of Montceau-les-Mines went on strike in August 1882. A number of incidents were provoked at the time by anarchists the blame for which was put on the miners. The workers were tried in October 1882 but had to be acquitted.   p. 170

[105] *The Central Labour Union in New York*—a federation of the New York labour unions which came into being in 1882 and grew into a workers' mass organisation in the eighties. It united within its ranks workers of American and foreign descent, both white and coloured. It was headed by socialists who realised that the working class needed both trade and political organisations to wage successfully the proletarian class struggle.   p. 171

[106] Engels replied in English.   p. 171

[107] Already in *The German Ideology*, written between 1845 and 1846, Marx and Engels described the role of the State as an instrument in the hands of the ruling class.   p. 172

[108] *Freiheit*—a German weekly of an anarchist trend, founded by Johann Most in London early in 1879. It was published from 1879 to 1882 in London, in 1882 in Switzerland, and from 1882 to 1908 in New York. Marx and Engels repeatedly criticised the anarchist ideas of Most and the paper he edited.   p. 173

[109] See Note 73.   p. 176

[110] The *Katheder-Socialists* represented a trend in bourgeois sociology and economics, which arose in Germany towards the end of the nineteenth century. From university chairs (called "Katheder" in German) the Katheder-Socialists (for example, Adolf Wagner, Gustav Schmoller, Lujo Brentano and Werner Sombart) advocated bourgeois reformism under the guise of socialism. They maintained that the State was a supra-class institution capable of reconciling the

hostile classes and gradually introducing "socialism" without infringing upon the interests of the capitalists.   p. 177

111 The Anti-Socialist Law was promulgated in Germany on October 21, 1878. This law banned all organisations of the Social-Democratic Party, all workers' mass organisations and the labour press; socialist literature was confiscated and many Social-Democrats were persecuted. Under pressure of the mass working-class movement the Anti-Socialist Law was abolished in 1890.   p. 177

112 Max Stirner, *Der Einzige und sein Eigenthum*, Leipzig 1845.   p. 179

113 To complete his commercial training Engels worked in Manchester from November 1842 to August 1844. During this period Engels's views developed rapidly. He passed from philosophical idealism to materialism and from revolutionary democratism to communism.
                                                          p. 179

114 In Brussels in 1845 and 1846 Marx and Engels wrote: *Die deutsche Ideologie. Kritik der neuesten deutschen Philosophie in ihren Repräsentanten Feuerbach, B. Bauer und Stirner, und des deutschen Sozialismus in seinen verschiedenen Propheten.* See Karl Marx and Frederick Engels, *The German Ideology*, Moscow 1968.   p. 179

115 Max Stirner's "rebellion" theory is examined by Marx and Engels in the section entitled Rebellion, Chapter III. Saint Max, of the *German Ideology* (pp. 411-425 of the English edition).   p. 179

116 *The Second International Socialist Workers' Congress* was held in Brussels from August 16 to 22, 1891. The Congress was attended by 337 delegates—in the main Marxists—from many European countries and the U.S.A. The anarchists who had come to attend the Congress were excluded from its deliberations by a majority vote.
    The items on the agenda included labour legislation, strikes, boycotts, militarism (which was the main question) and May Day celebrations.
    Domela Nieuwenhuis, a Dutch delegate who led the semi-anarchist elements within the Second International, spoke vehemently against the resolution on militarism and the fight against war tabled by Liebknecht, but the vast majority of delegates voted for Liebknecht's resolution.   p. 180

117 Engels refers to anarchist assaults in Spain which began in 1889 when a bomb exploded in the royal palace; similar incidents occurred in various parts of Spain during the following years.   p. 181

118 *Iskra*, founded by Lenin in 1900 as the organ of the R.S.D.L.P., was published abroad and distributed illegally in Russia. It played a decisive role in the formation of a revolutionary Marxist working-class party in Russia. After the Second Congress of the R.S.D.L.P. the Mensheviks gained control of *Iskra* and in October 1903 it became a Menshevik mouthpiece.
    Lenin here refers to the Menshevik *Iskra*, also known as the "new *Iskra*".   p. 187

[119] *Uperyod*—an illegal Bolshevik weekly, published in Geneva from December 22, 1904 (January 4, 1905) to May 5 (May 18), 1905. p. 187

[120] *Millerandism*—an opportunist trend in Social-Democracy so called after Alexandre Millerand, the French Socialist, who in 1899 became a minister in the reactionary bourgeois government of France and supported its unpopular policy.   p. 199

[121] The *Socialist-Revolutionaries* were a petty-bourgeois party which arose in Russia at the end of 1901 and beginning of 1902. The Socialist-Revolutionaries stood for the abolition of private ownership of land and the transfer of the land to village communes based on equalised tenure. Although they called themselves socialists, their programme was not really a socialist one, since capitalist exploitation cannot be done away with unless the proletariat seizes power and takes over control of the principal means of production—the big enterprises, railways and banks—in addition to the land. The S.R.s failed to perceive the class difference between the proletariat and the peasantry, they sought to play down the class stratification and contradictions existing within the peasantry, i.e., between the working peasants and the kulaks, and denied the leading role of the proletariat in the revolution. Their policy was characterised by adventurism in politics and individual terrorism adopted by them as the main weapon in the struggle with tsarism.

After the February Revolution of 1917, the S.R.s together with the Mensheviks were the mainstay of the bourgeois Provisional Government, and some of their leaders became members of this Government. The S.R.s refused to support the peasants' demand for the abolition of landlordism and as members of the Provisional Government they organised punitive actions against peasants who had seized land belonging to the landowners.

The S.R.s fought against the Soviet government during the foreign intervention and the civil war in Russia.   p. 200

[122] *Narodism*—a petty-bourgeois trend which came into being in the Russian revolutionary movement in the sixties and seventies of the last century. The Narodniks stood for the abolition of the autocracy and the transfer of the landowners' land to the peasants. They denied the necessity of capitalist development in Russia, and accordingly regarded the peasantry, and not the proletariat, as the principal revolutionary force, and the village commune as the embryo of socialism. The Narodniks therefore went into the villages, "among the people" (the term "Narodnik" is derived from "narod", people) to rouse the peasants to fight the autocracy, but they found little support among the masses.

Narodism passed through various stages, from revolutionary democratism to liberalism. In the 80s and 90s of the nineteenth century the Narodniks gave up the struggle for the revolutionary overthrow of tsarism, became reformists and fought against the Marxists.   p. 202

[123] Lenin refers to the St. Petersburg Soviet of Workers' Deputies, which was formed as a joint strike committee during the all-Russia

political strike of October 1905. A provisional Executive Committee
of the Soviet was elected on October 17 (30), 1905.   p. 203

124 *Cadets*—members of the Constitutional-Democratic Party, the main
party of the liberal-monarchist bourgeoisie in Russia. It was founded
in October 1905 and its membership was made up of the bourgeoisie,
landowners and bourgeois intellectuals. Although the Cadets called
themselves "the party of people's freedom", they virtually went no
further than a demand for a constitutional monarchy; during the
First World War they supported the expansionist foreign policy of
the tsarist government. During the February bourgeois-democratic
revolution they tried to save the monarchy, and in the Provisional
Government pursued a counter-revolutionary policy.

After the victory of the October Revolution the Cadets participated in armed counter-revolutionary actions against Soviet Russia
and supported the foreign intervention.   p. 205

125 *The Party of Law and Order*—a counter-revolutionary party of the
big commercial and industrial bourgeoisie and the higher bureaucracy,
founded in the autumn of 1905.   p. 205

126 Axelrod and other Mensheviks wanted to organise a congress of
representatives from various workers' organisations in order to set
up a "broad workers' party" which was to include Social-Democrats,
Socialist-Revolutionaries and anarchists. This would have actually
amounted to the dissolution of the R.S.D.L.P. and its replacement
by a non-party organisation.   p. 209

127 In 1907 *Osvobozhdeniye Truda* published a volume of articles, one
of which advocated a "workers' congress."   p. 209

128 The Second Conference of the R.S.D.L.P. (the First All-Russia Conference) was held in Tammerfors. In November 1906, the Conference, at which the Bolsheviks and their supporters were in the
minority, adopted a compromise resolution on the question of
campaigning for a workers' congress.   p. 209

129 Lenin refers to a meeting of St. Petersburg workers organised by the
St. Petersburg Social-Democratic Committee, and a conference of
Central Russian organisations of the Party organised by the Moscow
Social-Democratic Committee. The meeting and the conference passed
resolutions opposing "the workers' congress" advocated by the Mensheviks. The resolutions were published in the illegal Bolshevik
paper *Proletary*, which was edited by Lenin and published from
1906 to 1909.   p. 210

130 Lenin refers to Lunacharsky's pamphlet on the Party's attitude to
the trade unions. It was written in connection with the discussion
of this question at the Seventh, Stuttgart Congress of the Second
International, held from August 18 to 24, 1907, which Lunacharsky,
who was a member of the Russian delegation, attended as a representative of the Bolsheviks. Lenin wrote a preface to the pamphlet
(see this volume, pp 213-15, and V. I. Lenin, *Collected Works*, Vol.
13, pp. 161-68), but owing to the censorship the pamphlet was not
published.   p. 211

[131] *Mensheviks*—a faction in the R.S.D.L.P. It came into being at the Second Congress of the R.S.D.L.P. held in 1903. During the elections to the central organs of the Party the revolutionary Social-Democrats, headed by Lenin, received a majority (in Russian: *bolshinstvo*) of votes at this Congress, and the opportunist wing, headed by Martov, a minority (in Russian: *menshinstvo*). Hence the names Bolsheviks and Mensheviks.

During the first Russian Revolution (1905-1907) the Mensheviks came out against the hegemony of the proletariat in the revolution and against an alliance between the working class and the revolutionary peasants and advocated an agreement with the liberal bourgeoisie. After the defeat of the revolution the majority of Mensheviks demanded that the illegal revolutionary party of the working class should be dissolved and a legal party set up instead which would renounce the revolutionary struggle and adapt itself to the conditions which existed under the reactionary regime. They were called liquidators. These Mensheviks were expelled from the Party at the Sixth (Prague) All-Russia Conference of 1912.

After the February Revolution some of the Mensheviks became members of the Provisional Government and supported its policy. Following the October Revolution the Mensheviks became an openly counter-revolutionary party and took part in plots and uprisings against the Soviet government. p. 211

[132] A reference to the congress of the German Social-Democratic Party held in Essen from September 15 to 21, 1907, at which Bebel criticised Karl Liebknecht, who had denounced Noske's chauvinistic stand and the attitude of the German delegation at the Stuttgart Congress. Bebel also criticised Rosa Luxemburg and the German Left, who at the Stuttgart Congress supported the Bolsheviks in their fight against the social-chauvinists. p. 212

[133] *Obrazovaniye*—a literary monthly magazine published in St. Petersburg from 1892 to 1909. p. 212

[134] *Zarnitsy*—a Bolshevik symposium published in St. Petersburg in 1907. p. 212

[135] *Tovarishch*—a bourgeois daily published in St. Petersburg from March 15 (28), 1906 to December 30, 1907 (January 12, 1908). Virtually the mouthpiece of the "Left" Cadets, it published also contributions from Mensheviks. p. 212

[136] *Bernsteinism*—an anti-Marxist, opportunist trend in international Social-Democracy. It arose in Germany at the end of the nineteenth century. The name is derived from Eduard Bernstein, one of the most outspoken proponents of revisionism. p. 213

[137] *Uademecum for the Editorial Board of Rabocheye Dyelo*—a collection of articles and documents published by the Emancipation of Labour group with a preface by Plekhanov (Geneva, February 1900). It was directed against opportunist trends within the R.S.D.L.P. and especially against the Economism of the Union of Russian Social-Democrats Abroad and their organ *Rabocheye Dyelo*. p. 213

[138] A reference to the armed uprising of the workers in December 1905.   p. 214

[139] Lenin refers to the First Duma (April to July 1906) and the Second Duma (February to June 1907). The Duma was a representative body in tsarist Russia set up as a result of the Revolution of 1905-07. Although it was supposed to be a legislative assembly it had in fact no real power. The Duma was elected on the basis of indirect, unequal and non-universal suffrage. The working classes and the non-Russian nationalities possessed only limited franchise. A large section of workers and peasants had no vote.   p. 214

[140] *Economism*—an opportunist trend among Russian Social-Democrats at the turn of the century. According to the Economists the sole aim of the working class was to wage an economic struggle for higher wages, better working conditions, and so on. Political struggle, they contended, should be left to the liberal bourgeoisie; they denied the leading role of the working class party. Their belief in the spontaneity of the workers' movement led them to underrate the importance of revolutionary theory and to deny that the Marxist party had to impart a socialist consciousness to the workers' movement; they thus opened the door to bourgeois ideologies. By denying the need for a centralised working-class party the Economists defended disunity and amateurish methods within the Social-Democratic movement.   p. 215

[141] The *orthodox*—German Social-Democrats who opposed a revision of Marxism.   p. 216

[142] *Guesdists*—a Marxist trend in the French socialist movement at the turn of the century. It was headed by Jules Guesde and Paul Lafargue. The Socialist Party of France was founded by the Guesdists in 1901. In 1905 they united with the French Socialist Party formed by the Jaurèsists. During the First World War the leaders of the party became social chauvinists.   p. 216

[143] *Jaurèsists*—followers of Jean Jaurès, the French Socialist, who headed the reformist, Right wing of the French socialist movement. The French Socialist Party, which advocated reformists' views, was set up by the Jaurèsists in 1902.   p. 216

[144] *Broussists* or *Possibilists*—a petty-bourgeois, reformist trend which arose in the French socialist movement in the 1880s. The Possibilists, one of whose leaders was Paul Brousse, rejected the revolutionary programme and tactics of the proletariat and wanted to keep the fight of the workers within the bounds of the "possible". Most of them later joined the French Socialist Party.   p. 216

[145] *The Social Democratic Federation* was founded in Britain in 1884. Besides reformists and anarchists it had among its members revolutionary Social-Democrats, Marxists, such as Harry Quelch, Edward Aveling and Eleanor Marx-Aveling, who formed the Left wing of the British Socialist movement.   p. 216

[146] *Independent Labour Party*—founded in Britain in 1893; the party

12*

from the outset took a bourgeois reformist stand and concentrated
mainly on parliamentary forms of struggle.   p. 216

147 The *Integralists* were advocates of an "integral" socialism, a trend
within the Italian Socialist Party. Though on the whole they held
petty-bourgeois socialist views, on a number of issues the Integralists fought the Reformists, who adopted an extreme opportunist
attitude and collaborated with the reactionary bourgeoisie.   p. 216

148 *The Polish Socialist Party* (Polska Partia Socjalistyczna)—a reformist and nationalist party founded in 1892.
        In 1906 the chauvinist Right wing split away from the rest of
the party.   p. 218

149 *The International Socialist Congress in Stuttgart* (the Seventh
Congress of the Second International) was held from August 18 to
24, 1907.
        The Congress was attended by 886 delegates from socialist par-
ties and trade unions.   p. 220

150 See Karl Marx and Frederick Engels, *Manifesto of the Communist
Party*, Moscow 1969.   p. 221

151 The term *"A caricature of Bolshevism"* was applied by Lenin to
the trends of Otzovism and Ultimatumism which arose among the
Bolsheviks in 1908.
        The *Otzovists* (from the Russian word *otozvat*—to recall) declared
that under the conditions of reaction the Party could only wage
an underground struggle and therefore demanded that the Social-
Democratic deputies should be recalled from the Third Duma and
that work in the legal organisations—trade unions, co-operatives,
etc.—should be discontinued. A variant of Otzovism was *Ultimatumism*. Its advocates wanted to have the work of the Social-Democratic
group in the Duma directed by means of ultimatums, and if the
deputies failed to comply they were to be recalled.   p. 224

152 *Union of the Russian People*—an extremely reactionary monarchist
organisation, founded in St. Petersburg in October 1905 to combat
the revolutionary movement.   p. 224

153 A reference to the Third Duma (November 1907 to June 1912).
                                                                p. 224

154 Lenin refers to his article "Two Letters". (See Lenin, *Collected
Works*, Vol. 15, p. 286.)   p. 227

155 *Vekhi* (Landmarks)—a collection of articles by prominent Cadet
writers who belonged to the counter-revolutionary liberal bourgeoisie.
The book was published in Moscow in 1909.   p. 233

156 The words *The Faction of Supporters of Otzovism and God-Building*
refer to a group consisting of Otzovists, Ultimatumists and God-
Builders which was formed in the spring of 1909 to organise a
school on Capri. The school was in fact the centre of the faction's
anti-Party activity.

Some of the Otzovists (Bogdanov, Lunacharsky) and Menshevik-Liquidators (Valentinov, Yushkevich) published articles attacking dialectical and historical materialism, the theoretical basis of Marxism. Lunacharsky spoke of the necessity of founding a new religion and of combining socialism with religion. This trend was called god-building by Lenin.

In June 1909 a meeting of the enlarged editorial board of *Proletary* passed a resolution declaring that Bolshevism had nothing in common with Otzovism and Ultimatumism and calling on the Bolsheviks to wage a resolute struggle against them. Bogdanov was expelled from the Bolshevik organisation.   p. 235

[157] Lenin refers to the *Party of Octobrists* (or the Union of October Seventeenth) formed in Russia after the publication of the tsar's Manifesto of October 17, 1905, which promised the people civil liberties. It was a counter-revolutionary organisation which defended the interests of the big bourgeoisie and the landlords who ran their estates on capitalist lines. The Octobrists, who were the principal party in the Third Duma, supported the home and foreign policies of the tsarist government.   p. 235

[158] The July Conference of 1907, i.e., the Third (Second All-Russia) Conference of the R.S.D.L.P., was held in Kotka (Finland) from July 21 to 23 (August 3 to 5), 1907. The main issues discussed were whether to participate in the Third Duma and the tactics the Party was to adopt under the conditions of reaction following the dissolution of the Second Duma by the tsarist government and in view of the changes in the electoral law which increased the number of deputies returned to the Duma by the bourgeoisie and the landlords.

The majority of delegates at the July Conference voted for participation in the Duma and in the election campaign and for stepping up the fight against the Right wing parties and the Cadets.   p. 240

[159] The *"Young"*—a semi-anarchist opposition within German Social-Democracy. It consisted chiefly of young writers and students. p. 246

[160] Lenin refers to Vera Zasulich's article "Apropos of a Certain Question" published in the Menshevik Liquidators' paper *Zhivaya Zhizn* of July 19, 1913.

Liquidationism—a trend which became widespread among Mensheviks after the defeat of the Russian Revolution of 1905-1907. The Liquidators demanded the dissolution of the illegal revolutionary party of the working class, and wanted to set up in its place a legal opportunist organisation which was to confine its activities within the limits permitted by the tsarist government. The Liquidators were not supported by the bulk of the workers. The Prague Conference of the R.S.D.L.P. held in January 1912 expelled the Liquidators from the Party.   p. 251

[161] Lenin refers to the Congress of Commercial and Industrial Employees held in Moscow from June 29 to July 3 (July 12 to 16), 1913. The Liquidators were represented at the Congress by an insignificant group.   p. 254

[162] "The War and Russian Social-Democracy" was the first document of the C.C. of the R.S.D.L.P.(B.) expressing the attitude of the Bolsheviks to the First World War.   p. 255

[163] See Note 149.   p. 255

[164] *The Copenhagen Congress of the Second International*, which was held from August 28 to September 3, 1910, confirmed the resolution of the Stuttgart Congress of 1907, on "Militarism and International Conflicts", which demanded that the socialists of all countries should make use of the economic and political crisis created by war to overthrow the bourgeoisie. The resolutions of the Copenhagen Congress also bound the socialist parties and their parliamentary representatives to demand that their governments should carry through disarmament measures and that all international conflicts should be submitted to a court of arbitration, and called on the workers of all countries to organise protest demonstrations against the threat of war.   p. 255

[165] The International Socialist Congress held at Basle in November 1912 was specially convened in connection with the impending menace of a European war. The Manifesto, which was unanimously adopted at the Congress, analysed the predatory aims of the threatening world imperialist war and called upon the working class "to confront capitalist imperialism with the might of international proletarian solidarity".   p. 255

[166] See Karl Marx and Frederick Engels, *Manifesto of the Communist Party*, Moscow 1969.   p. 255

[167] *La Bataille Chauviniste*—an ironical allusion to the chauvinist stand taken by the anarcho-syndicalist daily *La Bataille Syndicaliste* during the First World War.   p. 258

[168] Lenin refers to Bukharin's article "Der imperialistische Raubstaat" published in *Jugend-Internationale*, Zürich 1916, No. 6.   p. 259

[169] *Letters from Afar*, which were written in Switzerland in March 1917, were occasioned by the outbreak of the Russian bourgeois revolution in February 1917.   p. 261

[170] See V. I. Lenin, "Several Theses", *Collected Works*, Vol. 21.
                                                                                         p. 261

[171] *"No tsar, but a workers' government"*—this slogan was one of the basic tenets of Trotsky's theory of permanent revolution—a revolution without the peasantry—as opposed to Lenin's theory of the transformation of the bourgeois democratic revolution into a socialist revolution carried through by the whole people headed by the proletariat.   p. 263

[172] See Karl Marx, *The Civil War in France* and Frederick Engels, "Introduction" to this work, Moscow 1961.   p. 263

[173] Lenin refers to his article "The Tasks of the Proletariat in the Present Revolution" published in *Pravda* on April 7, 1917. See V. I. Lenin, *Collected Works*, Vol. 24, p. 19.   p. 264

174 This refers to Plekhanov's pamphlet *Anarchism and Socialism*, first published (in German) in Berlin in 1894.   p. 264

175 See Karl Marx, *Critique of the Gotha Programme*, and Frederick Engels, "Vorwort zur Broschüre 'Internationales aus dem Volksstaat' (1871-75)".   p. 265

176 These words by Heine are quoted by Marx and Engels in *The German Ideology*.   p. 267

177 See Karl Marx, *The Civil War in France*.   p. 270

178 See Karl Marx, *The Civil War in France*.   p. 271

179 This refers to Karl Marx, "Der politische Indifferentismus" and Frederick Engels, "Von der Autoritat". (See pp. 94-99 of this volume.)   p. 275

180 See Karl Marx, *The Poverty of Philosophy*.   p.279

181 See Karl Marx, *Critique of the Gotha Programme*.   p. 280

182 This refers to the Resolution on Ratification of the Brest Treaty passed by the Fourth (Extraordinary) All-Russia Congress of Soviets, which was held in Moscow from March 14 to 16, 1918.   p. 289

183 In her letter Sylvia Pankhurst asked Lenin to give his opinion on the attitude towards parliamentarism. She lists the following parties and groups which existed in Britain at the time: (1) Trade unionists and labour politicians of the old type. (2) The Independent Labour Party. (3) The British Socialist Party. (4) Revolutionary industrialists. (5) The Socialist Labour Party. (6) The Socialist Labour Federation. (7) The South Wales Socialist Society. Lenin uses the same numbers in his reply.   p. 294

184 See pp. 279-86 of this volume.   p. 295

185 Lenin refers to the Inaugural Congress of the Communist Party of Germany, held in Berlin from December 30, 1918 to January 1, 1919. The Congress was convened by the Spartacus League, a revolutionary organisation of Left-wing Social-Democrats which was formed during the First World War by Karl Liebknecht, Rosa Luxemburg, Franz Mehring and others.   p. 295

186 Lenin refers to the Independent Social-Democratic Party of Germany—a Centrist party which was founded in April 1917.   p. 296

187 *The British Socialist Party* was founded in Manchester in 1911. Its propaganda was conducted in a Marxist spirit, but owing to its small membership and its weak links with the masses the Party was somewhat sectarian. During the First World War an intensive struggle was waged within the Party between the consistent internationalists and the chauvinists headed by Hyndman. The annual Conference of the B.S.P. held in Salford in April 1916 rejected the policy of Hyndman and his supporters and they quitted the Party

    The B.S.P. played an important role in the "Hands-off-Russia" campaign, the movement of the British workers in defence of Soviet

Russia. The overwhelming majority of the B.S.P. (98 organisations to 4) voted in 1919 for affiliation to the Communist International.   p. 296

188 *"Left-Wing" Communism—an Infantile Disorder* written in April and May 1920, was published in time for the opening of the Second Congress of the Communist International and handed out to all the delegates.   p. 304

189 This presumably refers to Lenin's article "What Should Not Be Copied from the German Labour Movement" published in the Bolshevik journal *Prosveshcheniye* in April 1914. (See V. I. Lenin, *Collected Works*, Vol. 20, pp. 254-58.) There Lenin critically analyses the actions of Legien during his visit to the United States in 1912. Legien, a prominent leader of the German trade unions and the Social-Democratic Party, addressed the U.S. Congress and, as Lenin writes, delivered "a purely liberal, bourgeois speech", talking "in such a way as not to offend 'capitalism' ".   p. 306

190 *The Treaty of Brest-Litovsk*, a peace treaty between Soviet Russia and the Quadruple Alliance (Germany, Austro-Hungary, Bulgaria and Turkey) was signed at Brest-Litovsk on March 3, 1918, and ratified on March 15, by the Fourth (Extraordinary) All-Russia Congress of Soviets. Soviet Russia had to accept extremely onerous terms.

  Trotsky and a group of "Left Communists" were against the Brest Treaty and it was due to Lenin's tremendous efforts that the treaty was finally signed.

  The Peace Treaty gave the Soviet state a breathing space and allowed it to demobilise the old disintegrating army and build a new Red Army, reconstruct the economy and gather strength for the struggle against the counter-revolutionary forces within the country and the foreign intervention. After the revolution in Germany, which overthrew the monarchy in November 1918, the All-Russia Central Executive Committee abrogated the Brest Treaty on November 13.   p. 307

191 The tsar's manifesto proclaiming the establishment of the Duma was issued on August 6 (19), 1905. This Duma had no legislative powers and was merely a deliberative body which could discuss certain questions. The Bolsheviks called upon the workers and peasants to boycott and actively oppose this Duma. The mounting tide of the revolution and the all-Russia political strike of October 1905 prevented the tsarist government from holding the elections to this Duma.   p. 307

192 *"Left Communists"*—a group formed early in 1918 during the negotiations for a peace treaty between Soviet Russia and Germany. Under the slogan of "a revolutionary war" the "Left Communists" demanded that the negotiations should be broken off and military operations continued, as they alleged, in the interests of the world revolution. See also Note 190.   p. 309

[193] *Fabians*—members of the Fabian Society, a British reformist organisation founded in 1884. Most of its members were bourgeois intellectuals, writers, scientists, and politicians (Sidney and Beatrice Webb, Ramsay MacDonald and Bernard Shaw). They denied the necessity of class struggle and of the socialist revolution and asserted that the transition from capitalism to socialism could be effected by minor reforms and the gradual transformation of society. The Fabian Society affiliated to the Labour Party in 1900.   p. 309

[194] This refers to the Bolshevik deputies Badayev, Muranov, Petrovsky, Samoilov and Shagov who voted against war credits at the Duma session of July 26 (August 8), 1914, and led a revolutionary propaganda campaign among the masses. The Bolshevik deputies were arrested in November 1914, tried in February 1915 and sentenced to exile for life in Eastern Siberia.   p. 311

[195] *Industrial Workers of the World*—a labour union founded in the U.S.A. in 1905. It led a number of successful mass strikes and fought against the policy of class collaboration pursued by the reformist leaders of the American Federation of Labor and by Right-wing socialists. Some of its activities, however, revealed anarcho-syndicalist tendencies, e.g., it repudiated the political struggle of the proletariat, the leading role of the party and the need for a proletarian dictatorship. After the First World War the I.W.W. rapidly declined.   p. 312

[196] *The Second Congress of the Communist International* was held from July 19 to August 7, 1920. It began its work in Petrograd but beginning with July 23 its meetings were held in Moscow. It was attended by over 200 delegates from communist parties and labour organisations of 37 countries.

At the first session Lenin made the "Report on the International Situation and the Fundamental Tasks of the Communist International". He participated in the sessions, commissions and discussions of the Congress and drafted some of its main theses and resolutions.   p. 316

[197] *The Communist Workers' Party of Germany* (Kommunistische Arbeiter Partei Deutschlands) was founded in April 1920 by "Left" Communists who were expelled from the Communist Party of Germany at the Heidelberg Congress in October 1919. The Communist Workers' Party of Germany subsequently degenerated into a small sectarian group.   p. 316

[198] This refers to the Provisional Bureau of the Communist International in Amsterdam.   p. 316

[199] The *Workers' Socialist Federation* was a small organisation which in May 1918 arose from the Women's Suffrage Federation.   p. 316

[200] This refers to the trade union controversy which began in November 1920. It was started by Trotsky who opposed the extension of democratic principles in the trade unions and called for the tightening of the screws of "War Communism" and the immediate "governmentalisation" of the unions. A pamphlet dealing with the

issues under discussion which Trotsky published on December 25 served other groups—e.g., the "buffer group" (led by Bukharin), the Workers' Opposition and the Democratic Centralists—as a signal for action.

Lenin was at the time against this discussion since it diverted the attention and forces of the Party from the urgent economic problems facing it. But after the various factions had started it he waged a determined fight against them. Lenin's views were backed by the majority of organisations of the Bolshevik Party.   p. 320

[201] *The Workers' Opposition*—an anti-Party anarcho-syndicalist group among whose members were Shlyapnikov, Medvedyev, Kollontai and Lutovinov. It proposed that the country's economy should be run by an all-Russia congress of producers, that is, the producers organised in trade unions were to elect a central body which was to manage the economy of the country. They demanded that all bodies controlling the national economy should be elected by the respective trade unions and that neither the Party nor the Soviets should have the right to reject those elected by the unions. These demands in fact denied the leading role of the Party and the dictatorship of the proletariat.   p. 324

[202] See V. I. Lenin, *Collected Works*, Vol. 32.   p. 330

[203] See Note 196.   p. 333

[204] Lenin refers to the resolution on the agrarian question passed by the Congress on August 4, 1920.   p. 334

[205] *The Third Congress of the Communist International* was held in Moscow from June 22 to July 12, 1921. Lenin made many important speeches at the sessions of the Congress and in various of its commissions and helped to draw up its principal documents.   p. 339

NAME INDEX

A

Adler, Friedrich (1879-1960)—leader of the opportunist wing of the Austrian Social-Democrats and of the Second International, an organiser of the Centrist Two-and-a-Half International and afterwards of what became known as the Labour and Socialist International.—309

Albarracin, Severino—Spanish anarchist, teacher, member of the Spanish Federal Council of the International (1872-73), one of the leaders of the uprising in Alcoy in 1873, after its defeat emigrated to Switzerland.—136

Alerini, Charles (b. 1842)—French anarchist, member of the Marseille Section of the International, an organiser of the Marseille Commune (April 1871), after its defeat emigrated to Italy and subsequently to Spain, where he propagated anarchist views, in 1873 was expelled from the International.—133, 134

Alexei Mikhailovich (1629-1676)

—Tsar of Russia (1645-1676).—112

Amadeo (1845-1890)—son of Victor Emmanuel II, King of Spain (1870-1873),—108, 126, 130, 190

Axelrod, P. B. (1850-1928)—Social-Democrat, in 1883 helped to form the Emancipation of Labour group, became a member of the *Iskra* editorial board in 1900, since the Second Congress of the R.S.D.L.P. a leader of the Russian Mensheviks.—209, 210

B

Bakunin, M. A. (1814-1876)—Russian revolutionary and publicist, took part in the German revolution of 1848-49, one of the ideologists of anarchism; being a member of the First International revealed himself as sworn enemy of Marxism and was expelled from the International for his schismatic activity by the Hague Congress in 1872.—45, 46, 47, 48, 49, 56, 61, 62, 63, 64, 68, 69, 70, 73, 74, 75, 77, 79, 80,

losopher, sociologist and economist. After the Second
Congress of the R.S.D.L.P.
(1903) he became a Bolshevik
and was an editor of the Bolshevik papers *Uperyod, Proletary* and *Novaya Zhizn*; tried
to create his own philosophical
system, empirio-monism (a
variant of Mach's subjective
idealist philosophy), which was
strongly criticised by Lenin in
his *Materialism and Empirio-
Criticism*; was expelled from
the Bolshevik Party in June
1909.—238, 239, 240

Bolte, Friedrich—American labour leader of German de-
scent, Secretary of the Federal
Council of the North American Sections of the International (1872), member of the
General Council of the International (1872-74).—55

Bracke, Wilhelm (1842-1880)—
German Social-Democrat, one
of the founders (1869) and
leaders of the Social-Democratic Workers' Party (Eise-
nachers); was close to Marx
and Engels.—154, 279

Branting, Carl Hjalmar (1860-
1925)—leader of the Social-
Democratic Party of Sweden;
one of the leaders of the
Second International; during
the First World War—social-
chauvinist; joined a coalition
government in 1917 and
supported military intervention
against Soviet Russia.—270

Bray, John Francis (1809-1895)
—British economist, utopian
socialist, follower of Robert
Owen.—96

Brouckère, Louis de (1870-1951)
—one of the leaders and theoreticians of the Workers' Party
of Belgium, headed its Left
wing up to the First World
War, subsequently a social-
chauvinist.—216

Brousse, Paul (1854-1912)—
French physician, petty-bourgeois socialist, took part in the
Paris Commune, after its
defeat emigrated and became
an anarchist; joined the French
Workers' Party in 1879, later
became one of the leaders of
the Possibilists.—134

Brutus, Lucius Junius (d. c. 509
B.C.)—according to tradition
the founder of the Roman
republic, sentenced his own
sons to death for conspiring
against the republic.—97

Bukharin, N. I. (pen-name Nota
Bene) (1888-1938)—a member
of the Bolshevik Party since
1906; during the First World
War opposed Lenin on a
number of problems, i.e., on
the state, the dictatorship of
the proletariat and the right
of nations to self-determina-
tion; after the October Revolution a member of the Polit-
bureau of the C.C. of the
R.C.P.(B.) and of the E.C.C.I.;
in 1918 one of the leaders of
the "Left Communists" and
later of the Right opposition;
was expelled from the Party
in 1937.—259, 260, 309, 319,
320, 322, 324

C

Cafiero, Carlo (1846-1892)—one
of the members of the Italian
labour movement; a member
of the International, in 1872
became a leader of the Italian
anarchists but rejected anarchism towards the end of the
seventies; in 1879 published a
brief summary in Italian of
the first volume of Marx's
Capital.—47, 78

the Civil War (1918-20) one of
the leaders of the whiteguard
movement, commander-in-chief
of the anti-Soviet armed
forces in the South of Russia,
after the defeat of his army
by the Soviet troops went
abroad (1920).—302, 311

Dubrovin, A. I. (1855-1918)—organiser and leader of the
reactionary Union of Russian
People; organised anti-Jewish
pogroms and terrorist acts
from 1905 to 1907.—224

Dufaure, Jules Armand Stanislas
(1798-1881)—French lawyer
and statesman, Orleanist, Minister of the Interior (1848 and
1849), Minister of Justice
(1871-73 and 1875-79) and
Chairman of the Council of
Ministers (1876, 1877-79),
hangman of the Paris Com-
mune.—73, 77

Dühring, Eugen (1833-1921)—
German philosopher and economist, propagated a petty-
bourgeois socialism; In his
philosophy combined positi-
vism, metaphysical materialism
and idealism; his views were
analysed in Engels's *Anti-
Dühring. Herr Eugen Düh-
ring's Revolution in Science,*
and by Lenin in *Materialism
and Empirio-Criticism.*—233,
247

Dupont, Eugène (c. 1831-1881)—
French worker who took part
in the revolutionary struggle
in France in 1848, lived in
London from 1862, was a
member of the General Council of the International (1864-
72) and a delegate to all its
Congresses; settled in the
U.S.A. in 1874.—122

Durand, Gustave (b. 1835)—
French goldsmith, police spy,
after the defeat of the Paris
Commune pretended to be an
émigré in London and became
Secretary of the French Section in 1871, but was soon
unmasked and expelled from
the International.—64

E

El—see *Luzin I. I.*

Engels, Frederick (1820-1895)—
47, 78, 88, 91, 122, 171, 172,
175, 176, 179, 188, 190, 192,
193, 194, 195, 196, 229, 230,
235, 247, 260, 262, 263, 264,
265, 267, 274, 275, 276, 278,
279, 280, 305, 329, 330, 334

Ewerbeck, August Hermann
(1816-1860)—German physi-
cian and writer, leader of the
Paris communities of the
League of the Just, later a
member of the Communist
League, from which he resigned in 1850.—40

F

Fanelli, Giuseppe (1826-1877)—
Italian bourgeois democrat,
took part in the Italian revolution of 1848-49 and in Garibaldi's campaign of 1860, he
was a follower of Mazzini, in
the middle sixties he became a
close friend of Bakunin and
a leader of the Alliance of
Socialist Democracy; he was
the first to organise sections
of the International and groups
of the Alliance in Spain (in
1868), in 1865 he became a
member of the Italian Parliament.—108

Farga Pellicer, Rafael (1840-
1890)—Spanish printer and
journalist, helped to organise
groups of the Alliance and the
first sections of the International in Spain, expelled from
the International in 1873.—133

Faucher, Julius (1820-1878)—

1875 President of the General Association of German Workers.—124

Hasselmann, *Wilhelm* (b. 1844) —a leader of the Lassallean General Association of German Workers, editor of the *Neuer Sozial-Demokrat* (1871-75), member of the German Social-Democratic Party from 1875 to 1880 when he was expelled from the Party as an anarchist.—124

Hegel, Georg Wilhelm Friedrich (1770-1831)—outstanding classical German philosopher, objective idealist.—30, 90

Henderson, Arthur (1863-1935) —a leader of the Labour Party and the British trade union movement; during the First World War took up a social-chauvinist stand; held various Cabinet posts in coalition and Labour Governments.—270

Hervé, Gustave (1871-1944)— French lawyer and journalist, member of the Socialist Party of France. He recommended semi-anarchist methods to fight militarism. During the First World War he became a social-chauvinist and was expelled from the Socialist Party in 1918.—221, 222, 223

Hildebrand, Max—German teacher in Berlin, follower of Max Stirner, collected biographical material on him.—179

Hilferding, Rudolf (1877-1941)— one of the opportunist leaders of the German Social-Democratic Party and the Second International, propounded the theory of "organised capitalism".—306

Höchberg, Karl (1853-1885)— German journalist, Right-wing Social-Democrat.—246

I

Iglesias, Pablo (1850-1925)—prominent figure in the Spanish working-class and socialist movement, printer, proletarian journalist, member of the Spanish Federal Council of the International (1871-72), one of the founders of the Spanish Socialist Workers' Party (1879), later he became a leader of its reformist wing. —181

Ikov, V. K. (Mirov, V.)—Russian Social-Democrat, Menshevik. He wrote for *Vozrozhdenie*, *Golos Sotzial-Demokrata* and other Menshevik periodicals.— 209

Iliodor (Trufanov, S. M.) (b. 1880)—a Russian monk, one of the leaders of the Black Hundreds.—224

Ivanovsky—see Shneerson I. A.

K

Kapp, Wolfgang (1858-1922)— German politician, in March 1920 he organised an uprising designed to set up a military dictatorship but was foiled by the workers who declared a general strike.—314

Kautsky, Karl (1854-1938)—one of the leaders of the German Social-Democratic Party and of the Second International, he was at first a Marxist but subsequently turned into an opportunist and centrist.—261, 262, 266, 271, 272, 281, 282, 283, 284, 296, 306

Kerensky, A. F. (1881-1970)— one of the leaders of the Party of the Socialist Revolutionaries, headed the Russian Provisional Government in Russia in 1917 and went abroad in 1918.—311

L

Labriola, Arturo (1873-1959)—
Italian political leader, lawyer
and economist; a leader of the
syndicalist movement in Italy.
He wrote several books on the
theory of syndicalism.—216

Lafargue, Paul (1842-1911)—
prominent figure in the French
and international working-class
movement and proponent of
Marxism; member of the General
Council of the International,
fought anarchism and
Bakuninism. One of the founders
of the Workers' Party in
France (1879), disciple and
associate of Marx and Engels.—42, 45, 58, 76, 180

Lagardelle, Juber (b. 1874)—
French petty-bourgeois politician,
a follower of Georges
Sorel, anarcho-syndicalist
theorist; wrote several works
on the history of anarcho-syndicalism
in France.—216

Lansbury, George (1859-1940)—
one of the leaders of the British
Labour Party. He was an
M.P. from 1910 to 1912 and
from 1922 to 1940; editor of
The Daily Herald from 1912
to 1922.—309

Larin, J. (Lurye, M. A.) (1882-
1932)—Social-Democrat, supported
the Menshevik programme
of municipalisation of
the land and the opportunist
idea of the convocation
of the "Workers' Congress".
He became a member of the
Bolshevik Party in August
1917.—209, 210

Lassalle, Ferdinand (1825-1864)
—German petty-bourgeois publicist
and lawyer; in 1848 and
1849 he took part in the democratic
movement in the
Rheinish Province; early in
the 1860s, joined the German
working-class movement; one
of the founders of the General
Association of German Workers
(1863). He advocated the
unification of Germany from
above under Prussian hegemony,
laid the beginning of
the opportunist trend in the
German working-class movement.—56, 147

Ledebour, Georg (1850-1947)—
German Social-Democrat.
During the First World War
he was for the re-establishment
of international links and belonged
to the Zimmerwald
Right. One of the founders of
the Independent Social-Democratic
Party of Germany.—
306

Ledru-Rollin, Alexandre Auguste
(1807-1874)—French lawyer
and politician, one of the leaders
of the petty-bourgeois
democrats, deputy of the Constituent
and the Legislative
Assembly where he headed the
Montagne; after the demonstration
of June 13, 1849, he
emigrated to Britain.—34

Legien, Karl (1861-1920)—German
Right-wing Social-Democrat,
a leader of the German
and international trade
union movement. He was a
revisionist and fought against
the revolutionary movement
of the proletariat.—270, 306

Le Moussu, A.—French engraver,
took part in the Paris Commune
and after its defeat
emigrated to London, member
of the General Council of the
International; supported the
fight of Marx and Engels
against the Bakuninists.—122

Lenin, Vladimir Ilyich (Ulyanov)
(1870-1924)—211, 263,
294, 322

Levi, Paul (1883-1930)—German
Social-Democrat, a mem-

counter-revolutionary officers. —283, 295

Luzin, I. I. (El) (d. c. 1914)—Russian Social-Democrat, Menshevik, wrote an article which was included in a symposium on a "workers' congress" published by Moscow Mensheviks in 1907.—209

Lvov. G. Y. Prince (1861-1925)—big Russian landowner, Cadet, from March to July 1917 Chairman of the Provisional Government and Minister of the Interior.—263

M

Maksimov, N.—see *Bogdanov, A.*

Malon, Benoît (1841-1893)—French socialist, member of the First International and Paris Commune, after its defeat he emigrated and became an anarchist, later he was a leader of the Possibilists.—77

Martinez de Campos, Arsenio (1831-1900)—Spanish general and reactionary politician, who put down the cantonalist uprising in Catalonia and Valencia in 1873. He headed the monarchist coup d'état which brought Alfonso XII to the throne (December 24, 1874) and was Minister of War (1881-1883).—140, 141, 142

Martov, L. (Tsederbaum, Y. O.) (1873-1923)—Social-Democrat, since 1900 member of the *Iskra* editorial board. After the Second Congress of the R.S.D.L.P. (1903) a leader of the Mensheviks. Following the October Revolution he was an opponent of the Soviet power and emigrated in 1920.—289

Martynov, A. (Piker, A. S.)— (1865-1935)—Menshevik, one of the leaders of Economism —Russian variant of Bern-

steinism. After the October Revolution he left the Mensheviks, and became a member of the Bolshevik Party in 1923, from 1924 was an editor of the journal *Communist International.*—199

Marx, Karl (1818-1883)—41, 43, 48, 55, 122, 153, 171, 172, 173, 176, 177, 179, 187, 189, 196, 216, 218, 229, 230, 231, 235, 247, 257, 259, 261, 262, 264, 265, 266, 267, 268, 271, 272, 273, 274, 275, 276, 278, 279, 280, 282, 289, 290, 295, 306, 307, 331, 332

Mazzini, Giuseppe (1805-1872)—Italian revolutionary, bourgeois democrat, a leader of the Italian national liberation movement. In 1864 when the International was formed he tried to bring it under his influence; in 1871 he attacked the Paris Commune and the International and impeded the development of an independent workers' movement in Italy.—163

Mirov, V.—see *Ikov, V. K.*

Moltke, Helmuth, Count (1800-1891)—Prussian fieldmarshal, one of the ideologists of Prussian militarism and chauvinism; during the Franco-Prussian war of 1870-71 actual commander-in-chief.—140

Most, Johann Joseph (1846-1906) —German anarchist, who joined the working-class movement in the 1860s; in 1878, after the promulgation of the Anti-Socialist Law, emigrated to England; because of his anarchist activity was expelled from the Social-Democratic Party in 1880 and emigrated to the U.S.A. in 1882 where continued his anarchist propaganda.—171, 173, 233, 246, 247

the Carlists and quelled the rising of the cantonalists in Andalusia; Captain-General of New Castilia (1873-74); led a monarchist coup d'état (January 2-3, 1874) in favour of Serrano, Senator since 1880.— 137, 140, 141

Peter I (1672-1725)—Tsar of Russia (1682-1725), Emperor of Russia since 1721.—112

Pi y Margall, Francisco (1824-1901)—Spanish politician, lawyer and writer, leader of the Left-wing federalist republicans, he was influenced by utopian-socialist ideas, took part in the bourgeois revolutions of 1854 to 1865 and 1868 to 1874, Minister of the Interior and provisional head of the republican government from June 11 to July 18, 1873.—126, 132, 137, 140, 191

Pio, Louis Albert François (1841-1894)—Danish socialist and propagator of Marxism, a founder of the Danish Sections of the International (1871), and of the Danish Social-Democratic Party (1876). He emigrated to America in 1877.—75

Pius IX (1792-1878)—pope (1846-1878)—60

Plekhanov, Georgi Valentinovich (1856-1918)—leader in the Russian and international working-class movement, first propagandist of Marxism in Russia; he formed the Emancipation of Labour group, the first Russian Marxist organisation, in Geneva in 1883. After the Second Congress of the R.S.D.L.P. he adopted a conciliating stand towards opportunism, and later joined the Mensheviks; during the first Russian revolution he shared the Menshevik views on all the major questions; during the First World War (1914-18) he was a social-chauvinist; he adopted a negative attitude towards the Great October Socialist Revolution, but did not take part in the struggle against the Soviet government.—189, 264, 266, 271, 272, 282, 306

Polovnev, A. V.—an agent of the tsarist Secret Police and one of the founders of the Union of the Russian People, a counter-revolutionary organisation.—224

Potel (pseudonym of Lucain)—a French émigré to Belgium, member of the International, delegate to the Hague Congress (1872) from the section of French émigrés in Brussels.—105

Prokopovich, S. N. (1871-1955)—bourgeois economist and writer, towards the close of the 1890s a prominent advocate of Economism, he was one of the first to propagate Bernsteinism in Russia. Later he was a member of the League of Emancipation, a liberal monarchist organisation, and in 1906 became a member of the C.C. of the Cadet Party. After the October Revolution he was sent out of the country for his anti-Soviet activities.—213

Proudhon, Pierre Joseph (1809-1865)—French journalist, economist and sociologist, an ideologist of the petty bourgeoisie and a founder of anarchism.—28, 32, 39, 43, 56, 88, 89, 90, 92, 93, 96, 97, 99, 151, 152, 153, 174, 176, 177, 178, 179, 272, 273, 279, 282

Purishkevich, V. M. (1870-1920)—big Russian landowner, who held extremely reactionary views monarchist, one of the organisers of the Union of the Russian People. He was a deputy of the Second, Third and Fourth Dumas and became notorious for the anti-Semitic speeches he made in the Duma.—224

Pyat, Félix (1810-1889)—French journalist, playwright and politician, petty-bourgeois democrat, took part in the 1848 revolution and had to emigrate in the following year; he was against an independent labour movement, and for a number of years carried on a slander campaign against Marx and the International and used the French Section in London for this purpose, a member of the Paris Commune.—51

R

Radek, K. B. (1885-1939)—from the beginning of the century he took part in the Social-Democratic movement in Galicia, Poland and Germany. He became a member of the Bolshevik Party in 1917, came out against Lenin on many occasions, was a "Left Communist" in 1918, and from 1923 took part in the Trotskyite opposition. In 1936 he was expelled from the Party for his anti-Party activity.—283, 309

Razin, S. T. (d. 1671)—leader of the greatest uprising of peasants and Cossacks which took place in Russia during the seventeenth century.—112

Renaudel, Pierre (1871-1935)—a reformist leader of the French Socialist Party.—270, 309

Ricardo, David (1772-1823)—outstanding British economist.—98

Richard, Albert (1846-1925)—French journalist, a leader of the Lyons Section of the International, and a member of the Secret Alliance, he took part in the Lyons rising of 1870, after the defeat of the Paris Commune he became a Bonapartist.—108

Rittinghausen, Moritz (1814-1890)—German journalist, petty-bourgeois democrat, he contributed to the *Neue Rheinische Zeitung* in 1848-49, was a member of the First International and later of the German Social-Democratic Party (until 1884).—24

Robespierre, Maximilian François Isidore de (1758-1794)—outstanding French revolutionist, leader of the Jacobins during the French Revolution of the end of the eighteenth century and head of the revolutionary government (1793-94).—32, 39, 156

Rodichev F. I. (b. 1856)—Russian landowner, a leader of the Cadets.—214

Romanov, Nicholas II (1868-1918)—last Tsar of Russia (1894-1917).—224

Rousseau, Jean Jacques (1712-1778)—outstanding French writer and philosopher of the Enlightenment.—32, 39

Ruge, Arnold (1802-1880)—German writer, a Young Hegelian and bourgeois radical; in 1848 he was a member of the Frankfurt National Assembly, where he belonged to the Left wing, in the fifties he was a leader of the German petty-bourgeois emigrants in England; after 1866 he was a National-Liberal.—32

Ryazanov (Goldendakh), D. B. (1870-1938)—Russian Social-Democrat, Menshevik, he became a member of the R.S.D.L.P.(B.) in 1917. After the October Revolution he held important trade union posts. He was expelled from the C.P.S.U.(B.) in 1931.—334

S

Sacase, François (1808-1884)— French civil servant, monarchist, member of the National Assembly since 1871.—73, 77

Sagasta, Praxedes Mateo (1827-1903)—Spanish statesman, leader of the Liberal Party, Minister for Internal Affairs (1871-72), Minister for Foreign Affairs (1874) and several times Prime Minister between 1881 and 1902.—144

Saint-Simon, Claude Henri de Rouvroy, Comte de (1760-1825)—French utopian socialist.—39, 45, 56, 96, 152

Salmeron y Alonso, Nicolas (1838-1908)—Spanish politician, professor of history and philosophy at Madrid University, a leader of the bourgeois republicans, President of the Spanish Republic from July 18 to September 7, 1873.—126, 191

Savinkov, B. V. (1879-1925)—a leader of the Socialist-Revolutionaries. Following the February Revolution of 1917 he was military governor-general of Petrograd. After the October Revolution he organised counter-revolutionary revolts and supported the interventionists, later a White émigré.—291

Scheidemann, Philipp (1865-1939)—a leader of the opportunist Right wing of the German Social-Democratic Party, Chancellor of Germany from February to June 1919; in 1918-21 he helped to put down the labour movement in Germany.—270, 295

Schweitzer, Johann Baptist von (1834-1875)—German lawyer,

Lassallean, President of the General Association of German Workers (1867-71), he was against the affiliation of the German workers to the First International; in 1872 when his relations with the Prussian authorities became known he was expelled from the General Association of German Workers.—56

Schwitzguébel, Adhémar (1844-1895)—Swiss engraver, a member of the International, anarchist, a leader of the Alliance of Social Democracy and of the Jura Federation, he was expelled from the International in 1873.—64, 68, 78, 86

Sembat, Marcel (1862-1922)— French journalist, a leader of the reformist wing of the French Socialist Party; he became a social-chauvinist during the First World War, from August 1914 to September 1917 he was Minister for Public Works in the French Government of National Defence.—270

Serraillier, Auguste (b. 1840)— participant of the French and international working-class movement, member of the General Council of the International (1869-1872) and of the Paris Commune, Marx's associate.—122

Shlyapnikov, A. G. (1885-1937)— a member of the Bolshevik Party from 1901, he held various posts in trade unions and the national economy after the October Revolution. From 1920 to 1922 he was a leader of the Workers' Opposition, in 1933 he was expelled from the Party.—319, 321, 324, 325, 336

Shneerson, I. A. (Ivanovsky, P.) (1878-1942)—Russian Social-

World War a centrist. Following the February Revolution of 1917 he returned to Russia from emigration and became a member of the Bolshevik Party at the Sixth Congress of the R.S.D.L.P.(B.) held from July 26 to August 3, 1917. But he did not accept the Bolshevik stand and led a secret and open struggle against Leninism and the Party policy. After the October Revolution he held various important posts. His anti-Party activity led to his expulsion from the Communist Party in 1927, and his expulsion from the U.S.S.R. and loss of his Soviet citizenship in 1924.—211, 320, 324

Trubetskoi, Y. N., Prince (1863-1920)—Russian idealist philosopher, one of the ideologists of Russian bourgeois liberalism. After the October Revolution he was an enemy of the Soviet regime and a supporter of Denikin.—302

Tsereteli, I. G. (1882-1959)—a leader of Menshevism in Russia, in May 1917 he became a member of the Russian Provisional Government and was one of the protagonists of the fight against the Bolsheviks. After the October Revolution he became a member of the counter-revolutionary Menshevik Government in Georgia. After the establishment of the Soviet power in Georgia he emigrated.—289

V

Van Patten, Philipp—American bourgeois who joined the socialist movement, since 1876 he was Secretary of the Working Men's Party of America, and since 1879 of the Socialist Labour Party of North America; in 1883 resigned his functions and became a government official.—171

Vandervelde, Emile (1866-1938) —leader of the Workers' Party of Belgium, President of the International Socialist Bureau of the Second International, extreme opportunist; supported armed intervention against Soviet Russia; from 1925 to 1927 he was Minister of Foreign Affairs.—216, 270

Van-Heddeghem (pseudonym of *Walter*) (b. c. 1847)—a police agent who managed to become a member of the Paris Section of the International; was a delegate to the Hague Congress of the International (1872) but was unmasked in 1873.—105

Velarde, José Maria—Spanish general, Captain-General of Catalonia from April to September 1873.—136

Victor Emmanuel II (1820-1878) —King of Sardinia (1849-61), and King of Italy (1861-78).—60

Viñas, Garcia José—Spanish medical student, anarchist, one of the organisers of the Alliance of Socialist Democracy in Spain (1868), took part in the revolutionary movement of 1873.—133

Vichard, Paul—participant of the French working-class movement; took part in the Paris Commune and represented the French Section in London at the Hague Congress of the International (1872).—105

Vollmar, Georg Heinrich (1850-1922)—one of the leaders of the reformist wing of the German Social-Democratic Party, he was a member of the Reichstag from 1881 to 1887 and

from 1890 to 1918; during the
First World War he was a
social-chauvinist.—220, 221

W

Walter—see *Van-Heddeghem*
Wilhelm II (1859-1941)—Emperor of Germany and King
of Prussia (1888-1918).—205

Y

Yezersky, F.—author of the article "French Workers' Strike"

published in 1907 in the journal *Obrazovaniye* No. 1.—212

Z

Zasulich, Vera Ivanovna (1849-
1919)—a prominent member of
the Narodniks and later of the
Social-Democratic   movement
in Russia; became a Menshevik
following the Second Congress
of the R.S.D.L.P. (1903).—251,
252

SUBJECT INDEX

A

Anarchism. Anarchists—47, 79, 86-87, 89, 96, 106, 113-14, 117, 118, 121, 123, 125, 127, 144-45, 152, 153, 156-58, 162-63, 174, 175-76, 179

—general characteristics—27-31, 74, 125, 170, 174, 242, 244, 252, 253, 287-88, 304-06, 317

—criticism of their political, economic and sociological views—74, 109, 185-86, 198-99, 201-02, 235-36, 261, 267, 272-73

—criticism of their views on the state—27-28, 45, 47-49, 69-71, 74, 94, 95, 103-04, 108-11, 128, 130, 145, 149-52, 167-68, 171-73, 179, 259-60, 261-62, 264, 273, 274-80, 281-85

—negation of the necessity of political struggle of the working class—94-96, 99, 158, 160, 162-63, 165, 170, 174, 176, 181, 186, 201-02, 204-06

—adventurism of their tactics—47-48, 74, 110-11, 117-18, 138, 160-61, 165, 181, 199, 205-06, 218-19, 220-23, 231-32, 233, 284-85

—their attitude to parliamentarism—196, 199-200, 201, 207-08, 226, 227-28, 235-36, 240-41, 270-71, 297

—their attitude to wars—220-23, 255-56

—their social-chauvinism during the imperialist world war of 1914-18—255, 258, 300

—in the West-European working-class movement—125, 205, 233, 294-95, 300-01, 317-18, 338-39

—in America—125

—in Austria—270, 233

—in Belgium—160

—in Germany—28, 172, 233, 246, 248, 249

—in France—170, 258

—in Italy—123, 159, 160, 163

—in Poland—218-19

—in Russia—203-06, 207, 209-10, 305-06

—in Spain—125, 127, 128, 159, 160, 162, 170

—in Switzerland—86, 159, 160, 165, 170

—Most's anarchist group—171-73, 233, 249

—semi-anarchist group of the "Young"—249

—struggle against the anarchists in the Second International—180, 205

See also *Authority; Anarcho-*